[pIʃü] *n.* The mark of evil that forecasts imminent death.

Pixu [脾虛] *(spleen deficient).* Term being used in Tradition Chinese Medicine (TCM). The word "spleen" does not necessarily refer to the organ, spleen. It is a term describing a group of physiological functions.

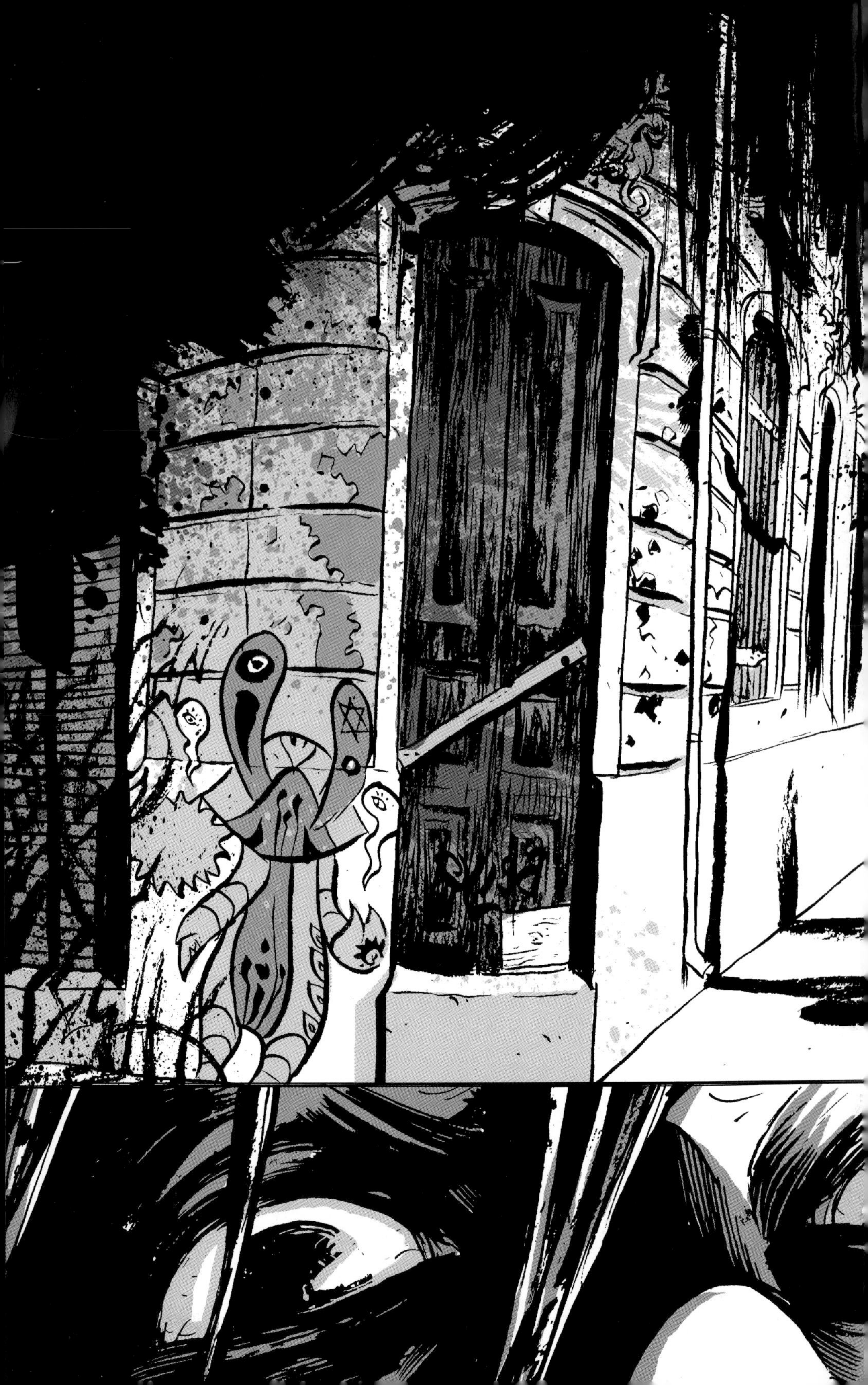

Pixu

Gabriel Bá
Becky Cloonan
Vasilis Lolos
Fábio Moon

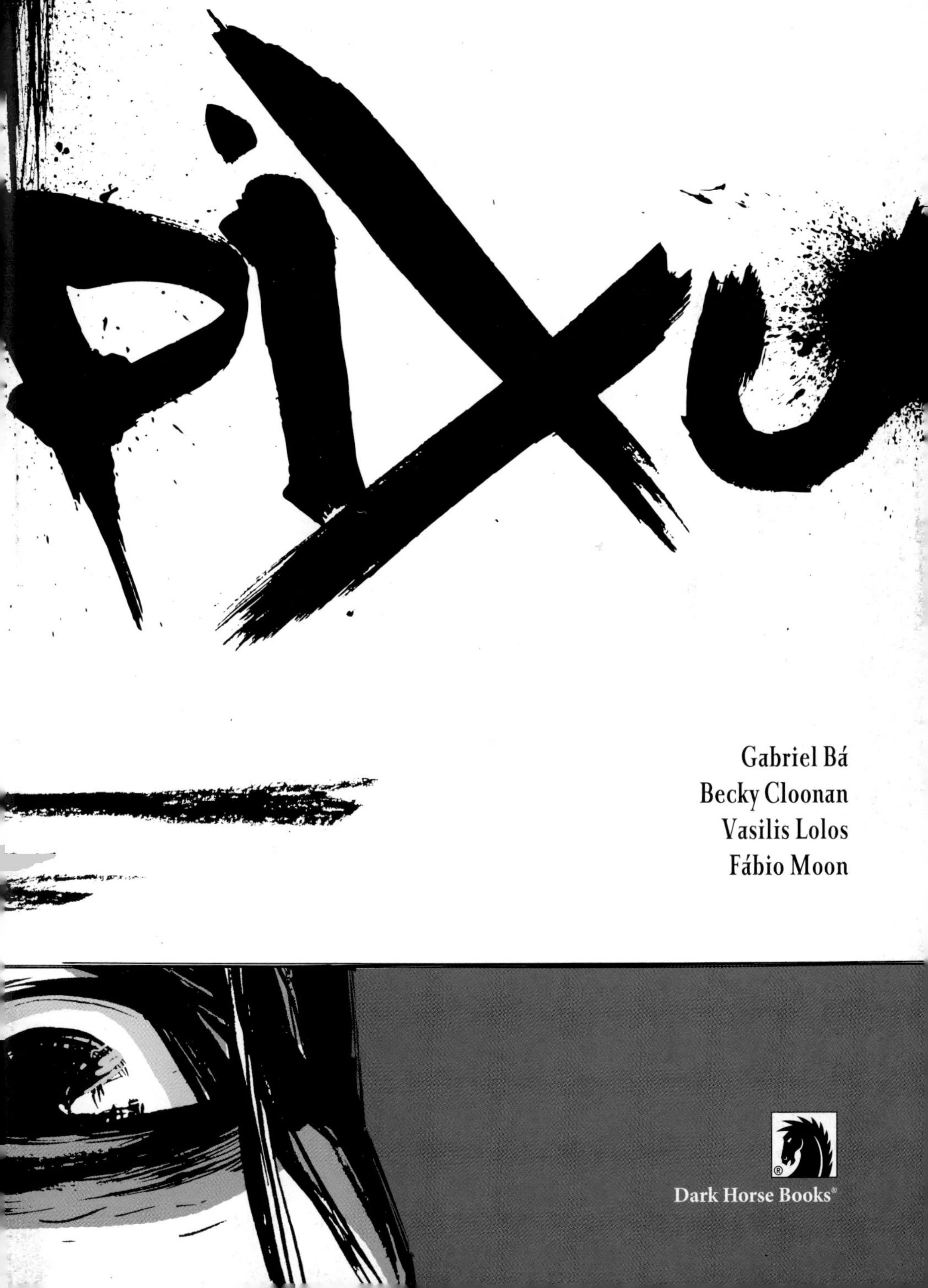

Dark Horse Books®

President & Publisher
Mike Richardson

Editor
Sierra Hahn

Collection Designer
Scott Cook

Special thanks to Scott Allie.

PIXU: The Mark of Evil

Published by Dark Horse Books, a division of Dark Horse Comics, Inc. 10956 SE Main Street, Milwaukie, OR 97222

To find a comics shop in your area, call the Comic Shop Locator Service toll-free at (888) 266-4226.

First edition: July 2009
ISBN 978-1-59582-340-3

10 9 8 7 6 5 4 3 2
Printed in China

NEIL HANKERSON *executive vice president* TOM WEDDLE *chief financial officer* RANDY STRADLEY *vice president of publishing* MICHAEL MAR TENS *vice president of business development* ANITA NELSON *vice president of marketing, sales, and licensing* DAVID SCROGGY *vice president of product development* DALE LAFOUNTAIN *vice president of information technology* DARLENE VOGEL *director of purchasing* KEN LIZZI *general counsel* DAVEY ESTRADA *editorial director* SCOTT ALLIE *senior managing editor* CHRIS WARNER *senior books editor, Dark Horse Books* DIANA SCHUTZ *executive editor* CARY GRAZZINI *director of design and production* LIA RIBACCHI *art director* CARA NIECE *director of scheduling*

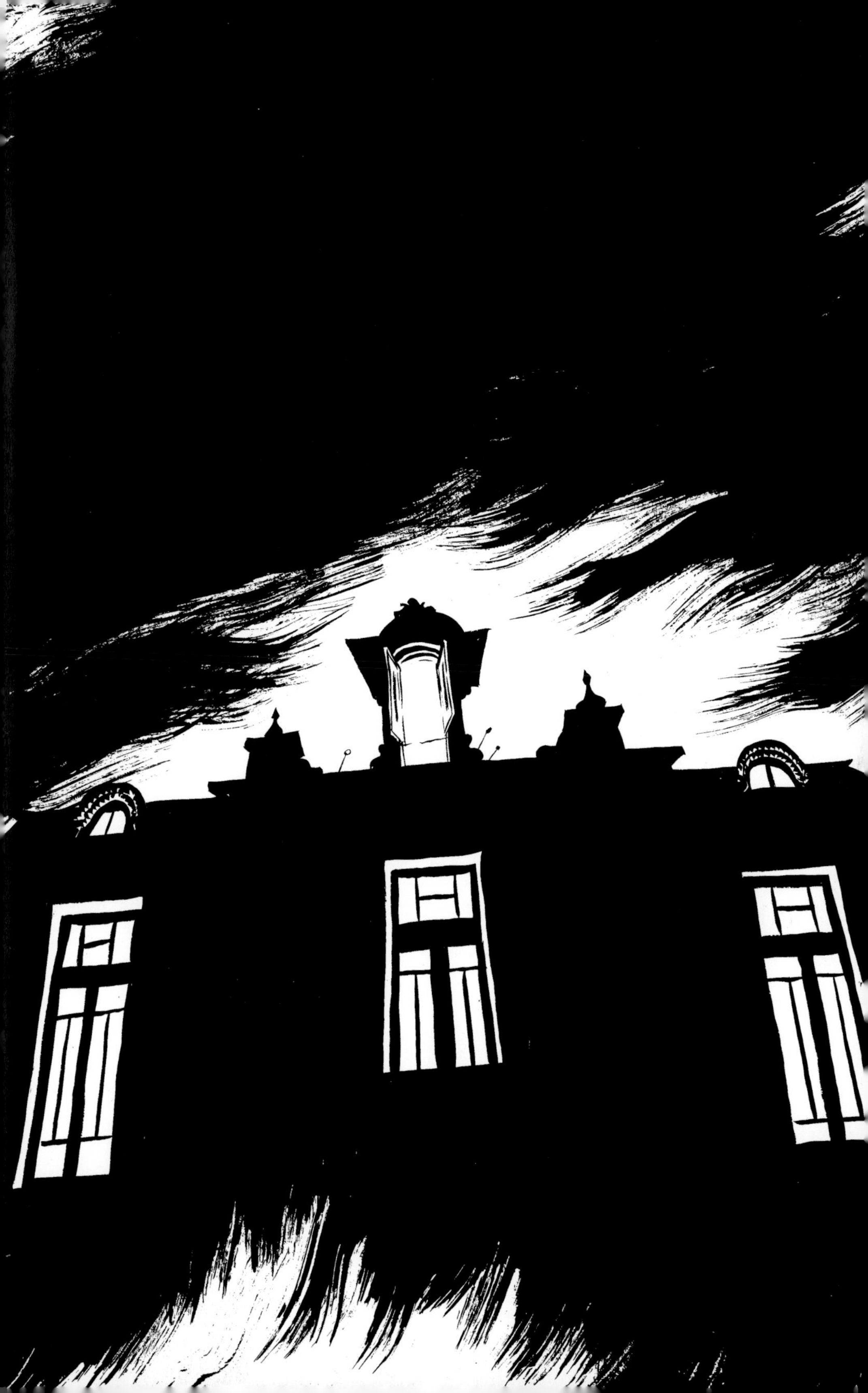

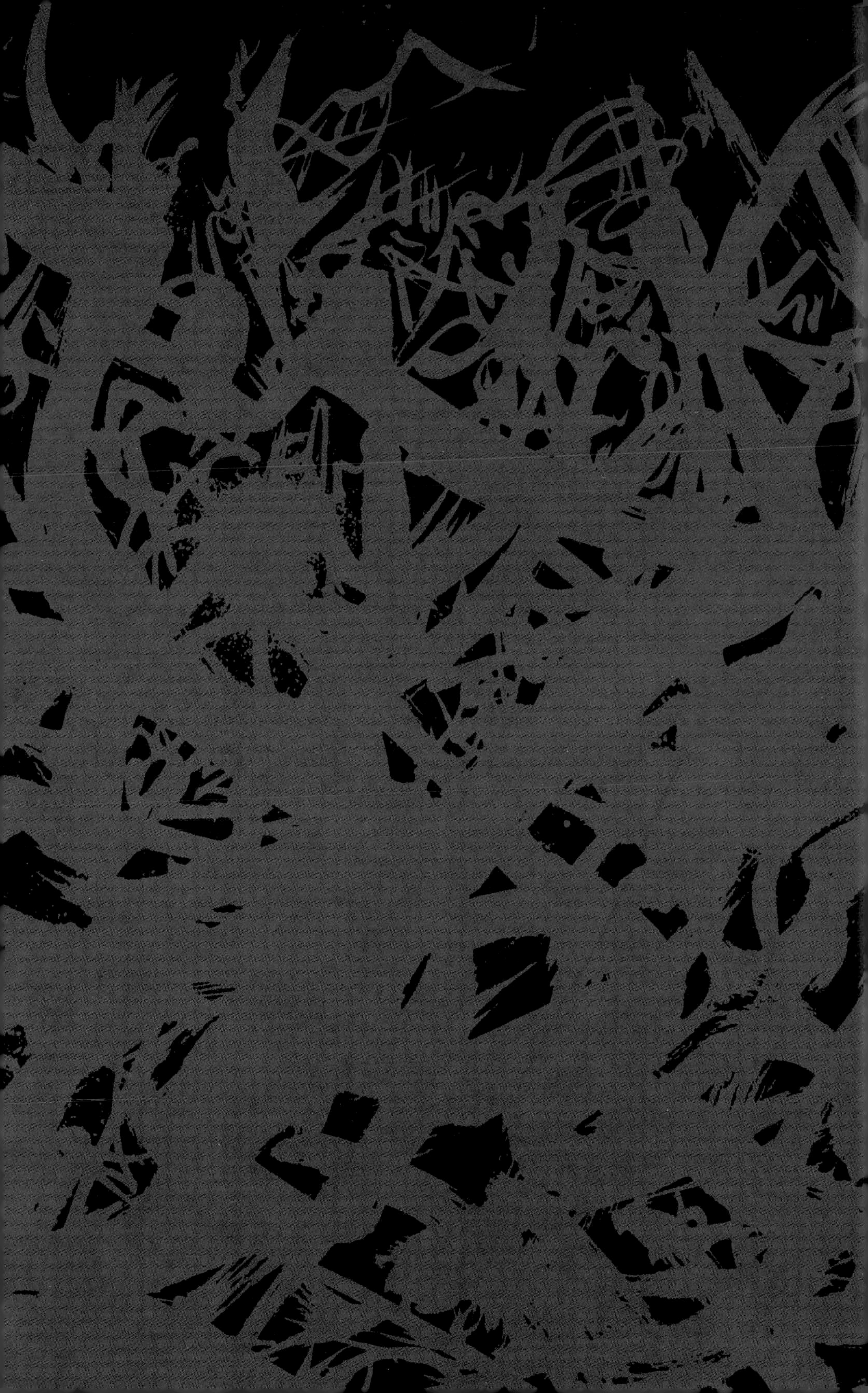

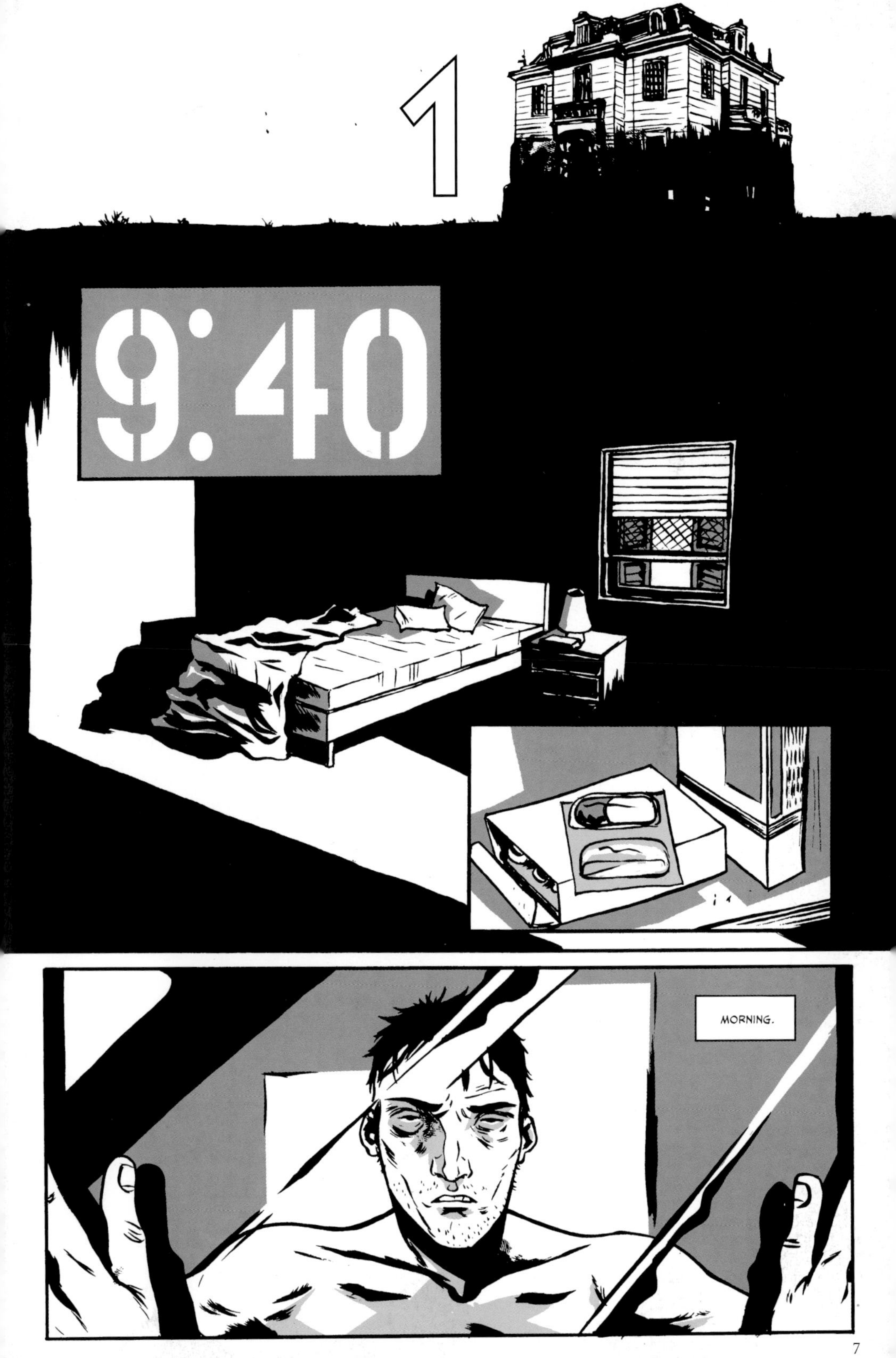
1
9:40
MORNING.

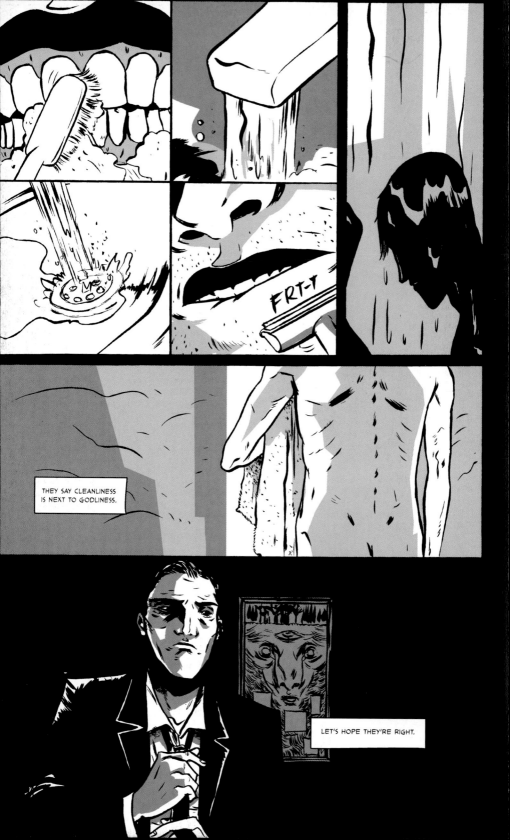

FRT-Y

THEY SAY CLEANLINESS IS NEXT TO GODLINESS.

LET'S HOPE THEY'RE RIGHT.

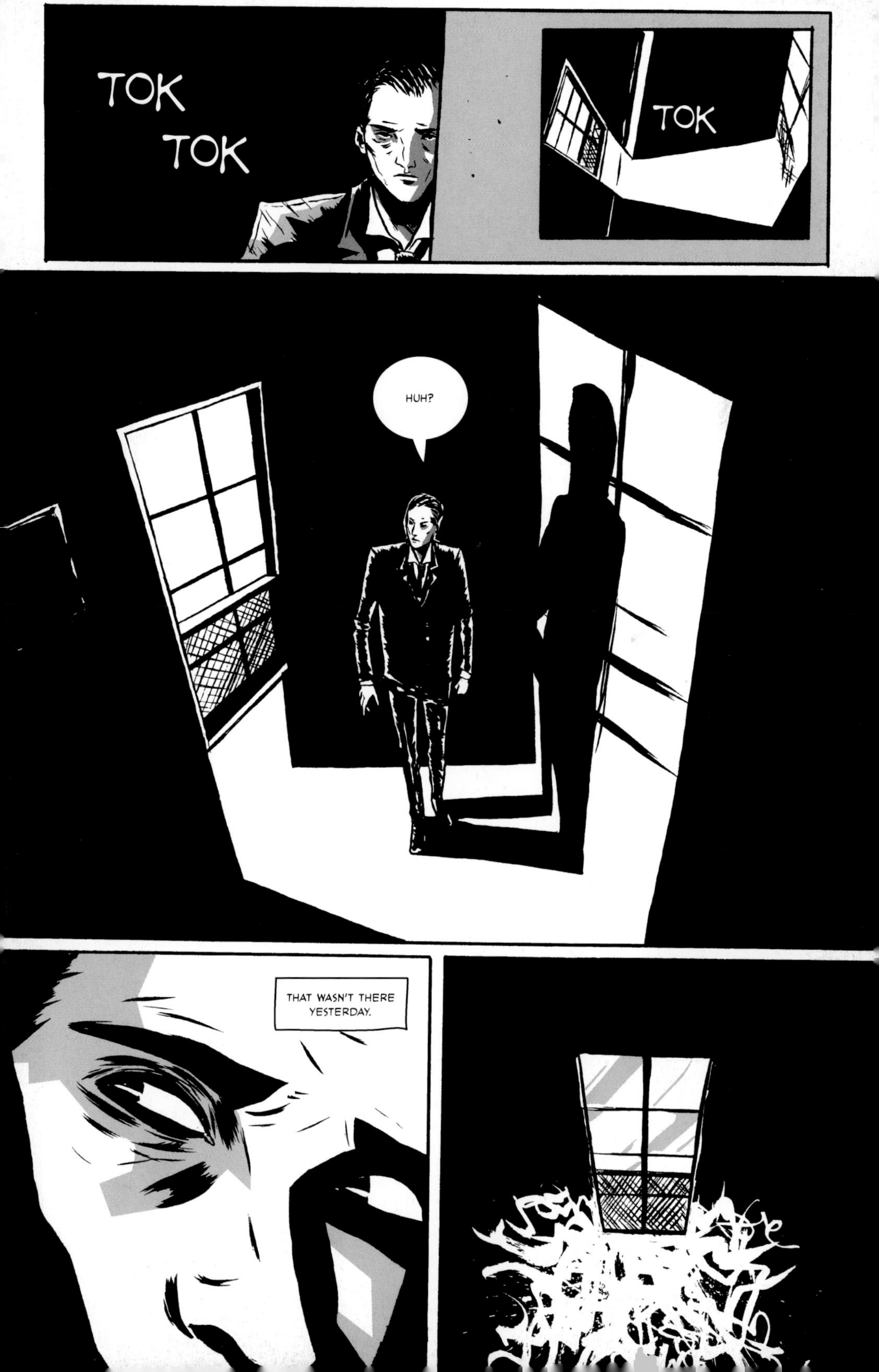
TOK
TOK
TOK
HUH?
THAT WASN'T THERE YESTERDAY.

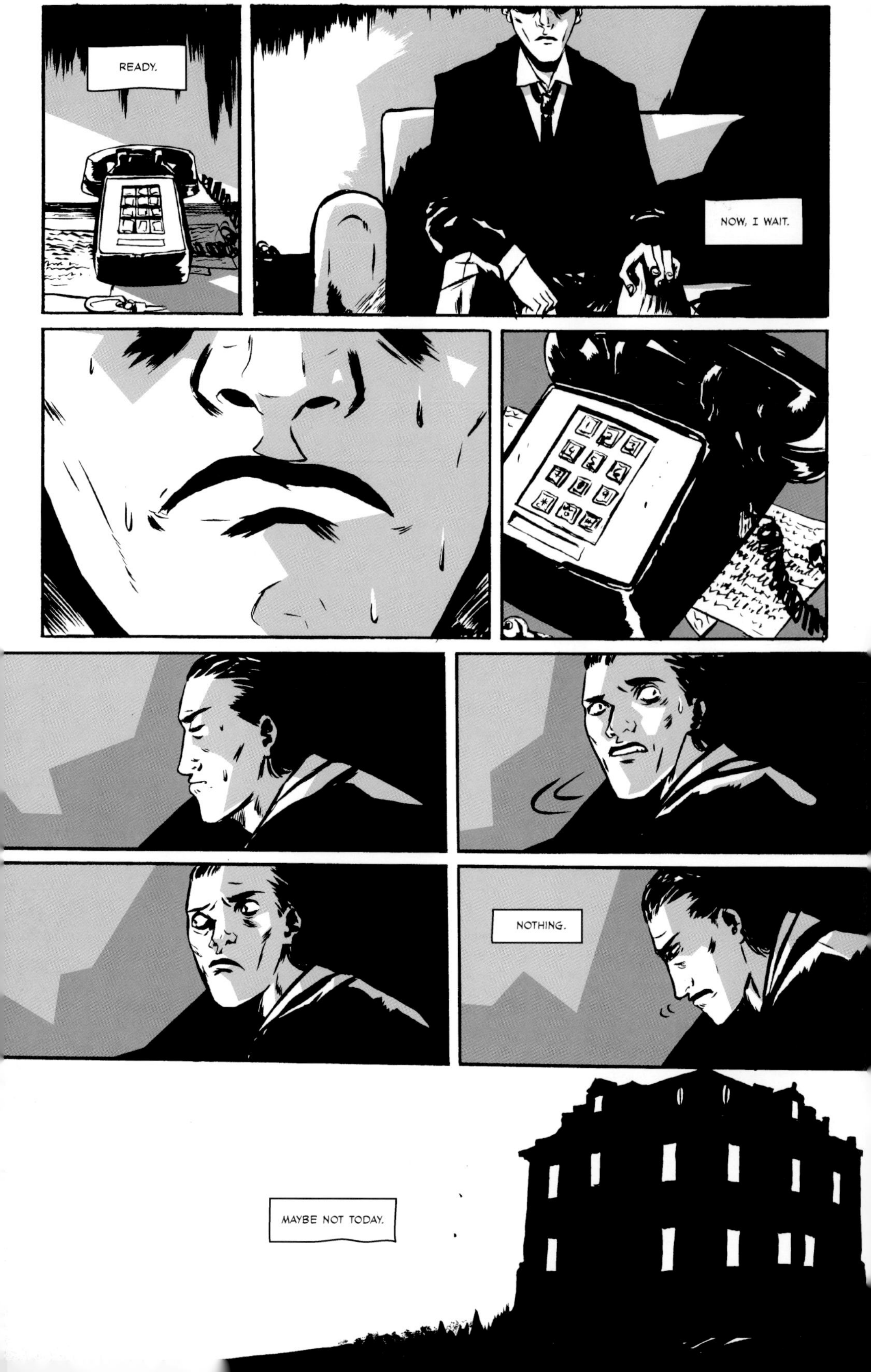
READY.
NOW, I WAIT.
NOTHING.
MAYBE NOT TODAY.

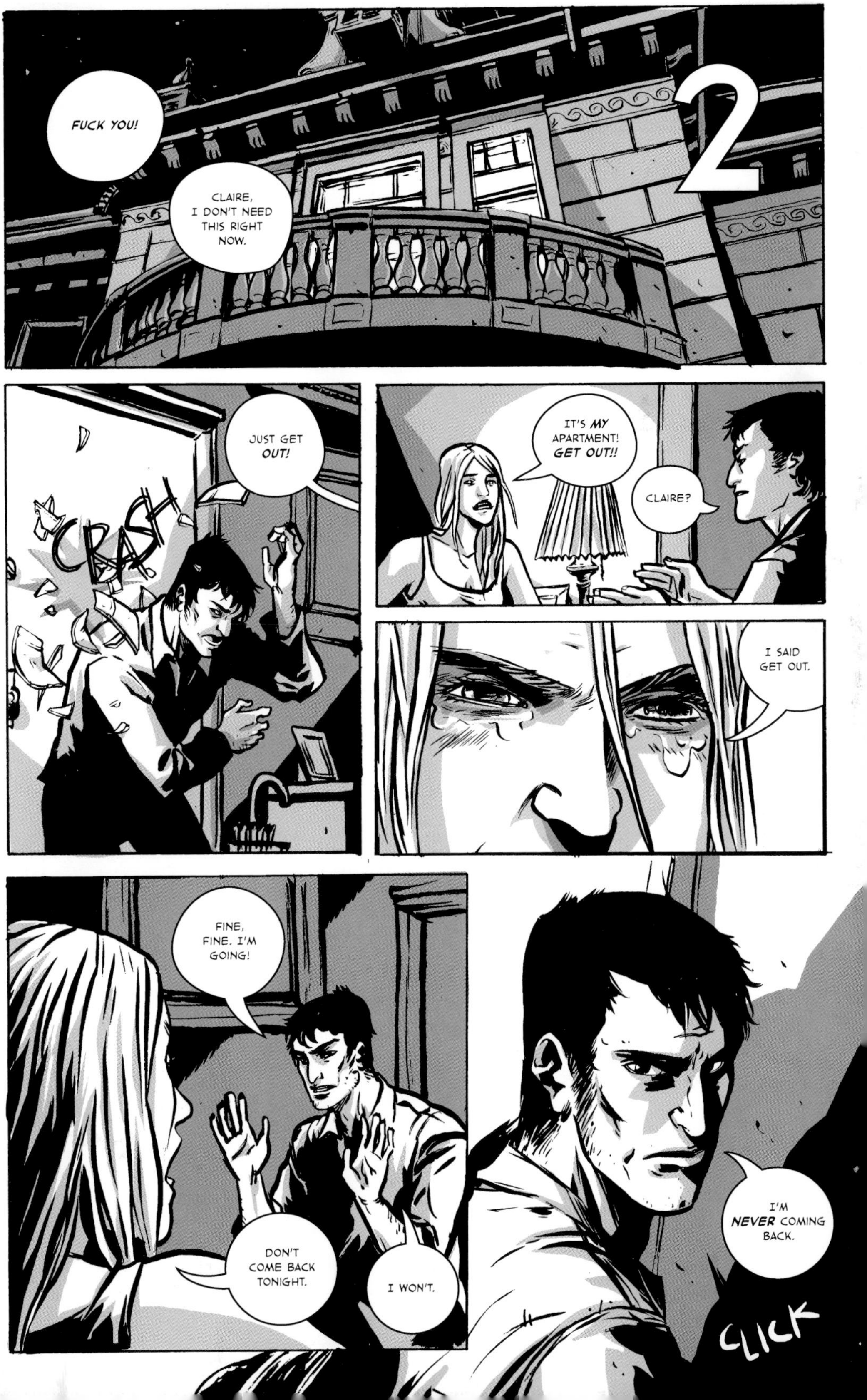
2
FUCK YOU!
CLAIRE, I DON'T NEED THIS RIGHT NOW.
JUST GET OUT!
CRASH
IT'S MY APARTMENT! GET OUT!!
CLAIRE?
I SAID GET OUT.
FINE, FINE. I'M GOING!
DON'T COME BACK TONIGHT.
I WON'T.
I'M NEVER COMING BACK.
CLICK

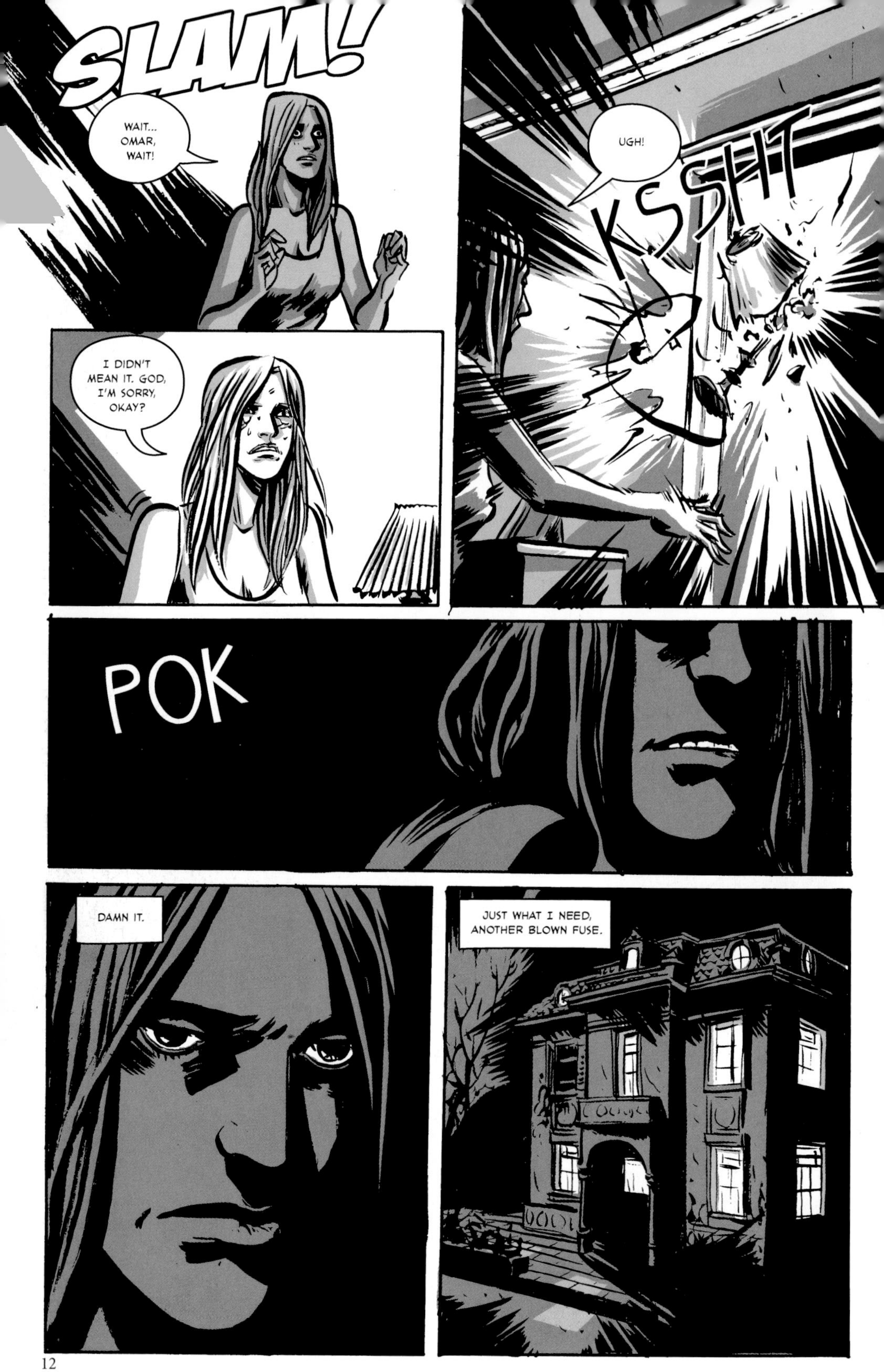
SLAM!
WAIT... OMAR, WAIT!
UGH!
KSSHT
I DIDN'T MEAN IT. GOD, I'M SORRY, OKAY?
POK
DAMN IT.
JUST WHAT I NEED, ANOTHER BLOWN FUSE.

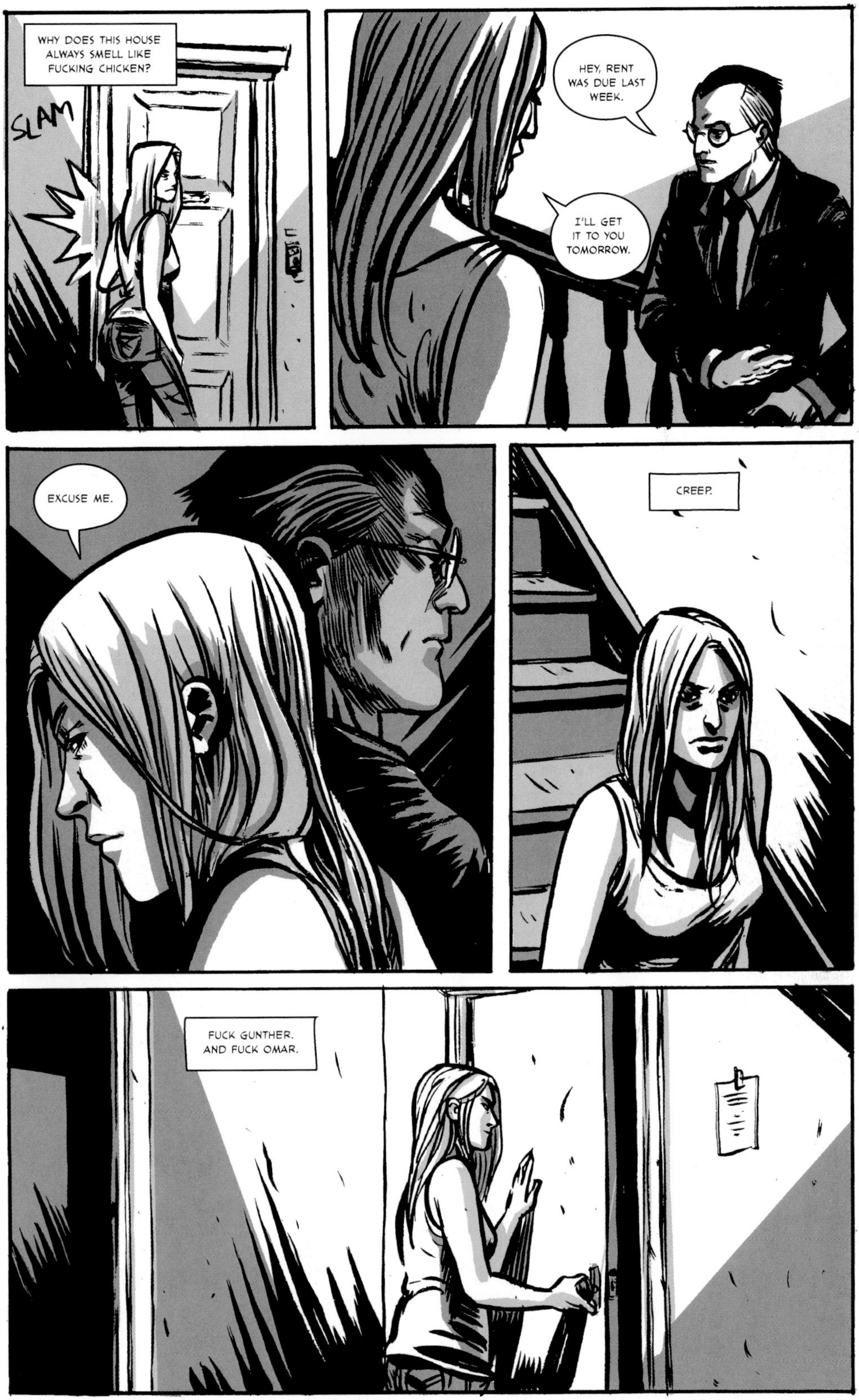
WHY DOES THIS HOUSE ALWAYS SMELL LIKE FUCKING CHICKEN?
SLAM
HEY, RENT WAS DUE LAST WEEK.
I'LL GET IT TO YOU TOMORROW.
EXCUSE ME.
CREEP.
FUCK GUNTHER. AND FUCK OMAR.

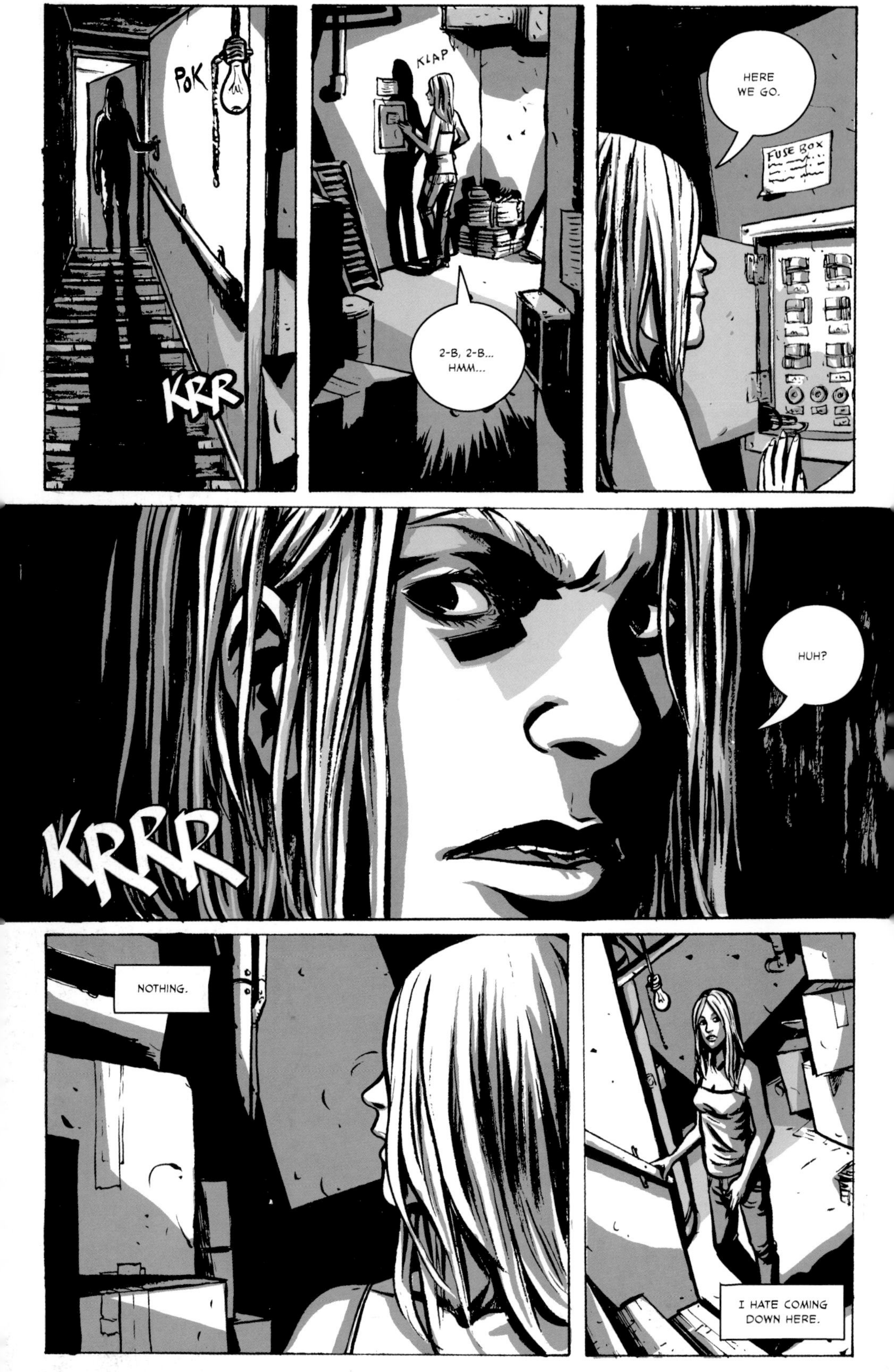
POK
KRR
KLAP
2-B, 2-B... HMM...
HERE WE GO.
FUSE BOX
HUH?
KRRR
NOTHING.
I HATE COMING DOWN HERE.

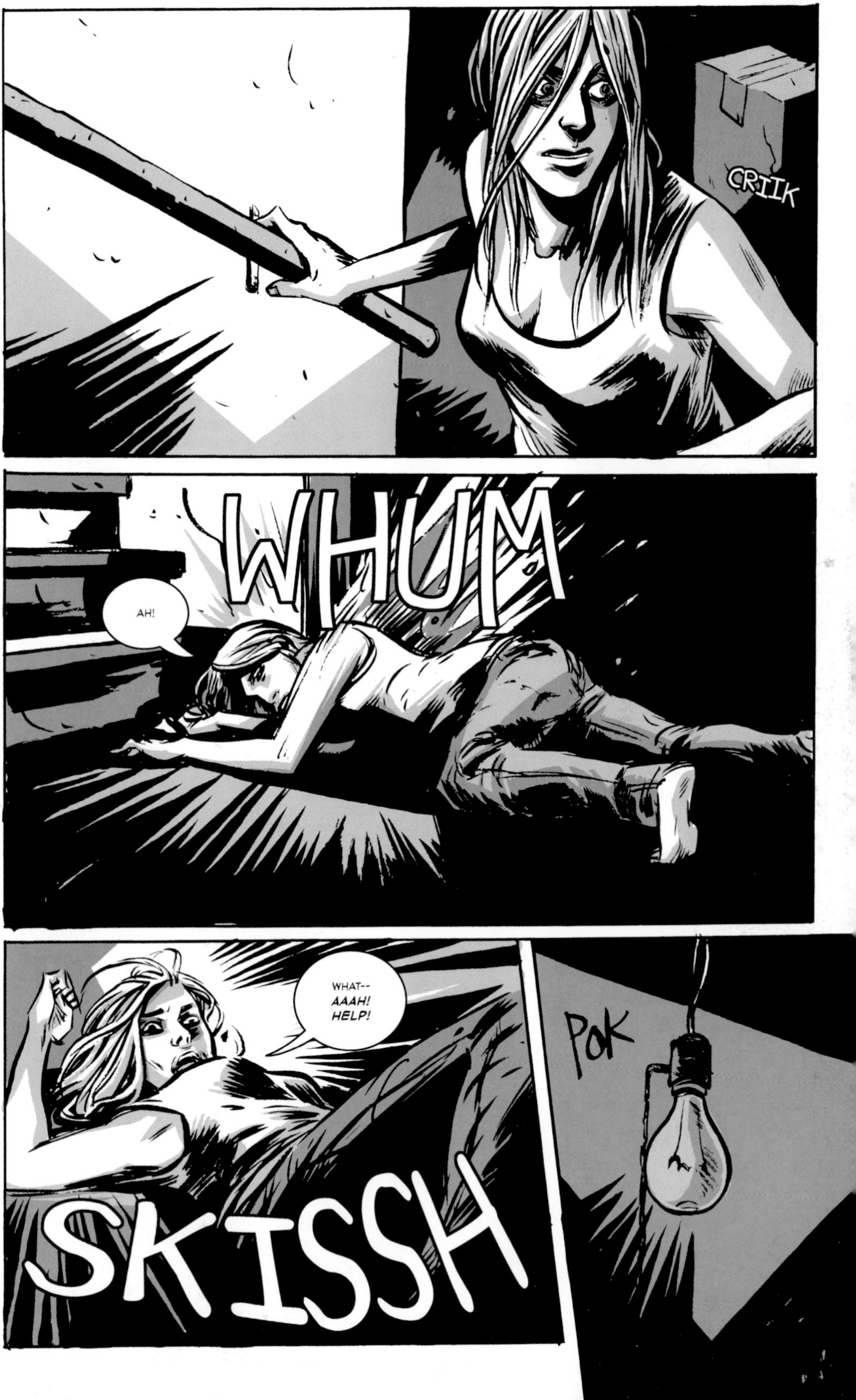
CRIK
WHUM
AH!
WHAT-- AAAH! HELP!
SKISSH
POK

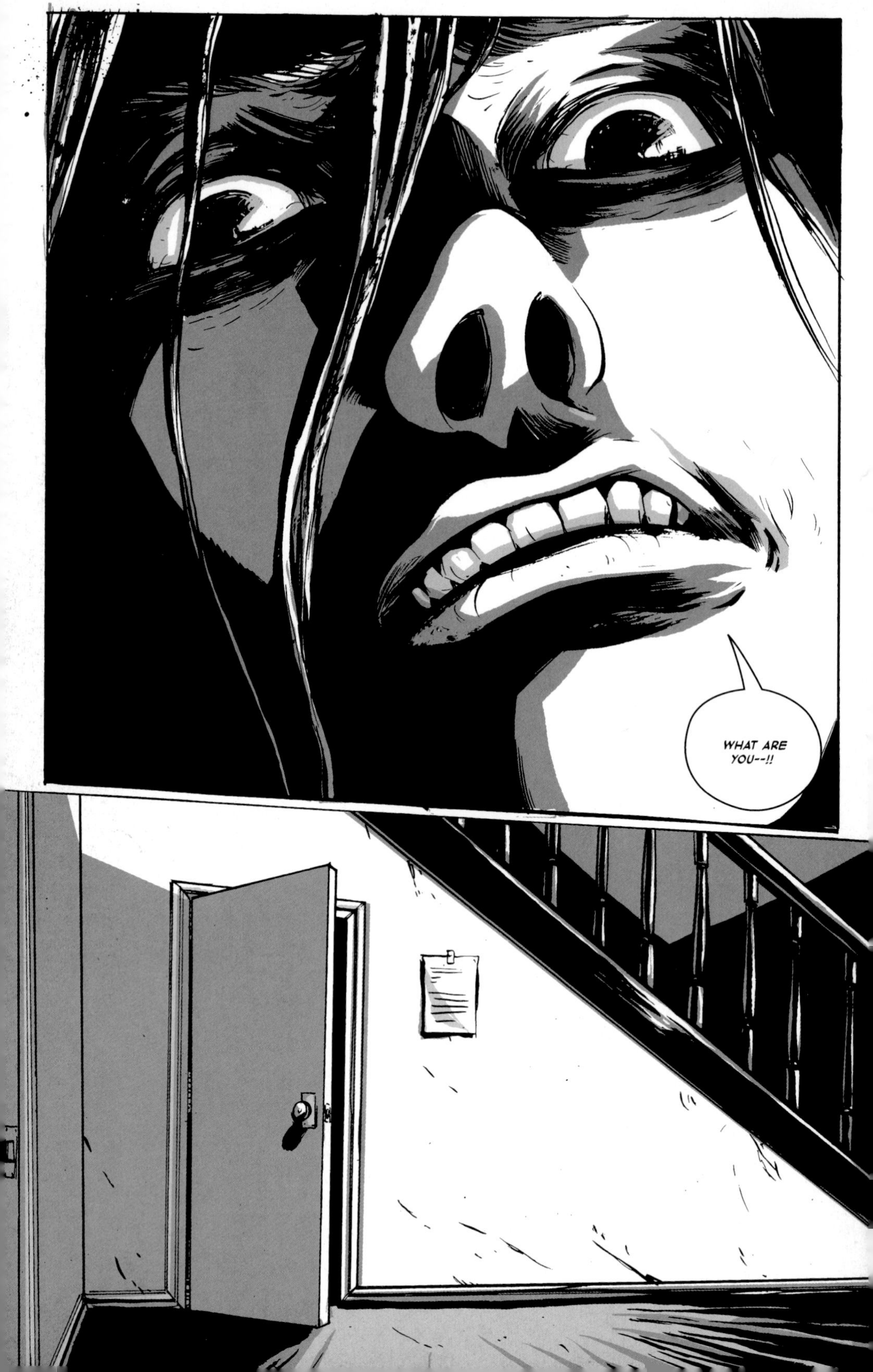
WHAT ARE YOU--!!

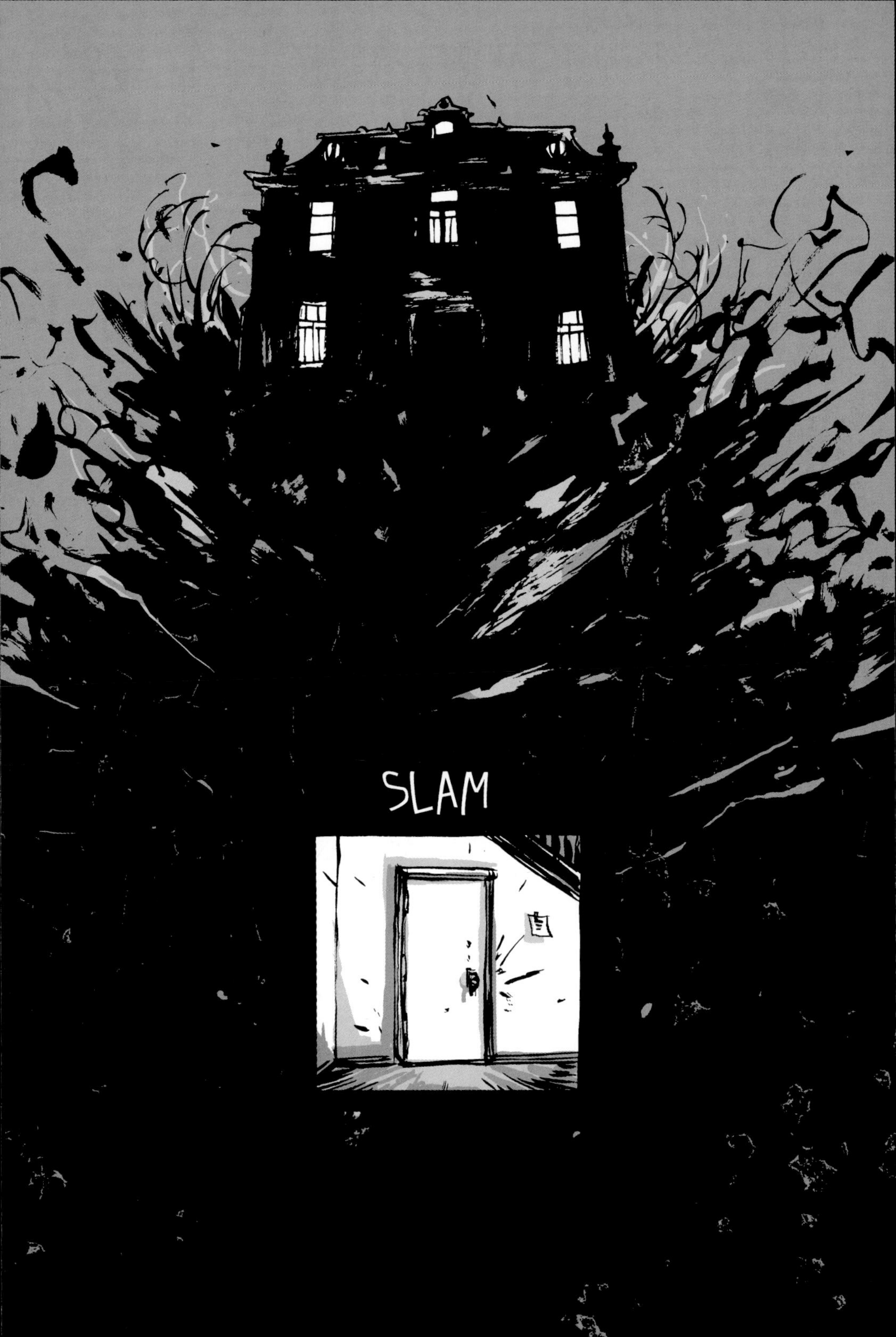
SLAM

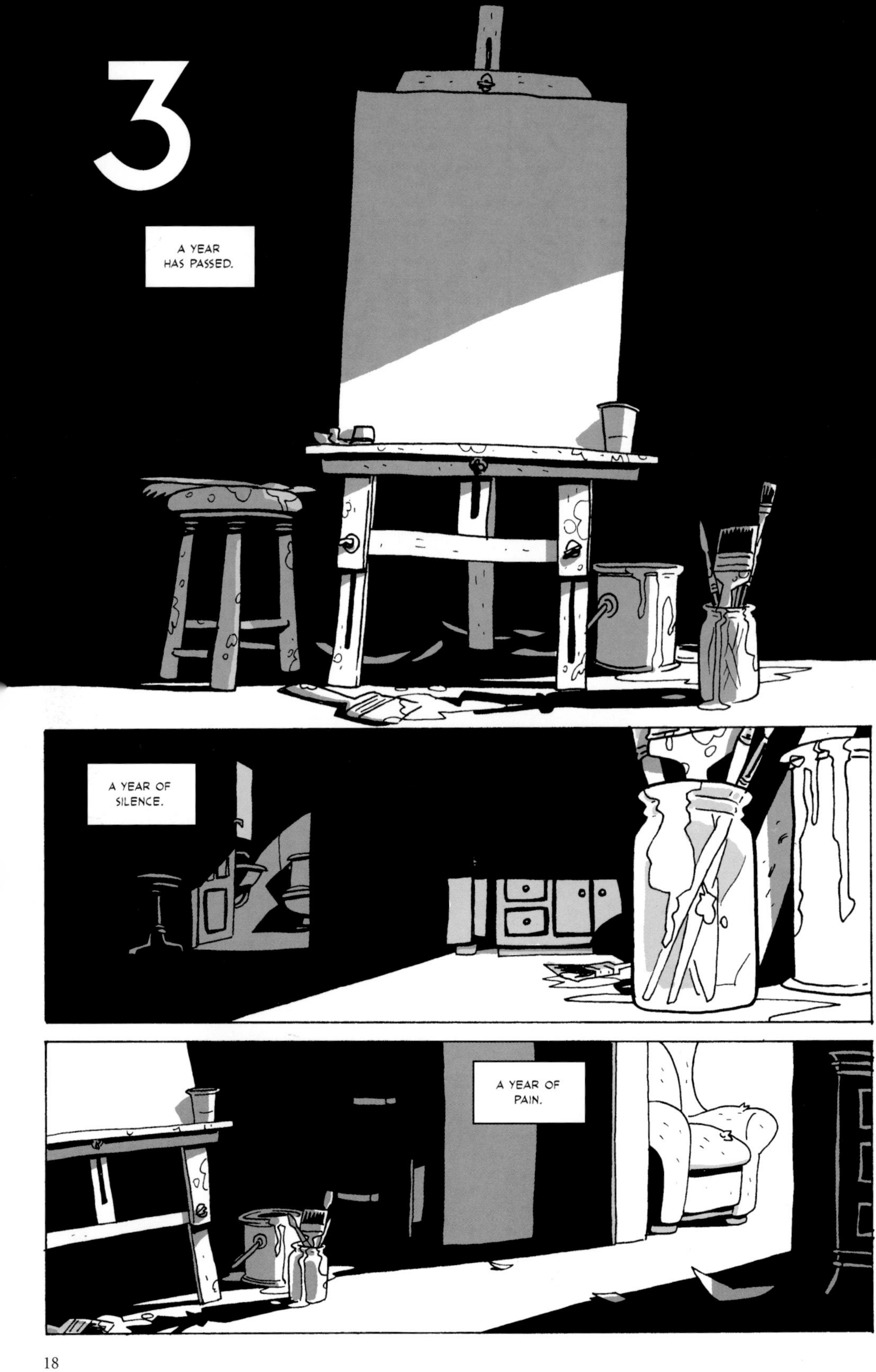
3
A YEAR HAS PASSED.
A YEAR OF SILENCE.
A YEAR OF PAIN.

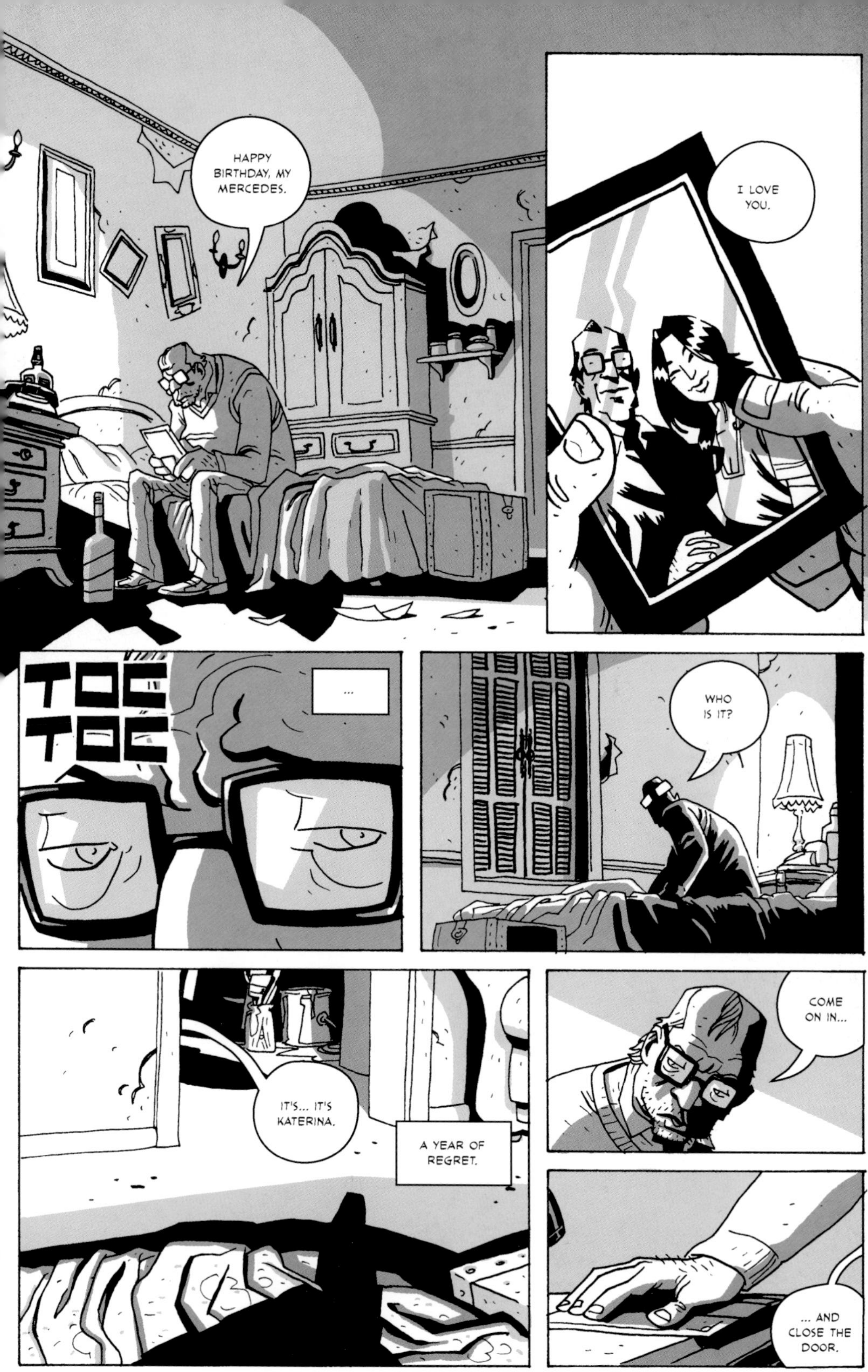
HAPPY BIRTHDAY, MY MERCEDES.
I LOVE YOU.
TOC TOC
...
WHO IS IT?
IT'S... IT'S KATERINA.
A YEAR OF REGRET.
COME ON IN...
... AND CLOSE THE DOOR.

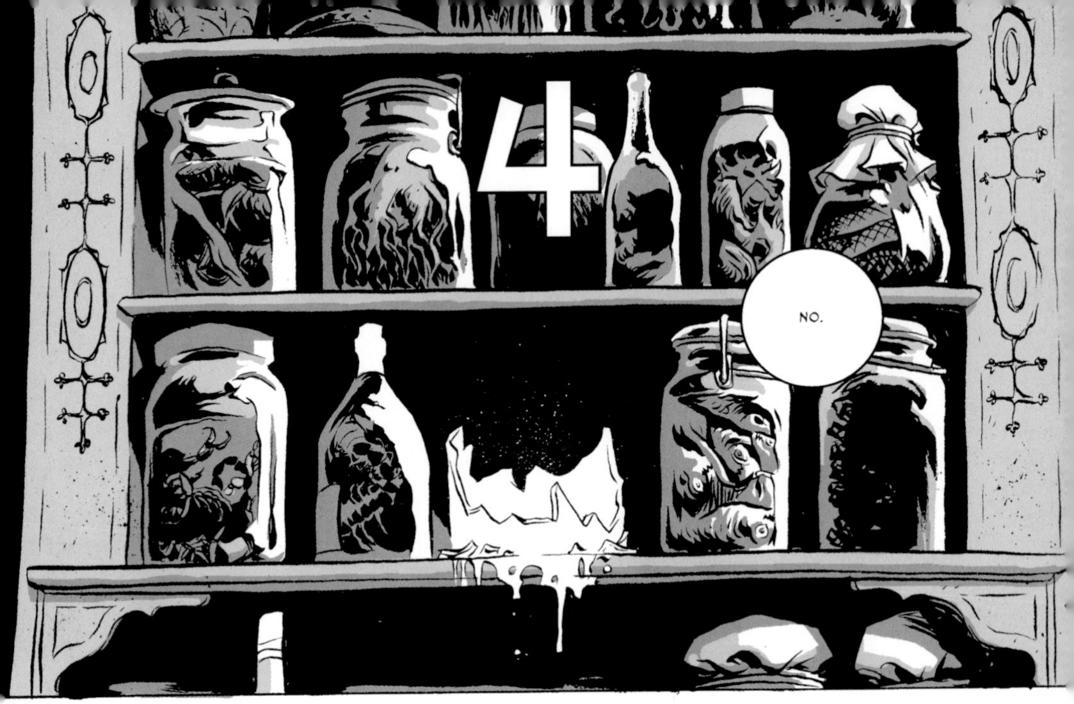
4
NO.

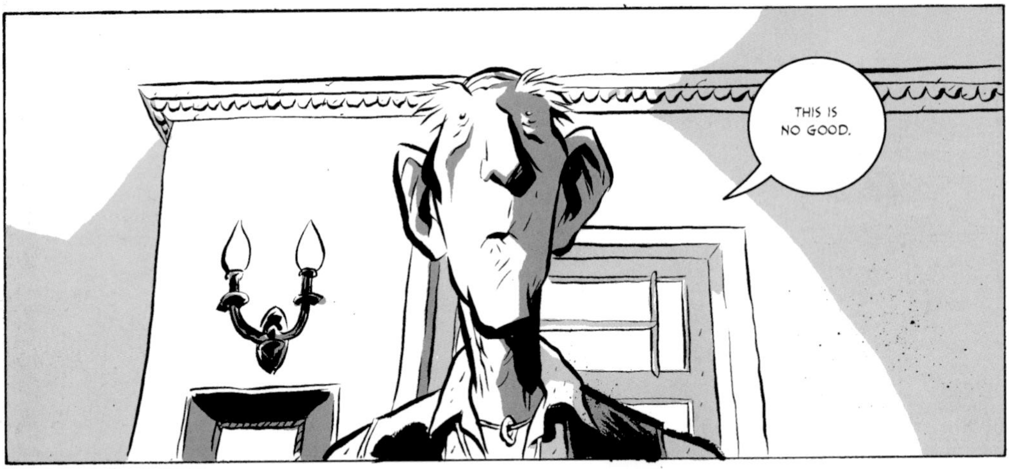
THIS IS NO GOOD.

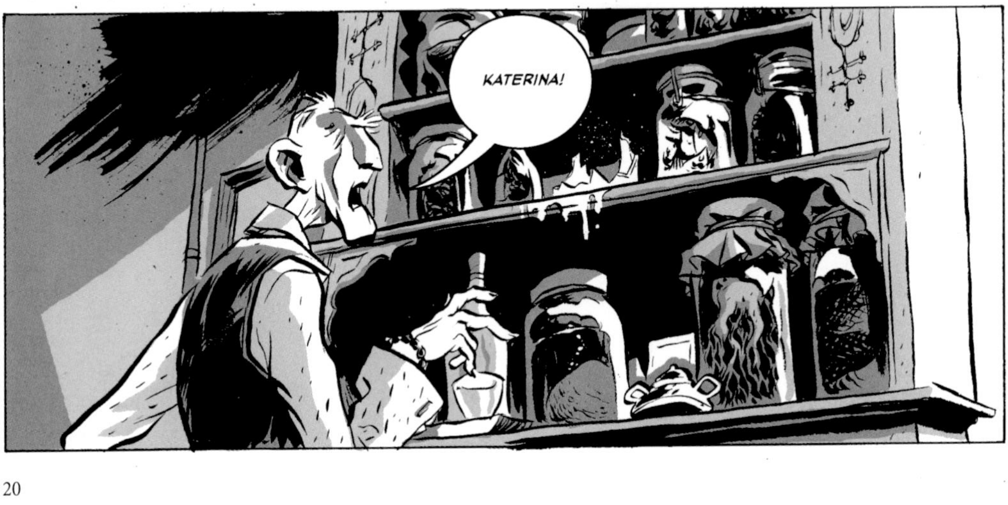
KATERINA!

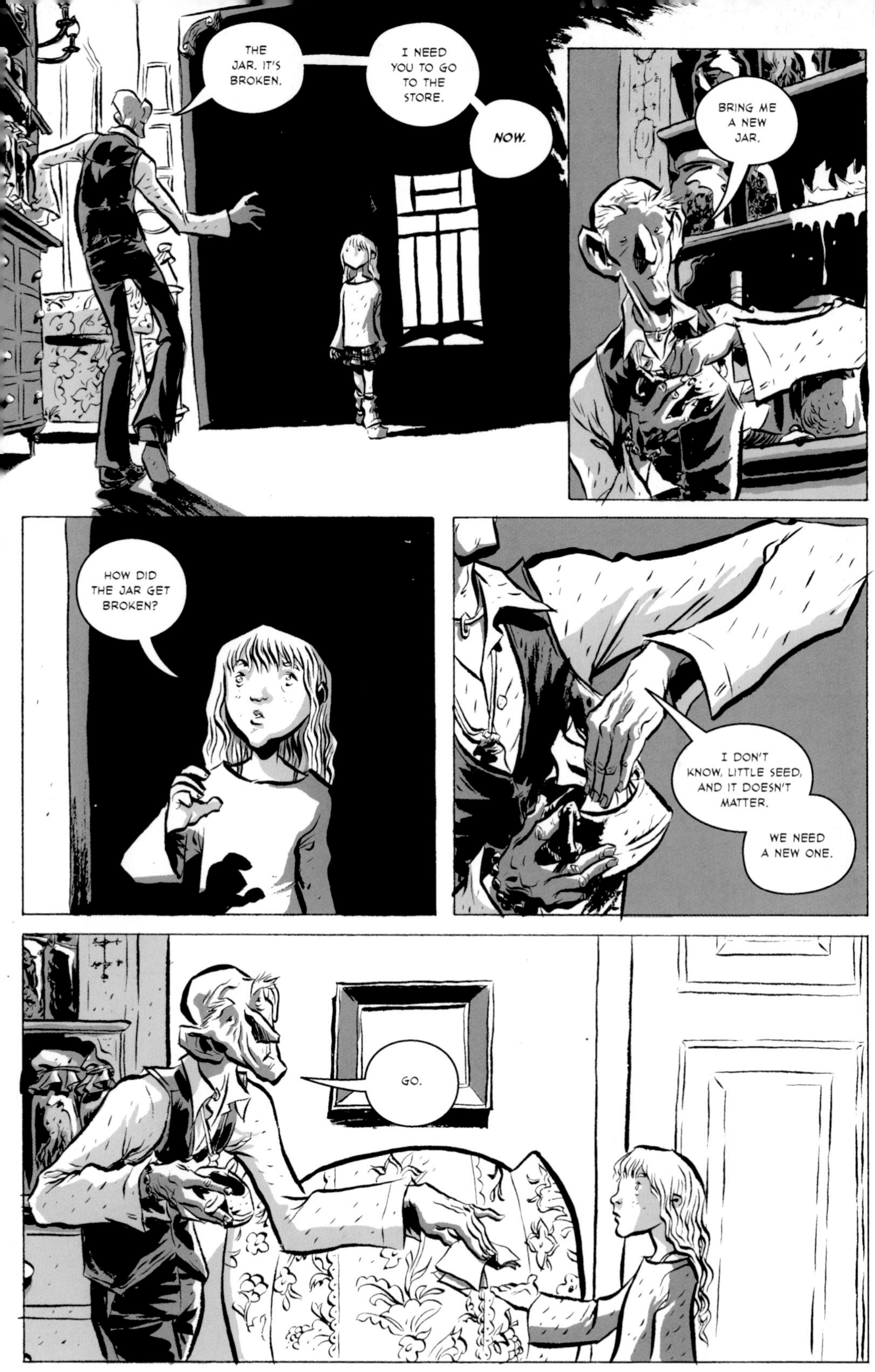
THE JAR. IT'S BROKEN.
I NEED YOU TO GO TO THE STORE.
NOW.
BRING ME A NEW JAR.
HOW DID THE JAR GET BROKEN?
I DON'T KNOW, LITTLE SEED, AND IT DOESN'T MATTER.
WE NEED A NEW ONE.
GO.

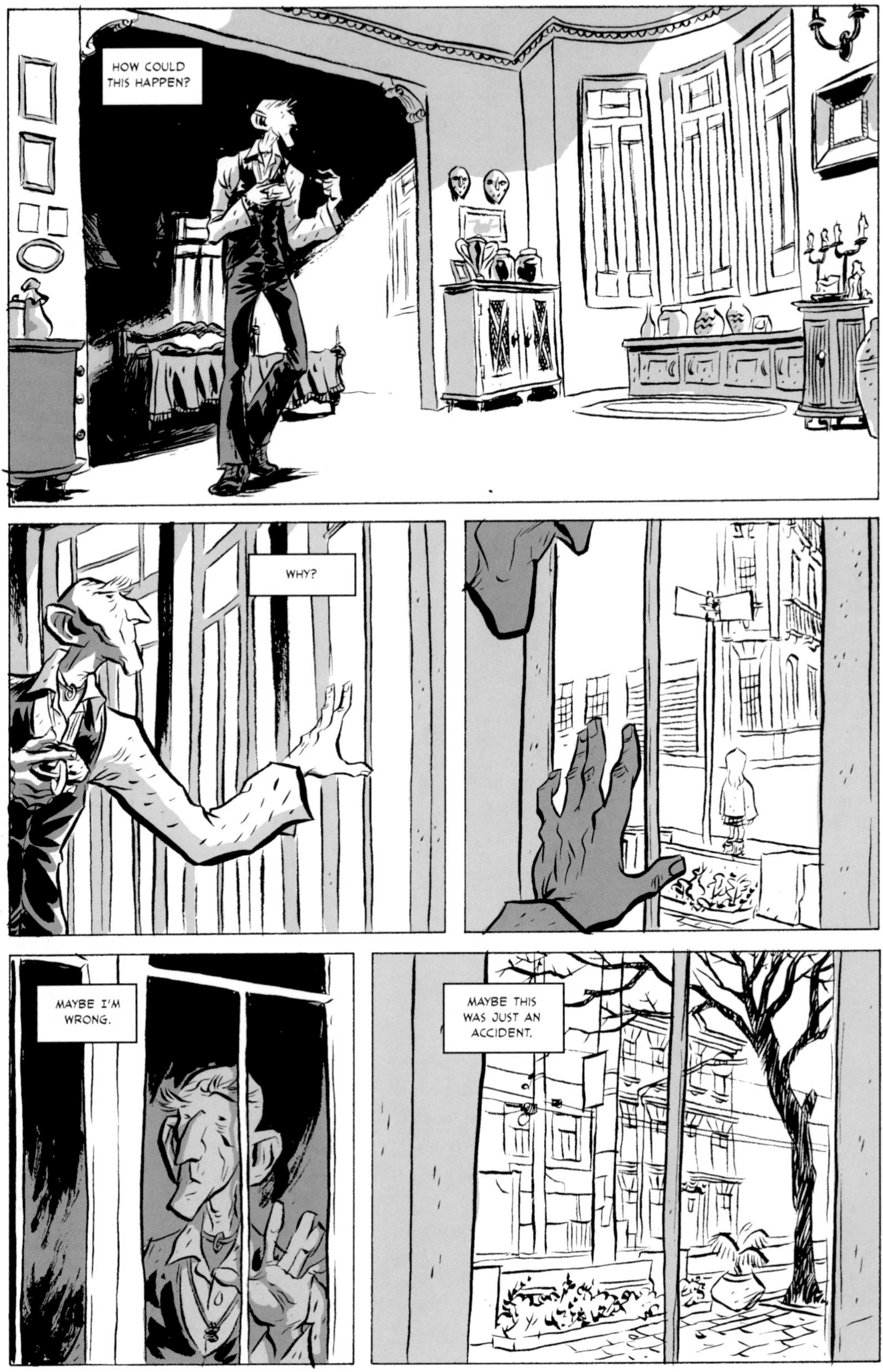
HOW COULD THIS HAPPEN?
WHY?
MAYBE I'M WRONG.
MAYBE THIS WAS JUST AN ACCIDENT.

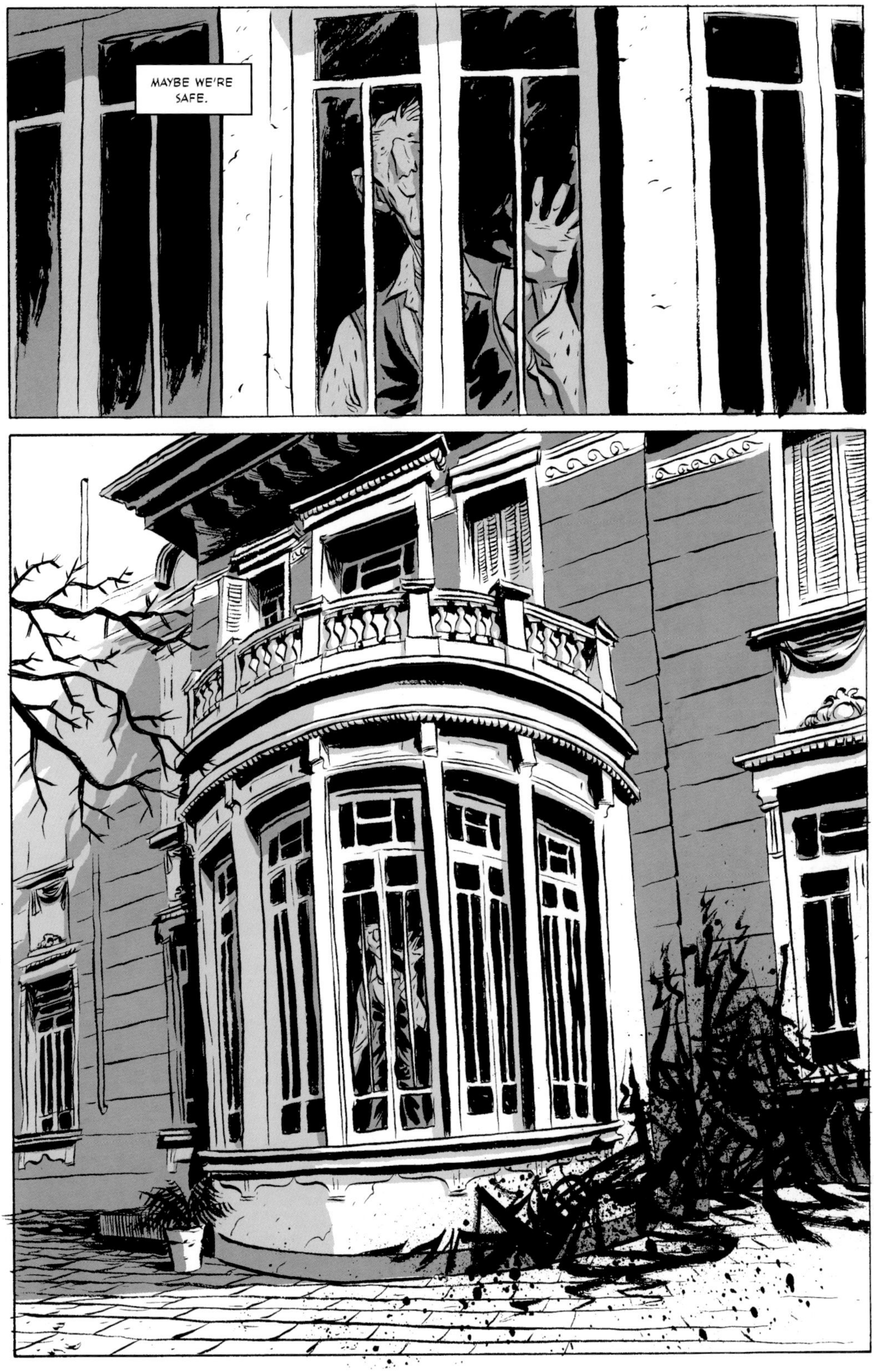
MAYBE WE'RE SAFE.

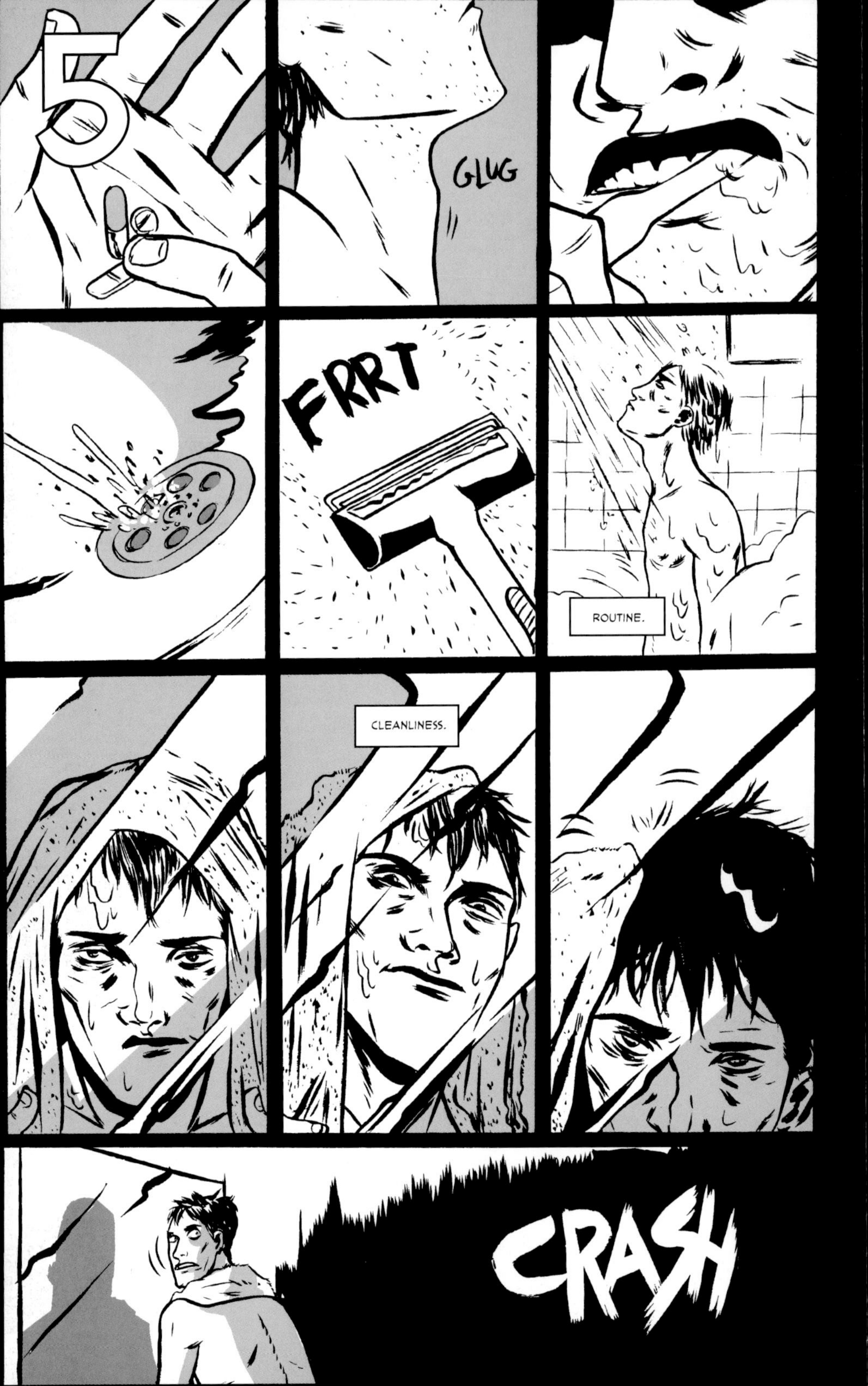
5
GLUG
FRRT
ROUTINE.
CLEANLINESS.
CRASH

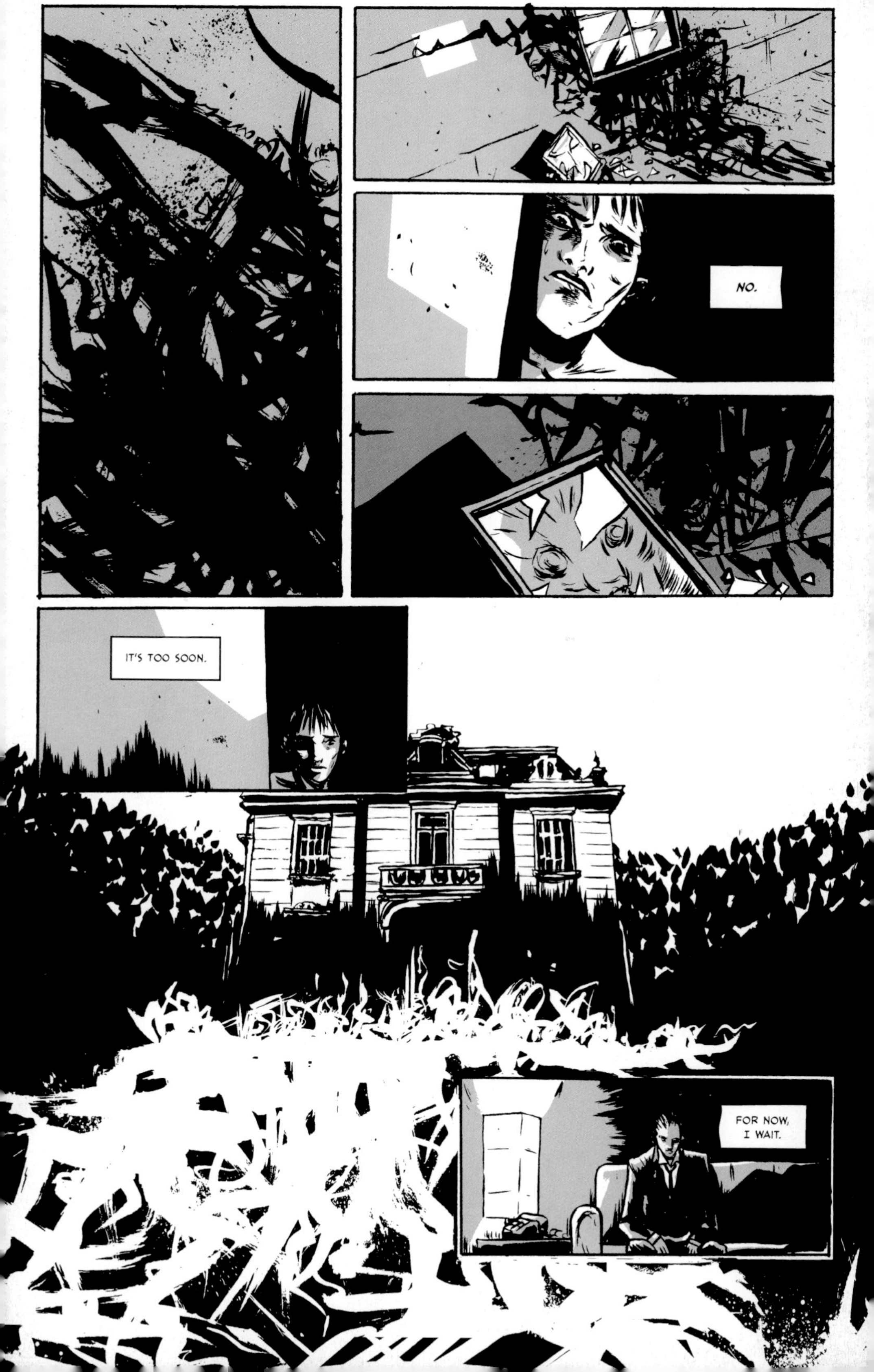
NO.
IT'S TOO SOON.
FOR NOW, I WAIT.

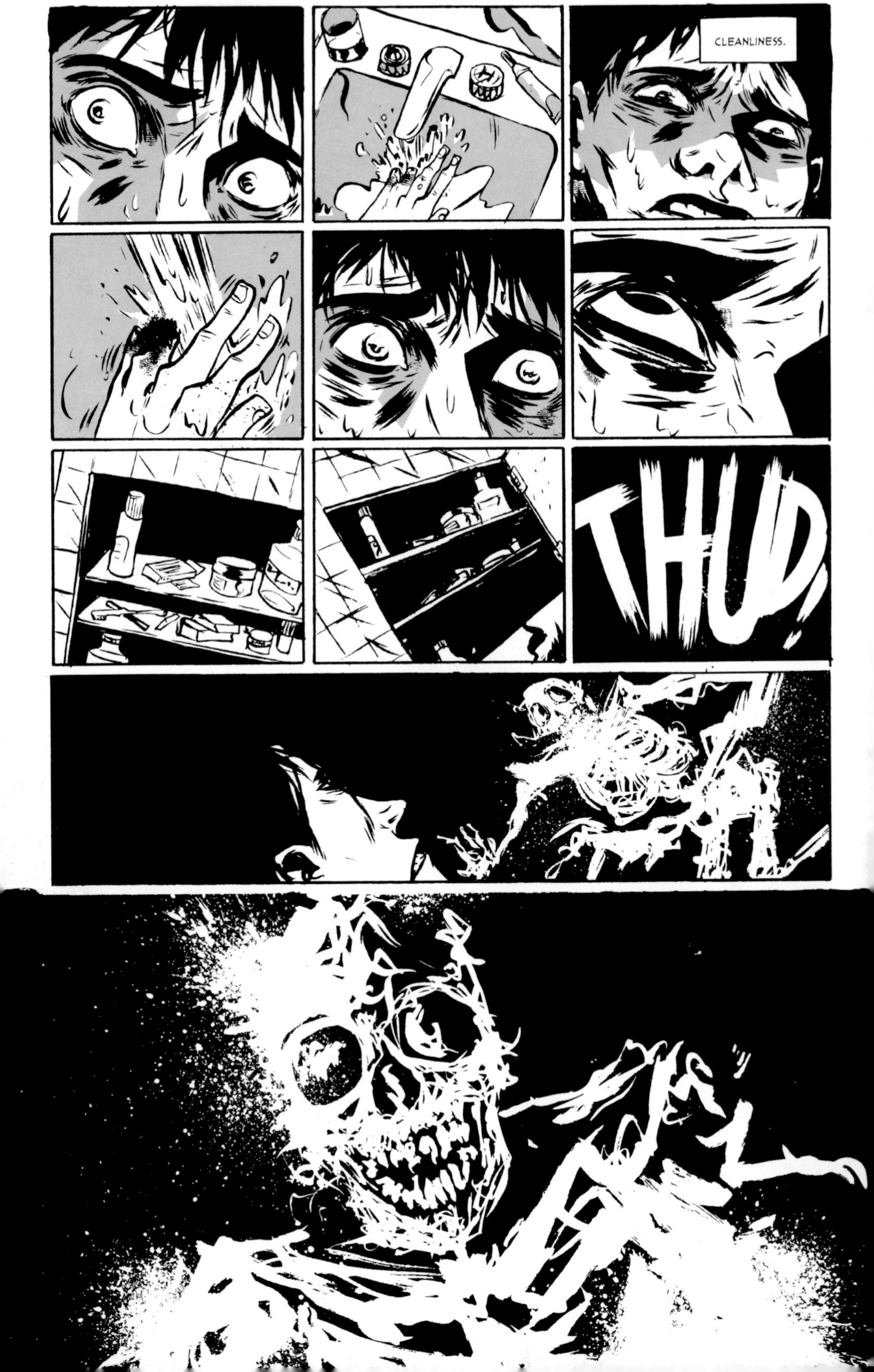
CLEANLINESS.
THUD.

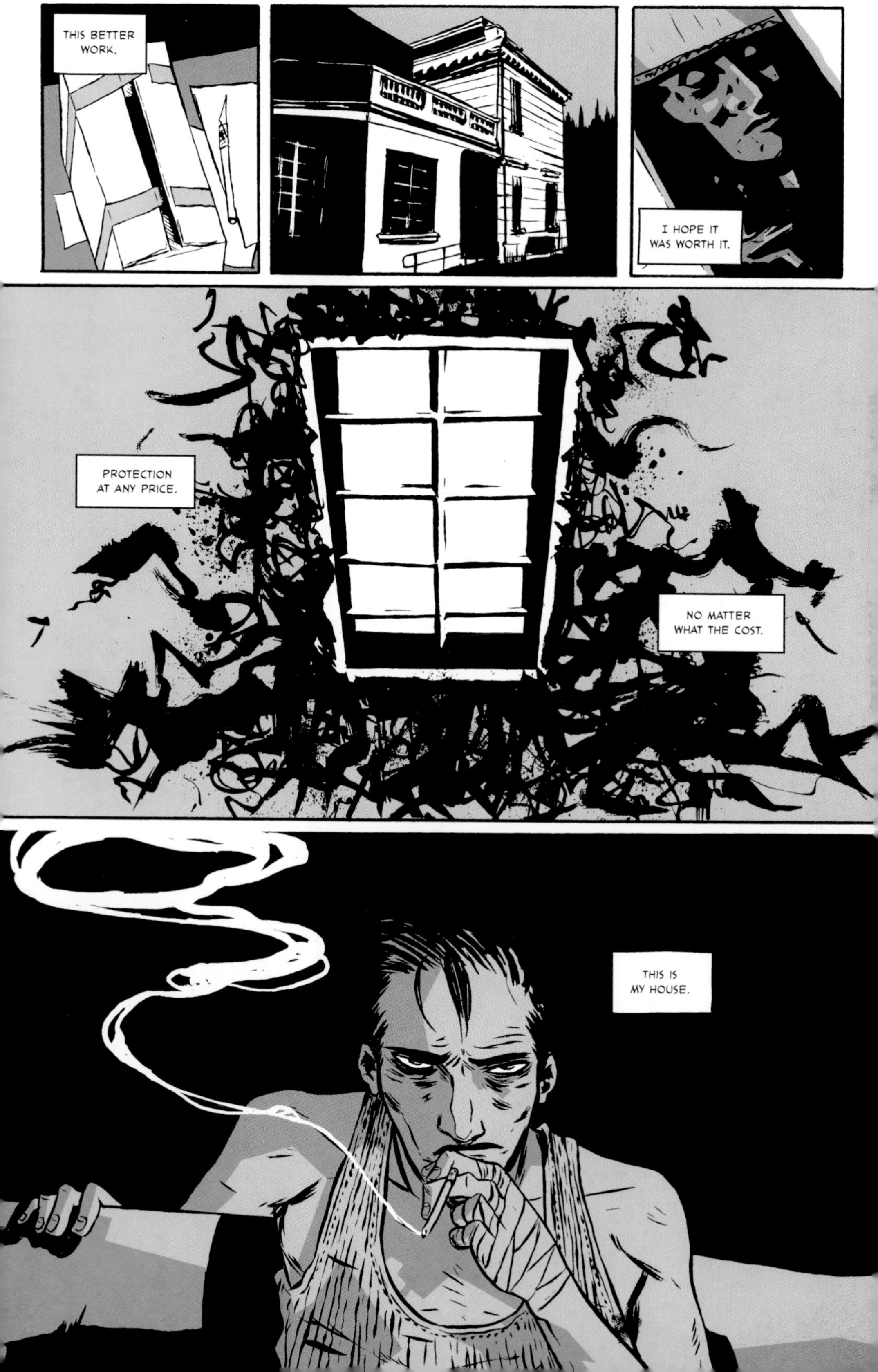
THIS BETTER WORK.
I HOPE IT WAS WORTH IT.
PROTECTION AT ANY PRICE.
NO MATTER WHAT THE COST.
THIS IS MY HOUSE.

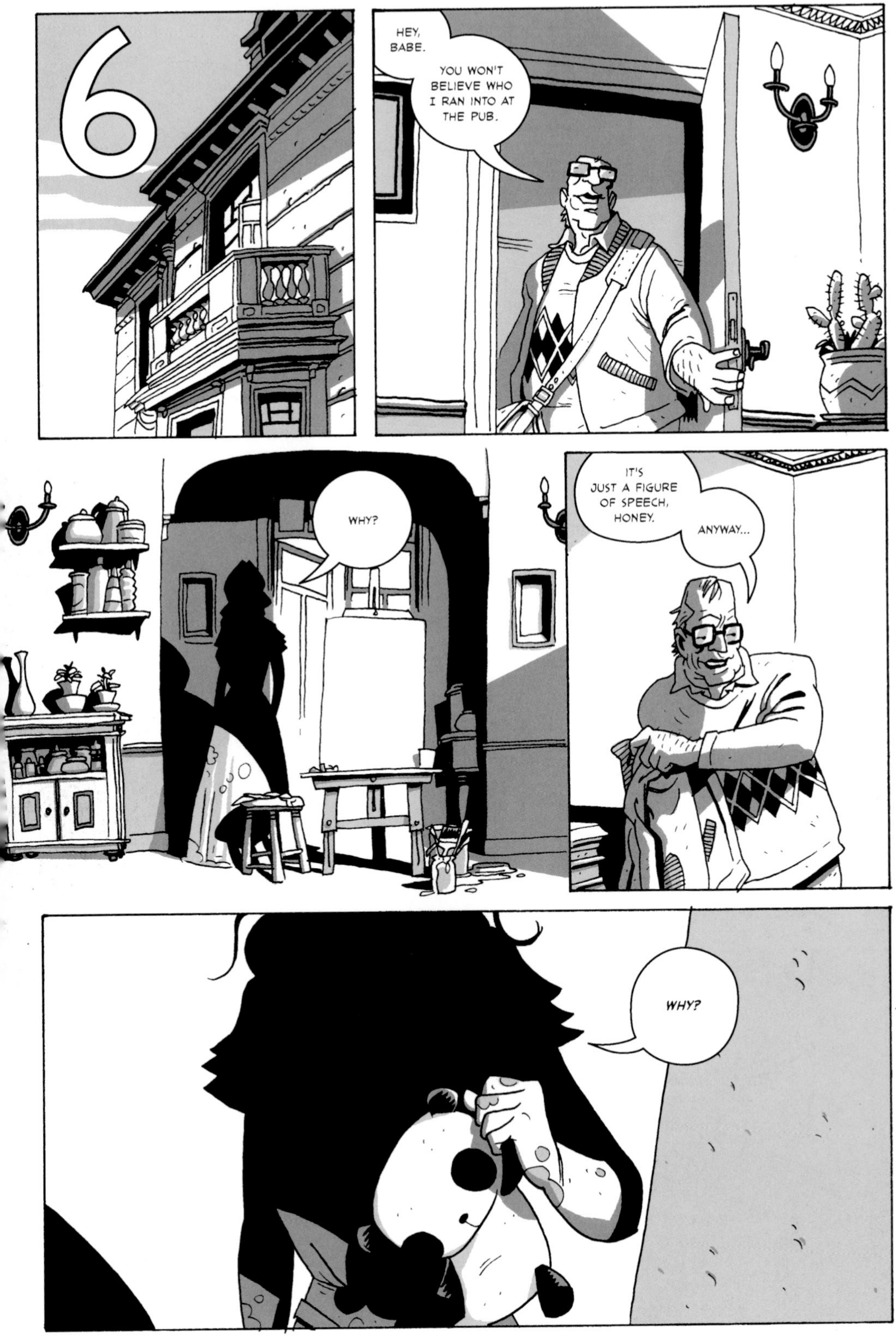
6
HEY, BABE.
YOU WON'T BELIEVE WHO I RAN INTO AT THE PUB.
WHY?
IT'S JUST A FIGURE OF SPEECH, HONEY.
ANYWAY...
WHY?

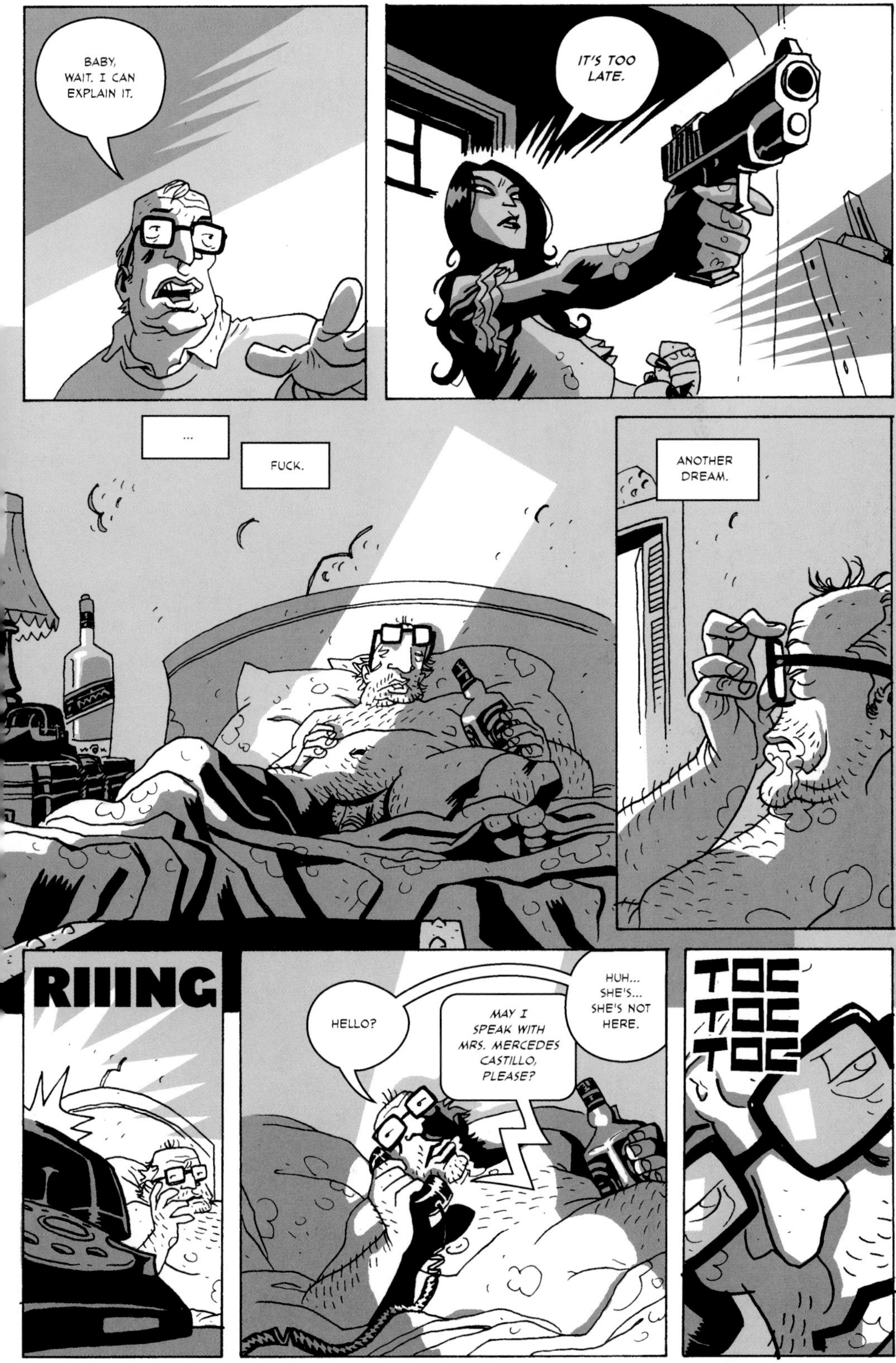
BABY, WAIT. I CAN EXPLAIN IT.
IT'S TOO LATE.
...
FUCK.
ANOTHER DREAM.
RIIING
HELLO?
MAY I SPEAK WITH MRS. MERCEDES CASTILLO, PLEASE?
HUH... SHE'S... SHE'S NOT HERE.
TOC TOC TOC

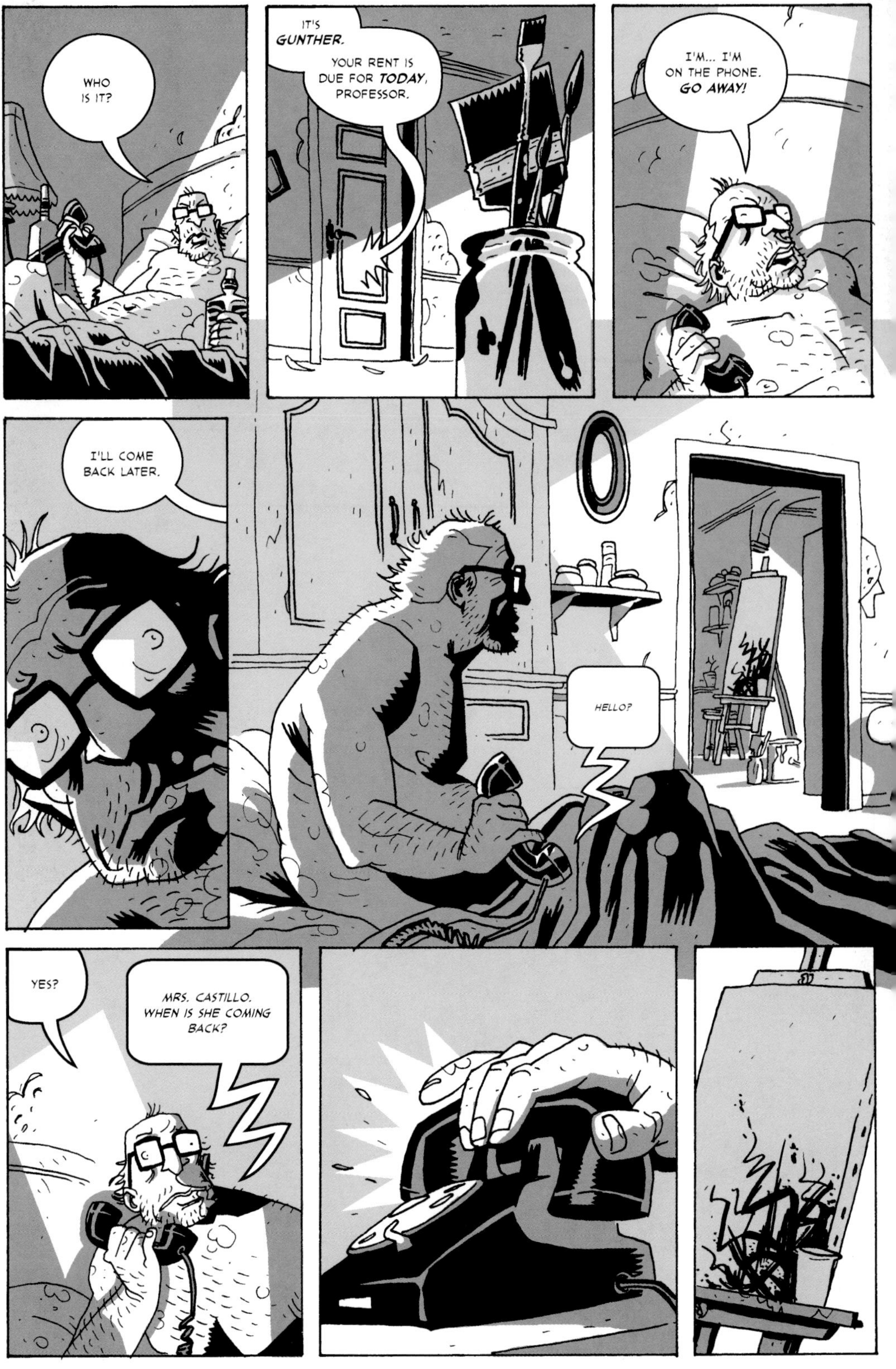
WHO IS IT?
IT'S GUNTHER.
YOUR RENT IS DUE FOR TODAY, PROFESSOR.
I'M... I'M ON THE PHONE. GO AWAY!
I'LL COME BACK LATER.
HELLO?
YES?
MRS. CASTILLO. WHEN IS SHE COMING BACK?

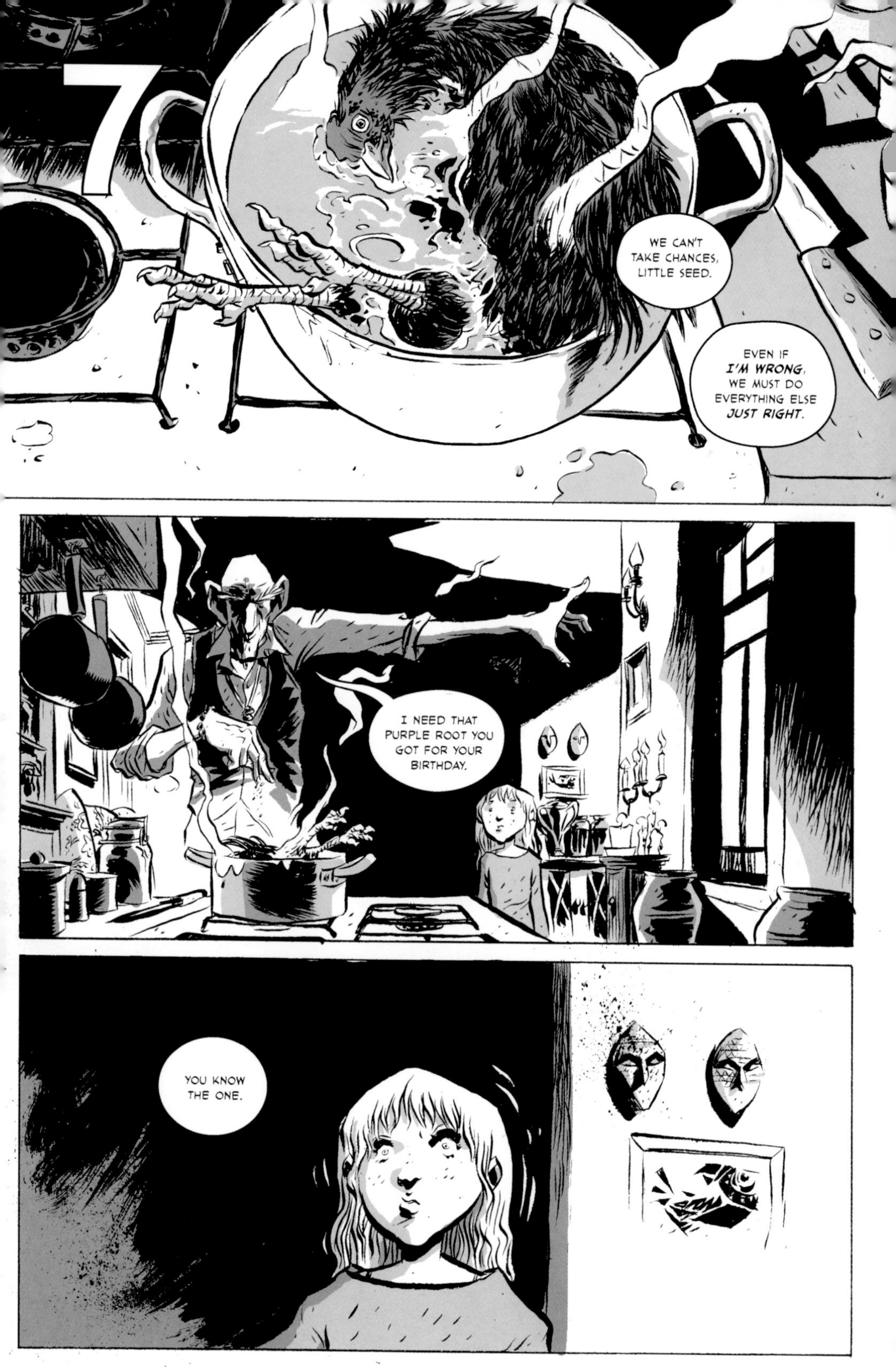
7
WE CAN'T TAKE CHANCES, LITTLE SEED.
EVEN IF *I'M WRONG*, WE MUST DO EVERYTHING ELSE *JUST RIGHT*.
I NEED THAT PURPLE ROOT YOU GOT FOR YOUR BIRTHDAY.
YOU KNOW THE ONE.

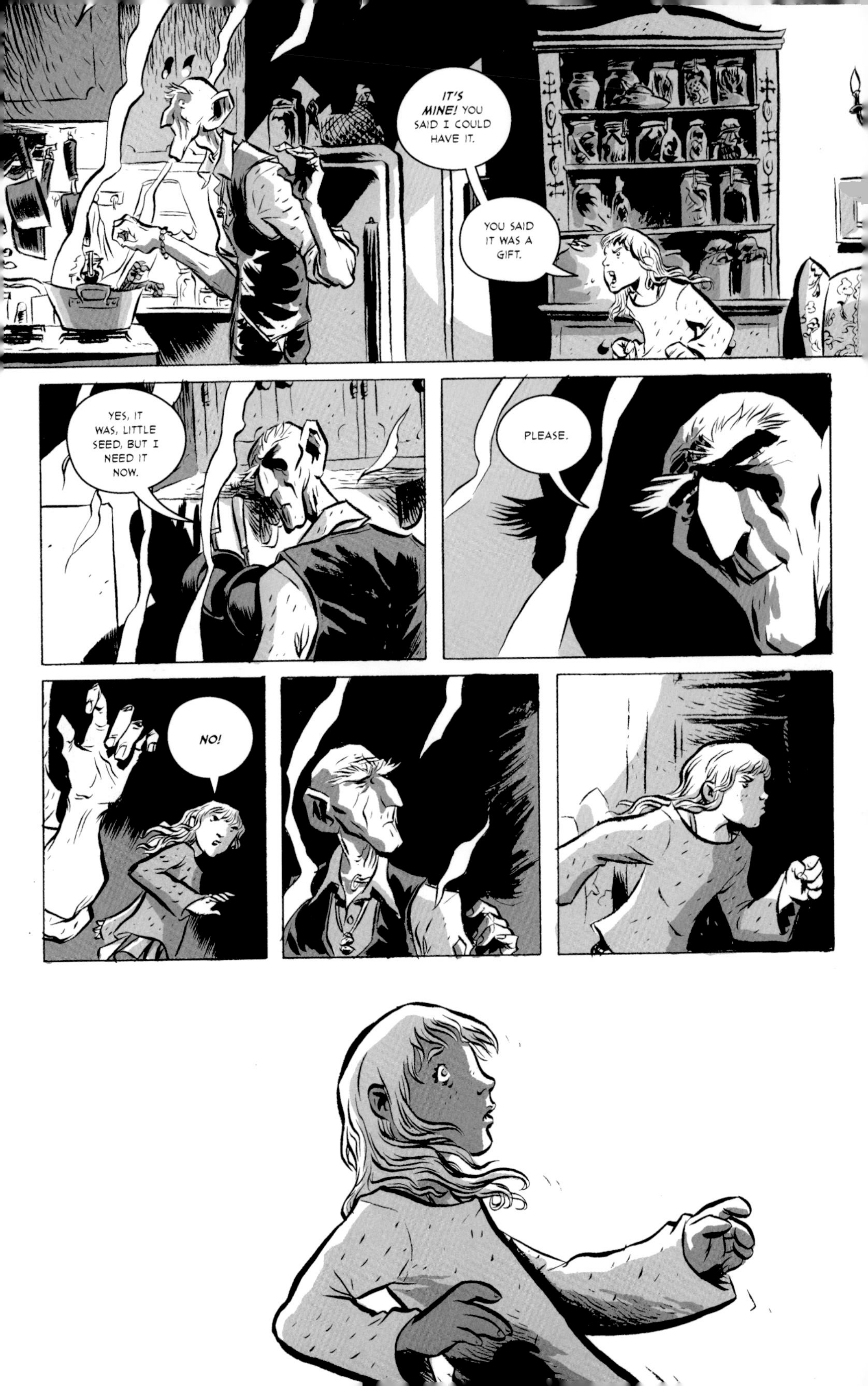
IT'S MINE! YOU SAID I COULD HAVE IT.
YOU SAID IT WAS A GIFT.
YES, IT WAS, LITTLE SEED, BUT I NEED IT NOW.
PLEASE.
NO!

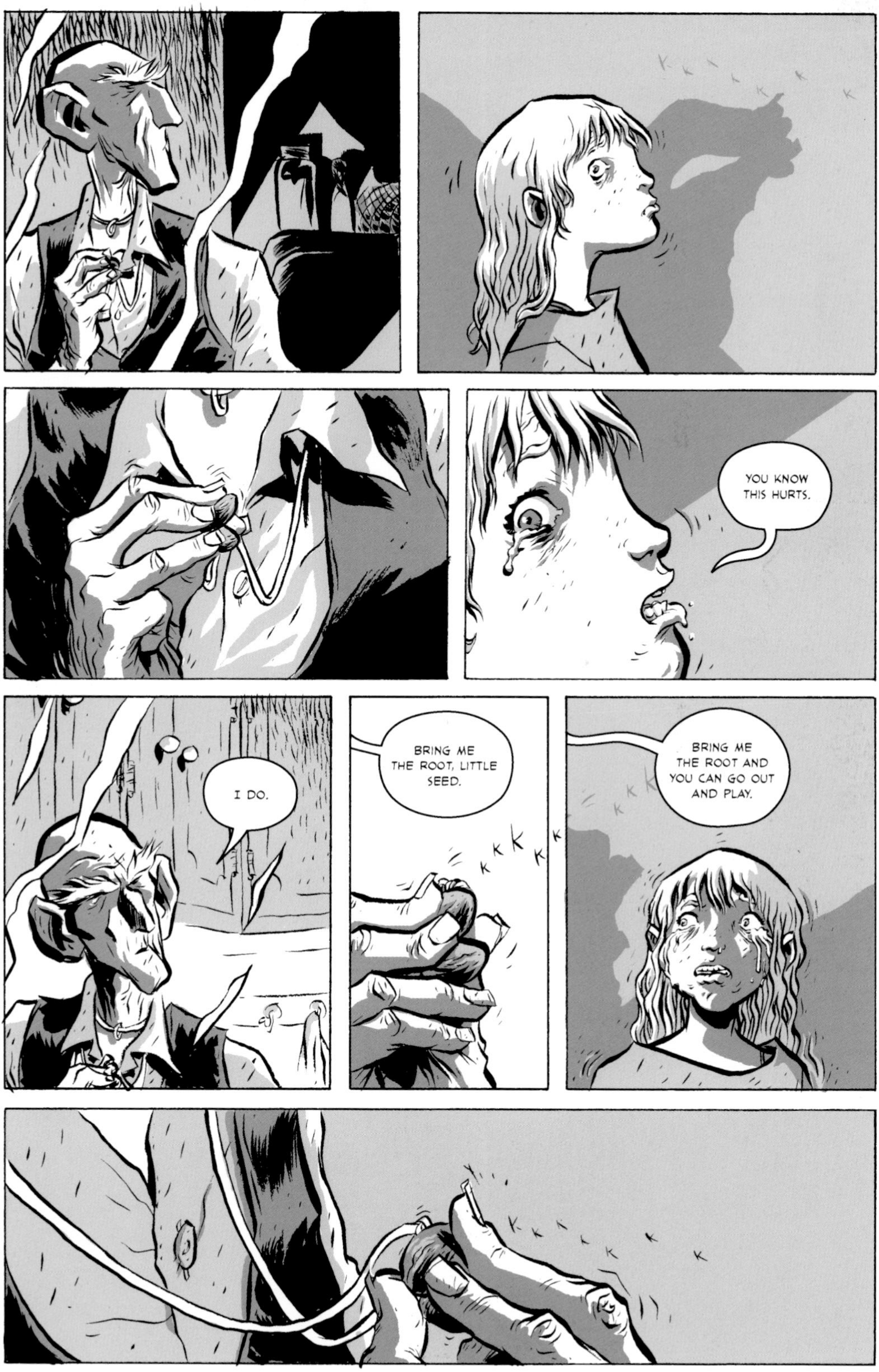
YOU KNOW THIS HURTS.
I DO.
BRING ME THE ROOT, LITTLE SEED.
BRING ME THE ROOT AND YOU CAN GO OUT AND PLAY.

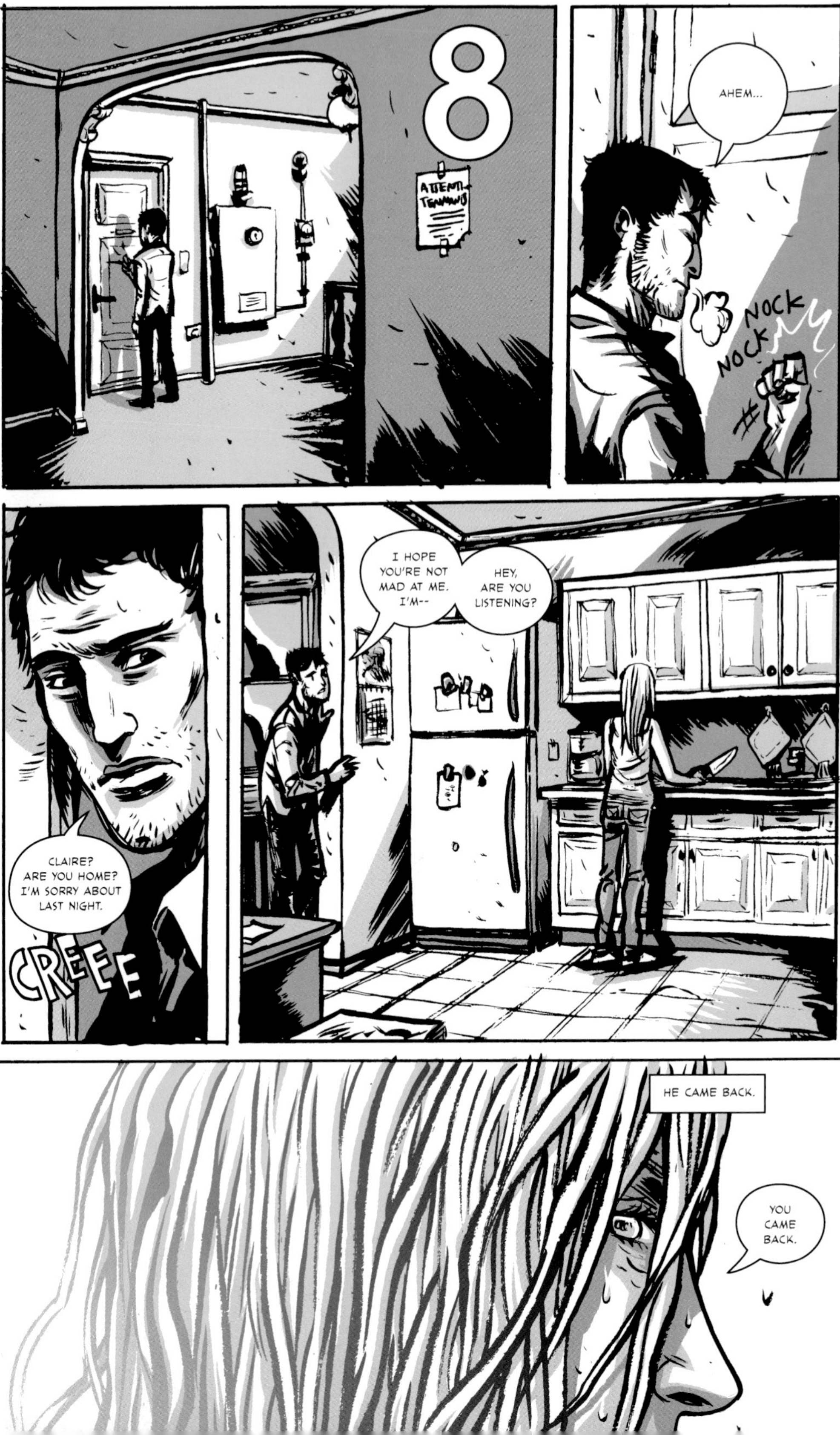
8
ATTENTI... TENANTS
AHEM...
NOCK NOCK
CLAIRE? ARE YOU HOME? I'M SORRY ABOUT LAST NIGHT.
CREEE
I HOPE YOU'RE NOT MAD AT ME. I'M--
HEY, ARE YOU LISTENING?
HE CAME BACK.
YOU CAME BACK.

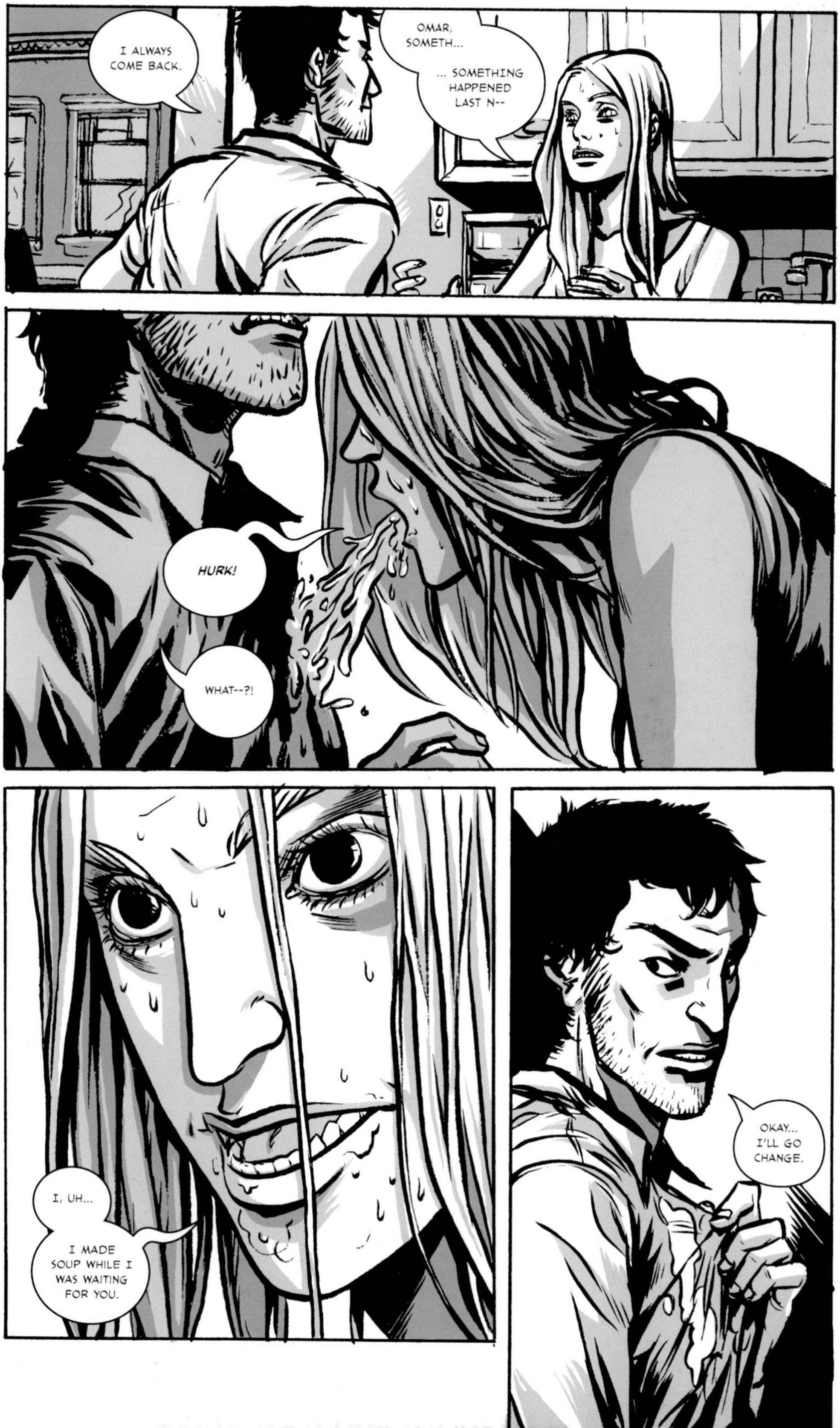
I ALWAYS COME BACK.
OMAR, SOMETH...
... SOMETHING HAPPENED LAST N--
HURK!
WHAT--?!
I, UH...
I MADE SOUP WHILE I WAS WAITING FOR YOU.
OKAY... I'LL GO CHANGE.

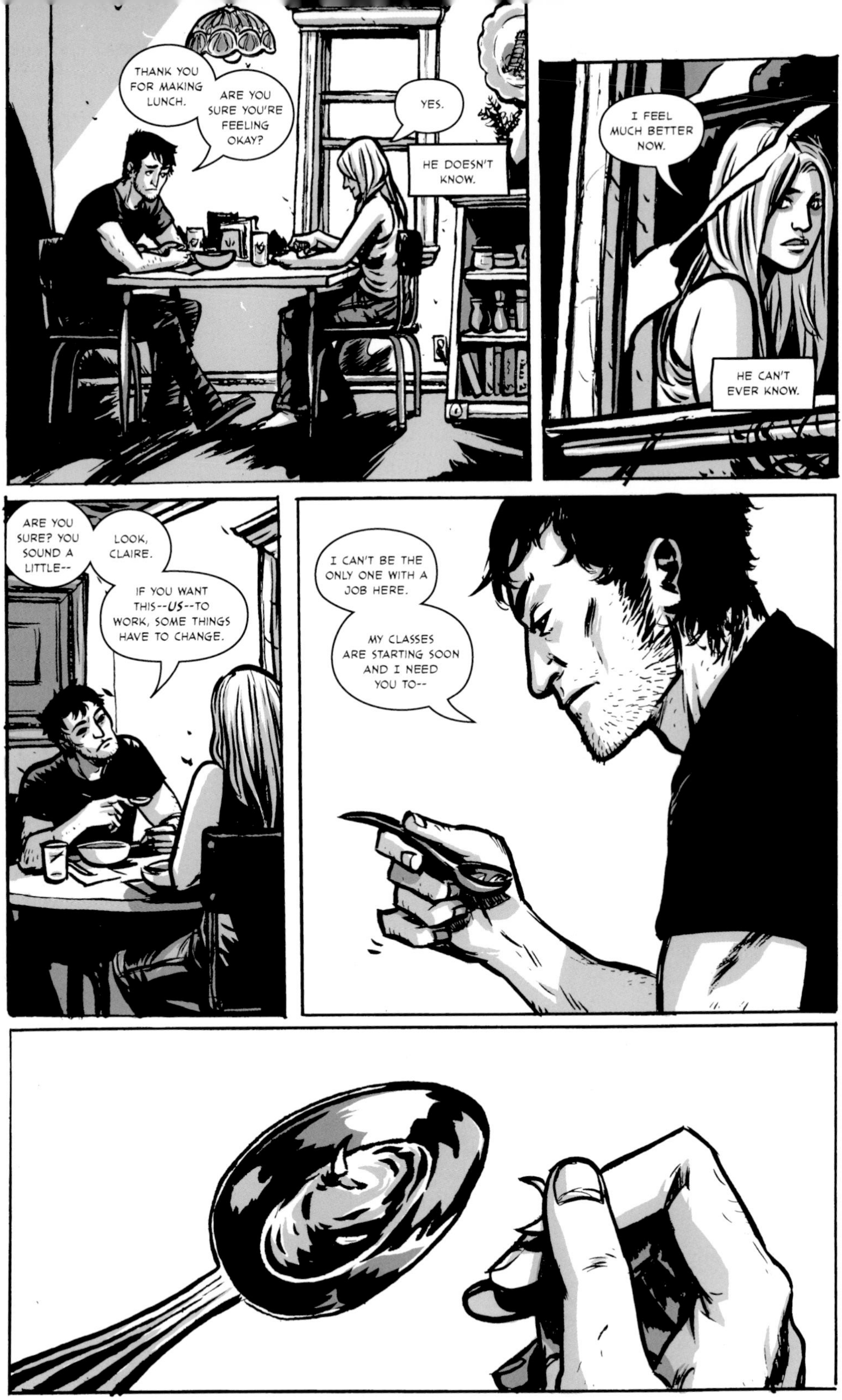
THANK YOU FOR MAKING LUNCH.
ARE YOU SURE YOU'RE FEELING OKAY?
YES.
HE DOESN'T KNOW.
I FEEL MUCH BETTER NOW.
HE CAN'T EVER KNOW.
ARE YOU SURE? YOU SOUND A LITTLE--
LOOK, CLAIRE.
IF YOU WANT THIS--*US*--TO WORK, SOME THINGS HAVE TO CHANGE.
I CAN'T BE THE ONLY ONE WITH A JOB HERE.
MY CLASSES ARE STARTING SOON AND I NEED YOU TO--

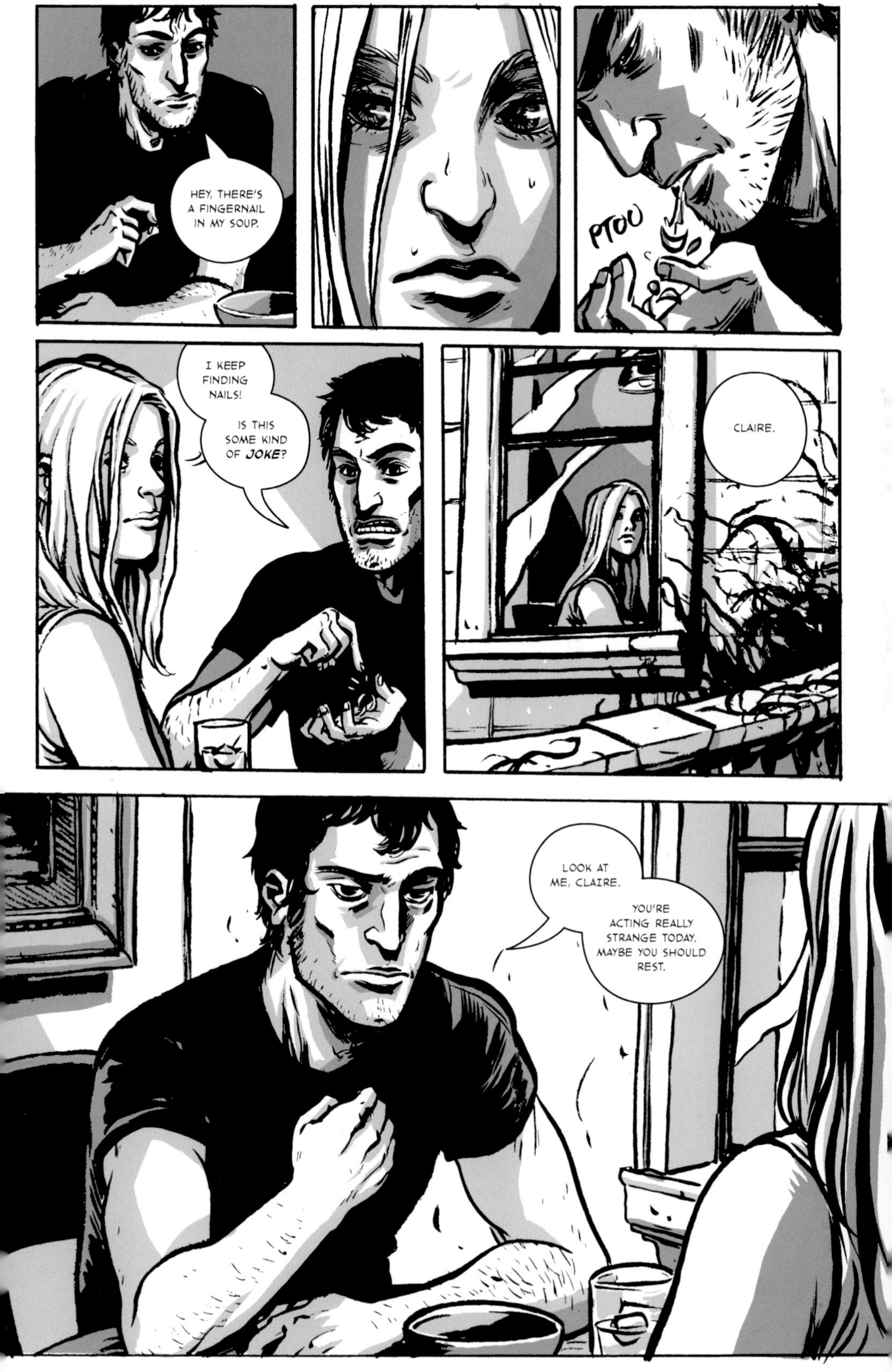
HEY, THERE'S A FINGERNAIL IN MY SOUP.
PTOU
I KEEP FINDING NAILS!
IS THIS SOME KIND OF *JOKE*?
CLAIRE.
LOOK AT ME, CLAIRE.
YOU'RE ACTING REALLY STRANGE TODAY. MAYBE YOU SHOULD REST.

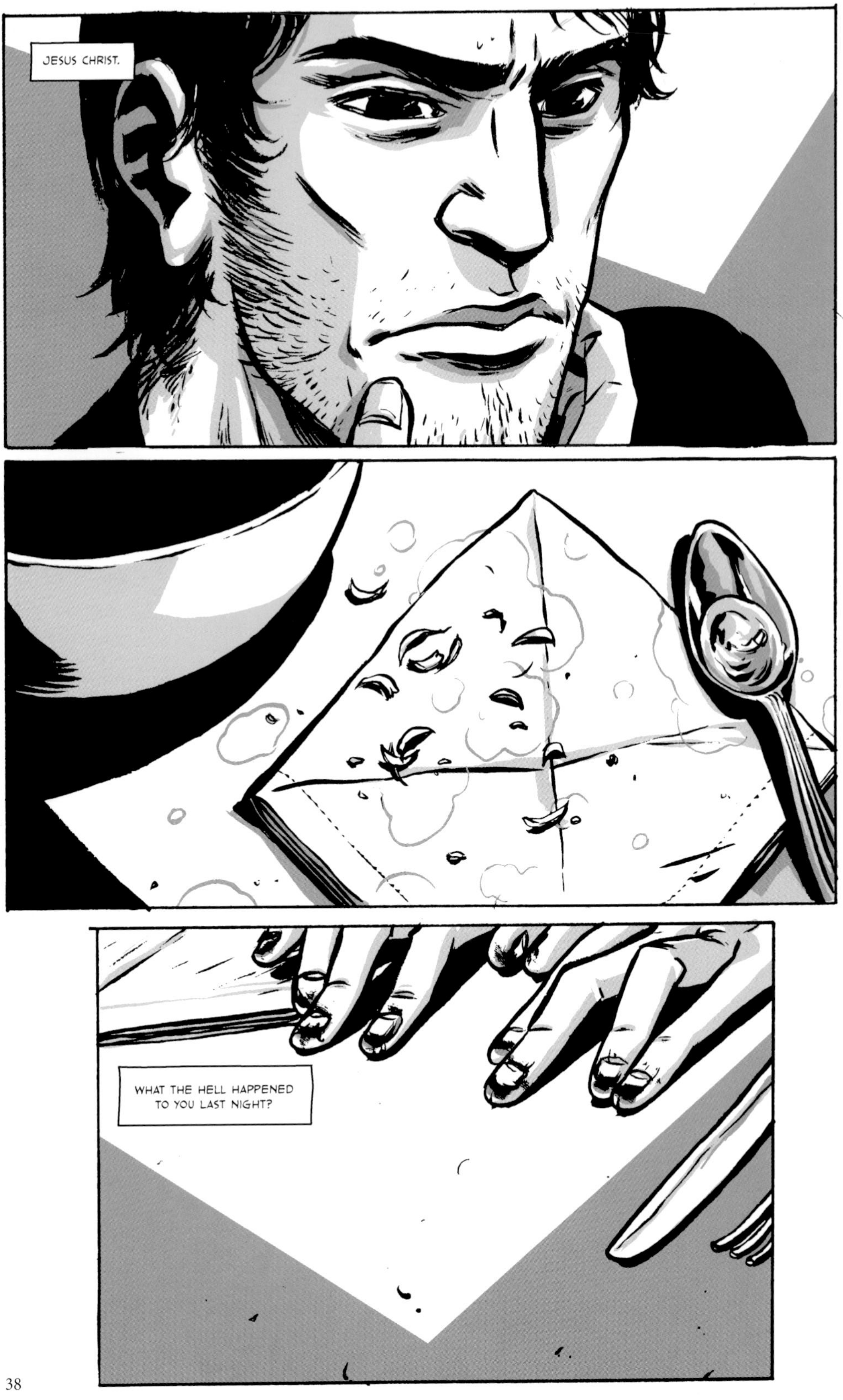
JESUS CHRIST.
WHAT THE HELL HAPPENED TO YOU LAST NIGHT?

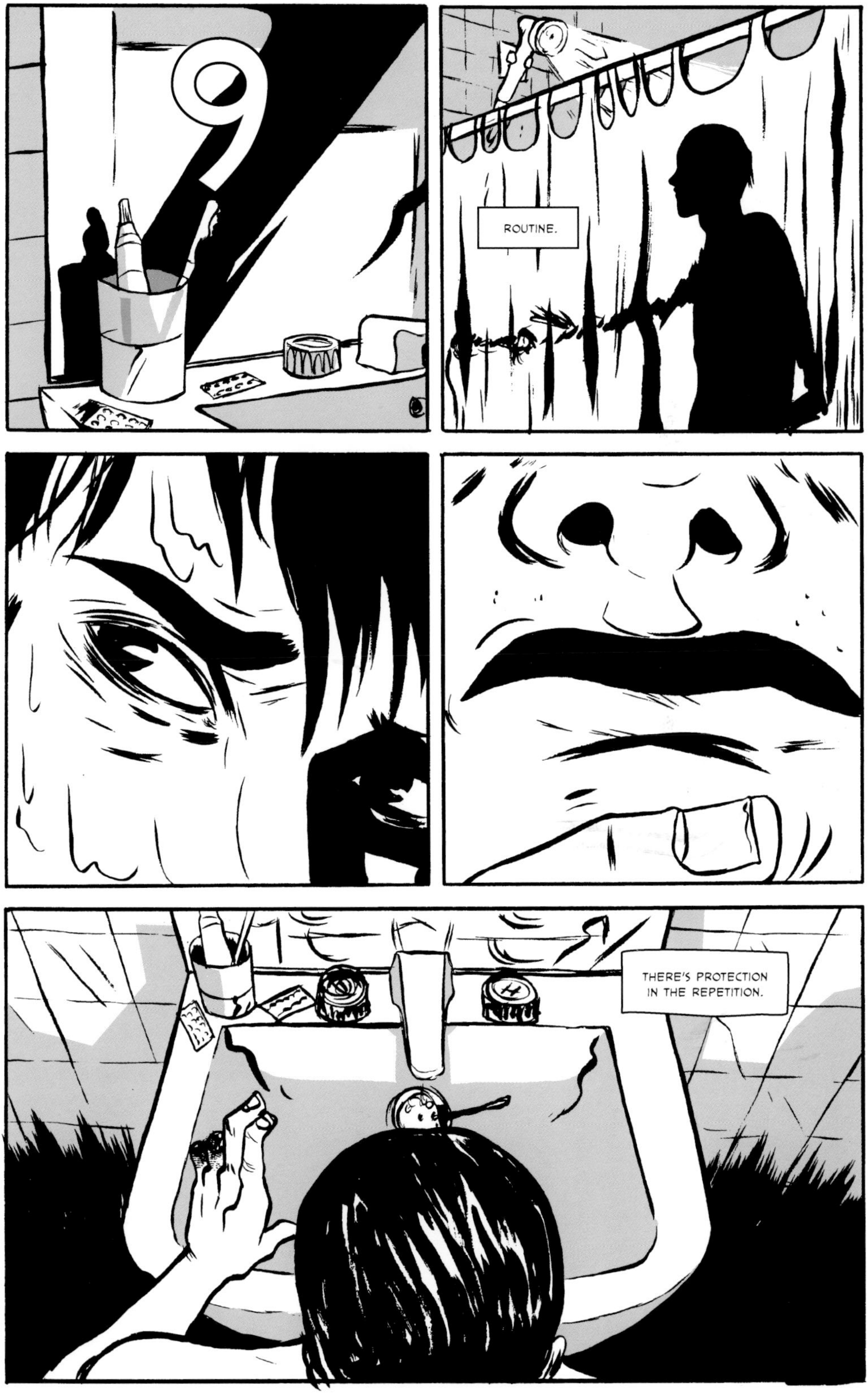
ROUTINE.
THERE'S PROTECTION IN THE REPETITION.

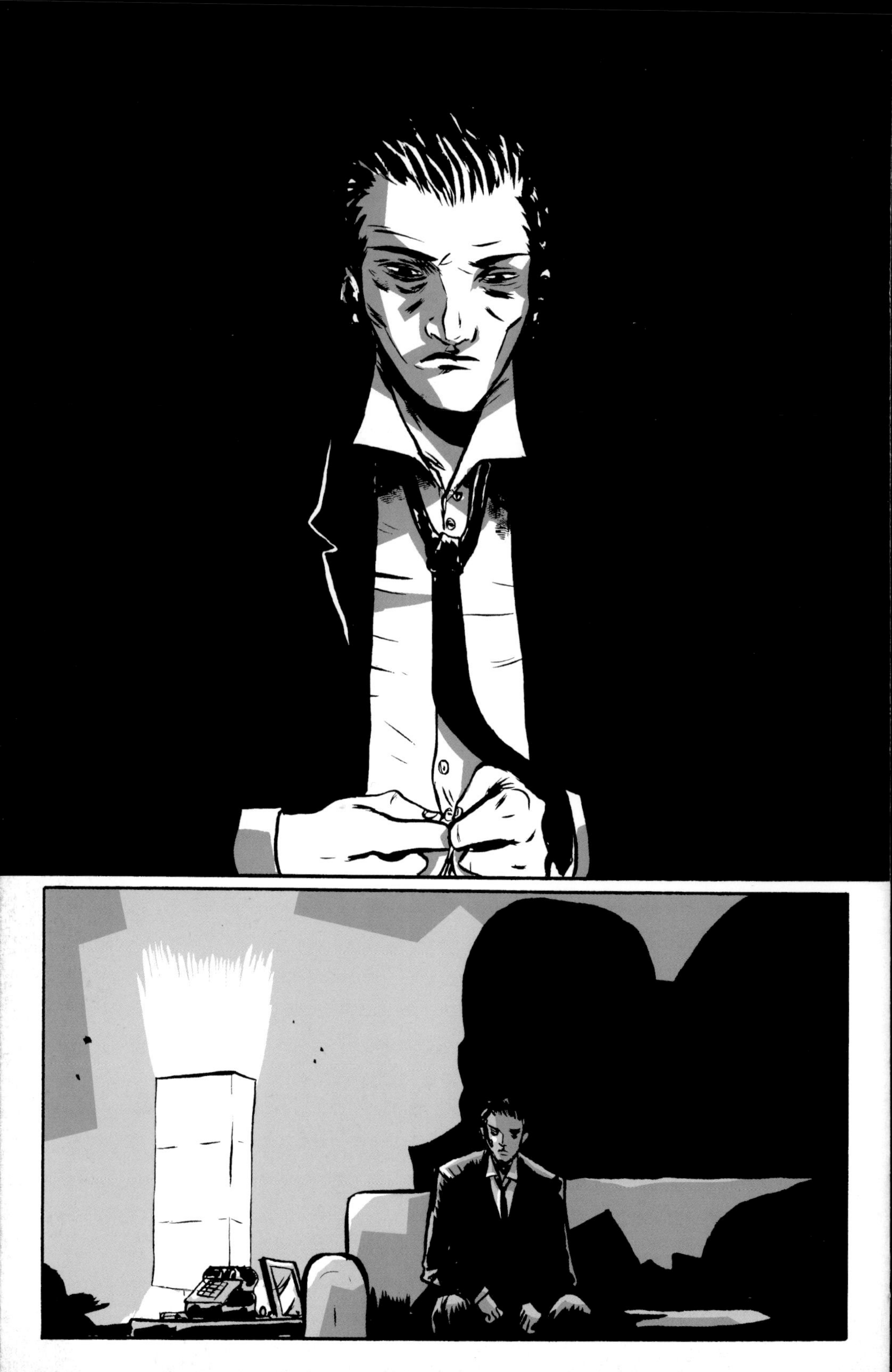

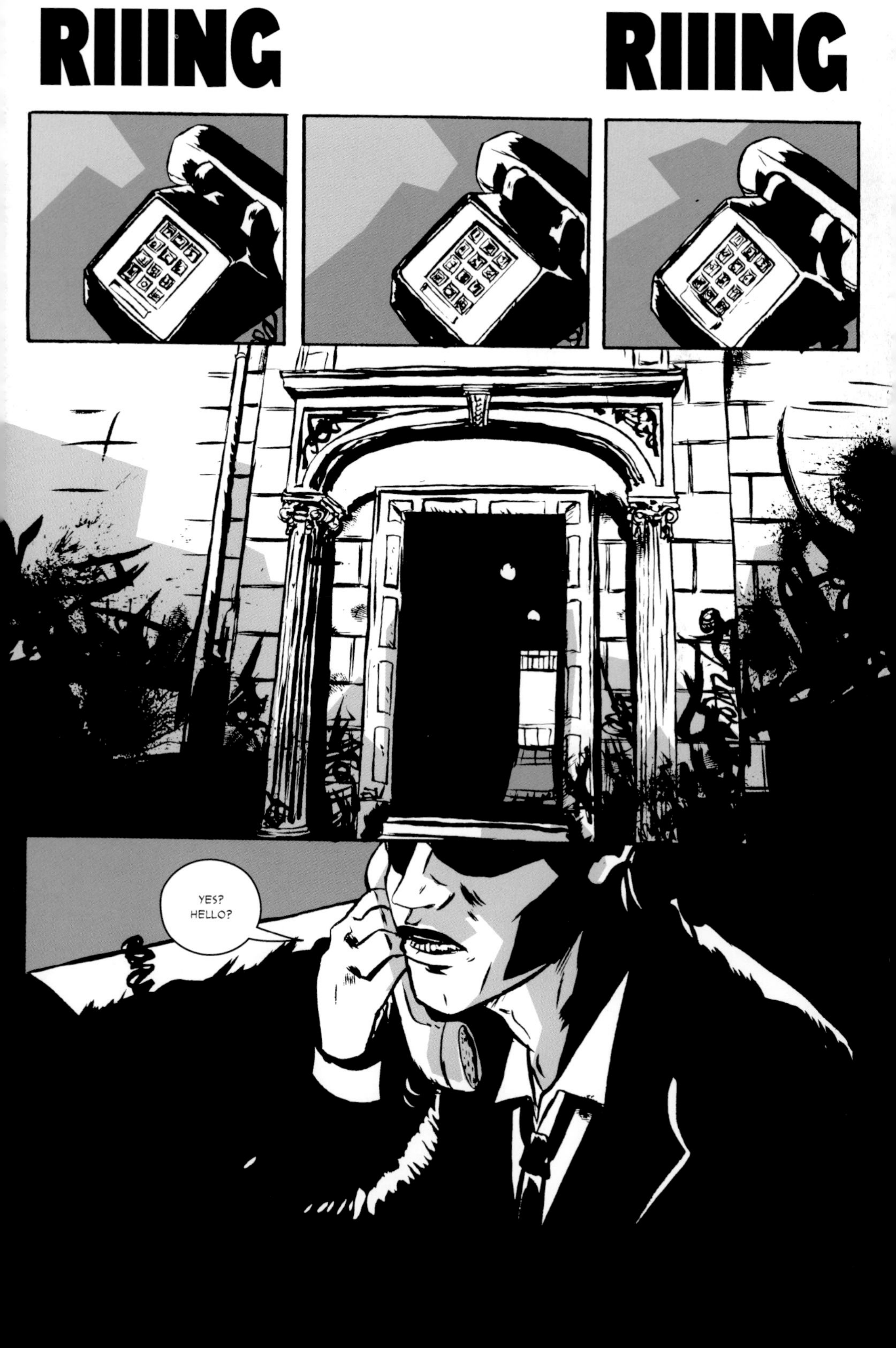
RIIING
RIIING
YES? HELLO?

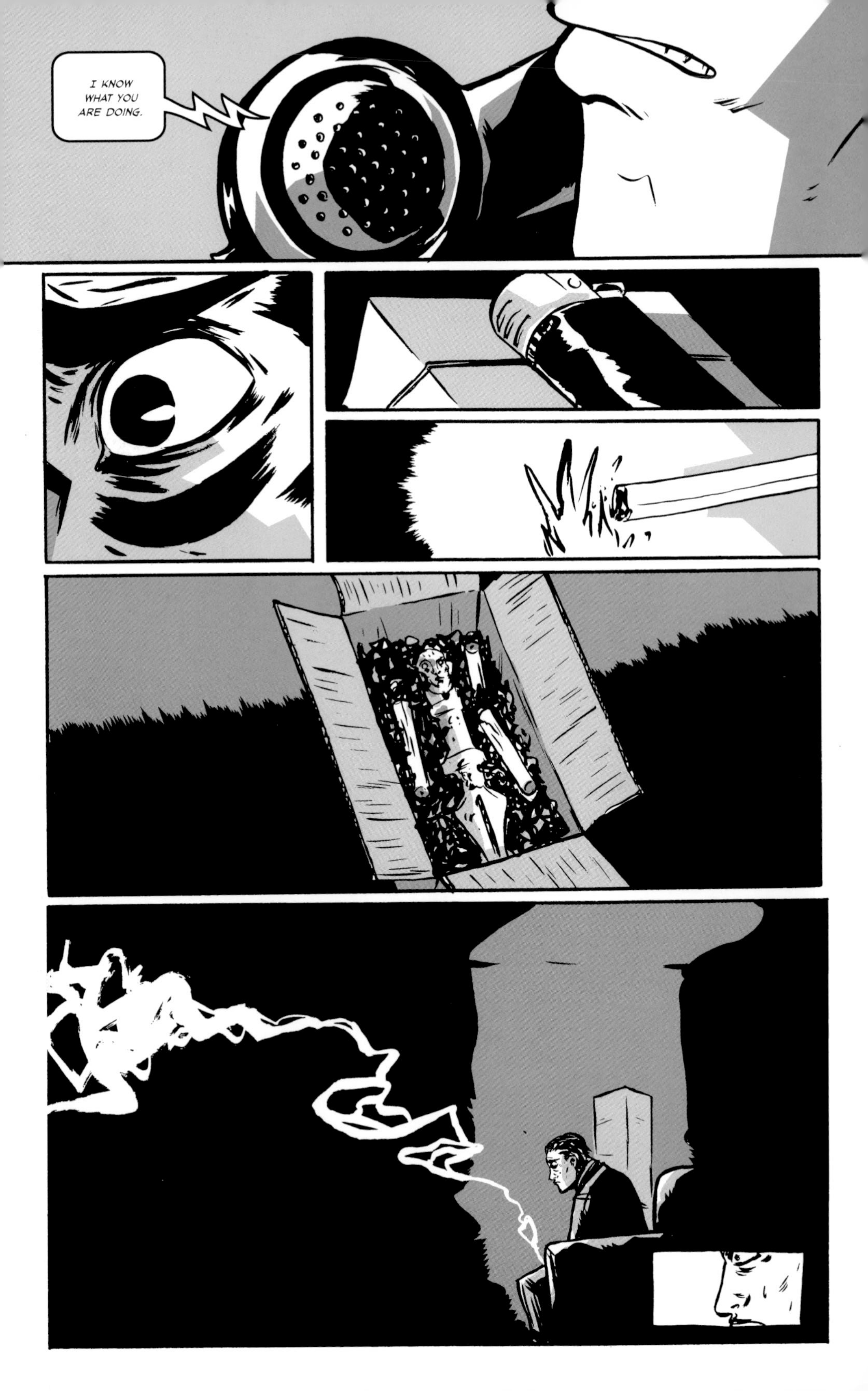
I KNOW WHAT YOU ARE DOING.

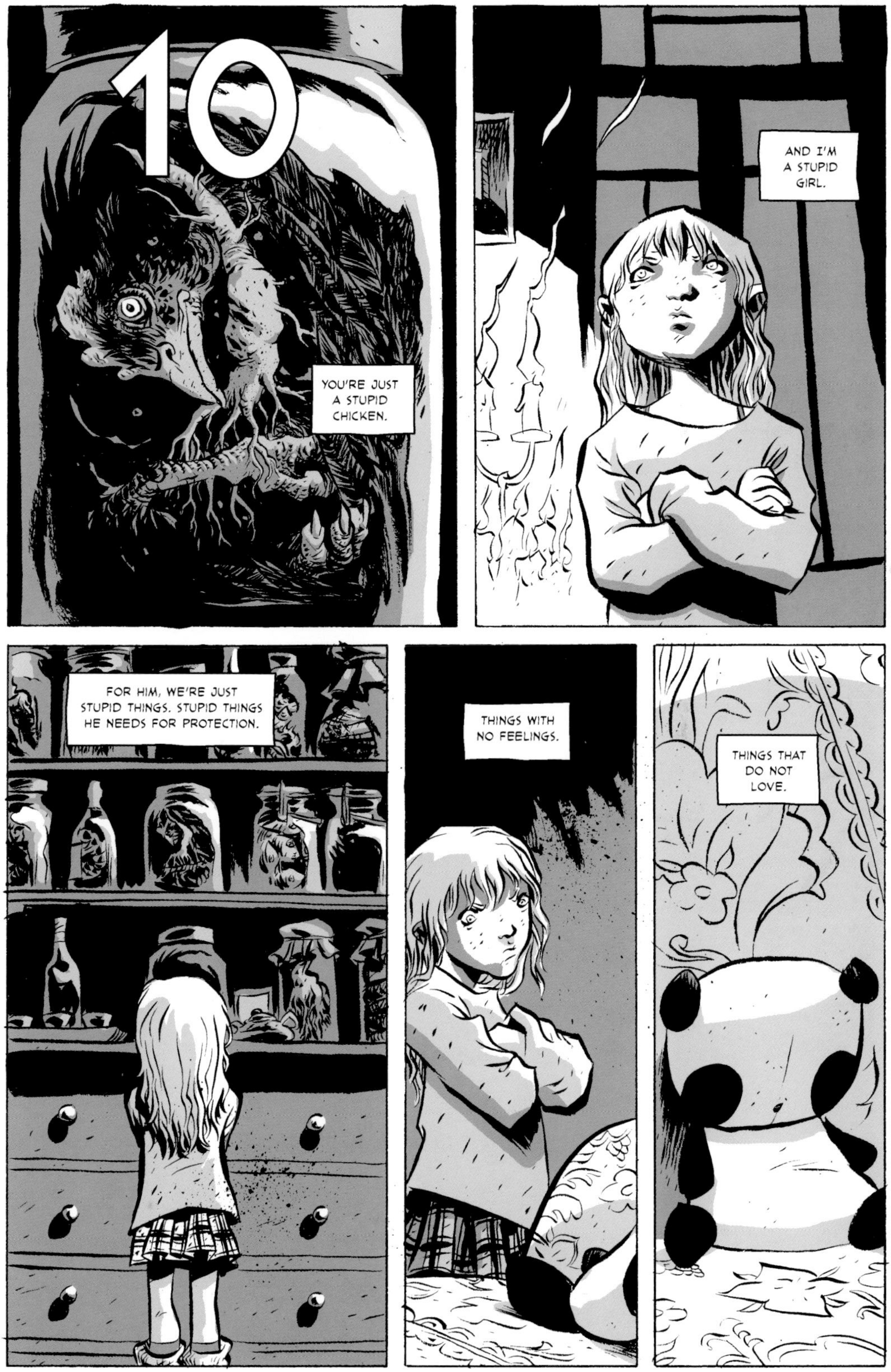
10
YOU'RE JUST A STUPID CHICKEN.
AND I'M A STUPID GIRL.
FOR HIM, WE'RE JUST STUPID THINGS. STUPID THINGS HE NEEDS FOR PROTECTION.
THINGS WITH NO FEELINGS.
THINGS THAT DO NOT LOVE.

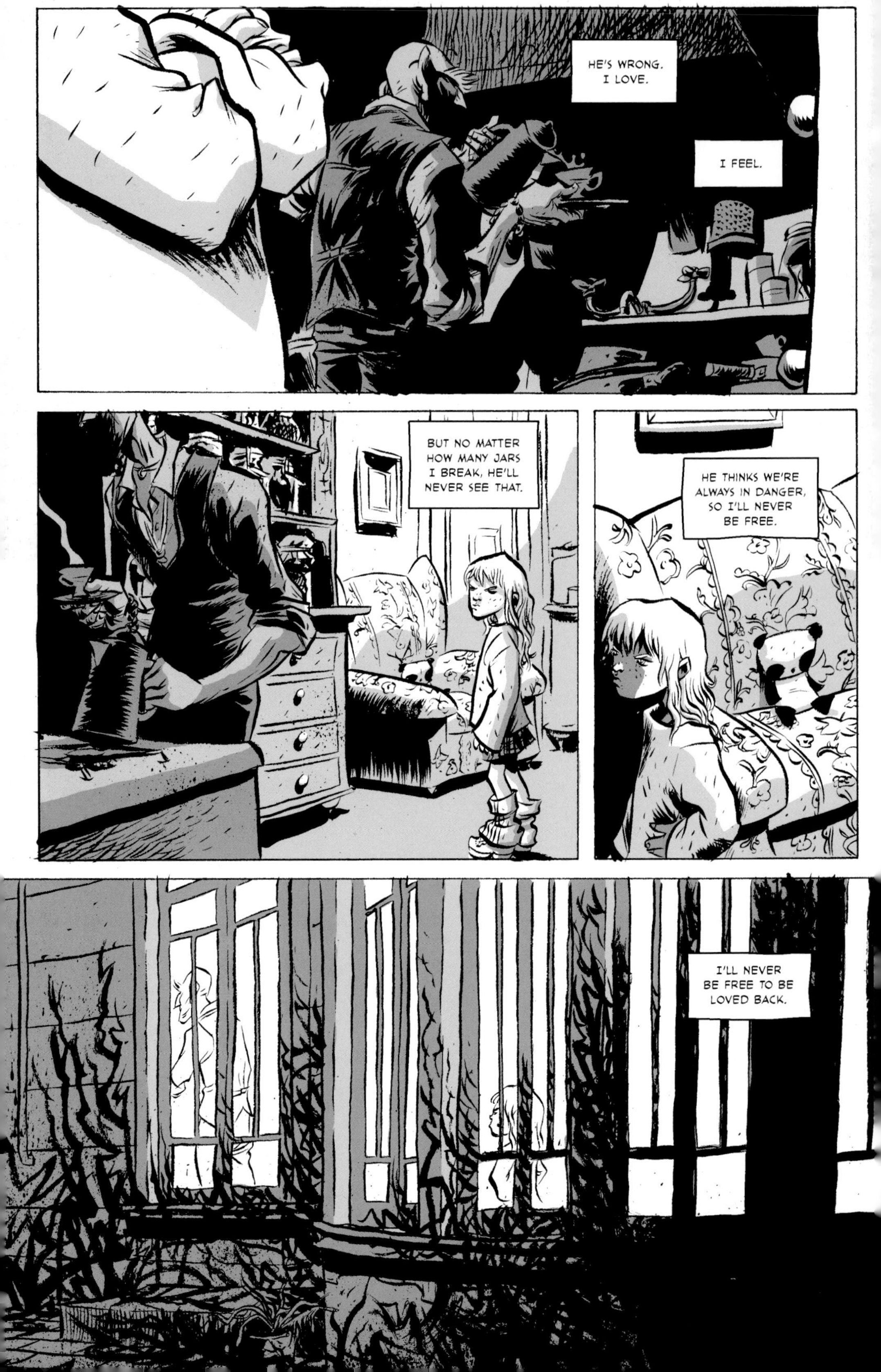
HE'S WRONG. I LOVE.
I FEEL.
BUT NO MATTER HOW MANY JARS I BREAK, HE'LL NEVER SEE THAT.
HE THINKS WE'RE ALWAYS IN DANGER, SO I'LL NEVER BE FREE.
I'LL NEVER BE FREE TO BE LOVED BACK.

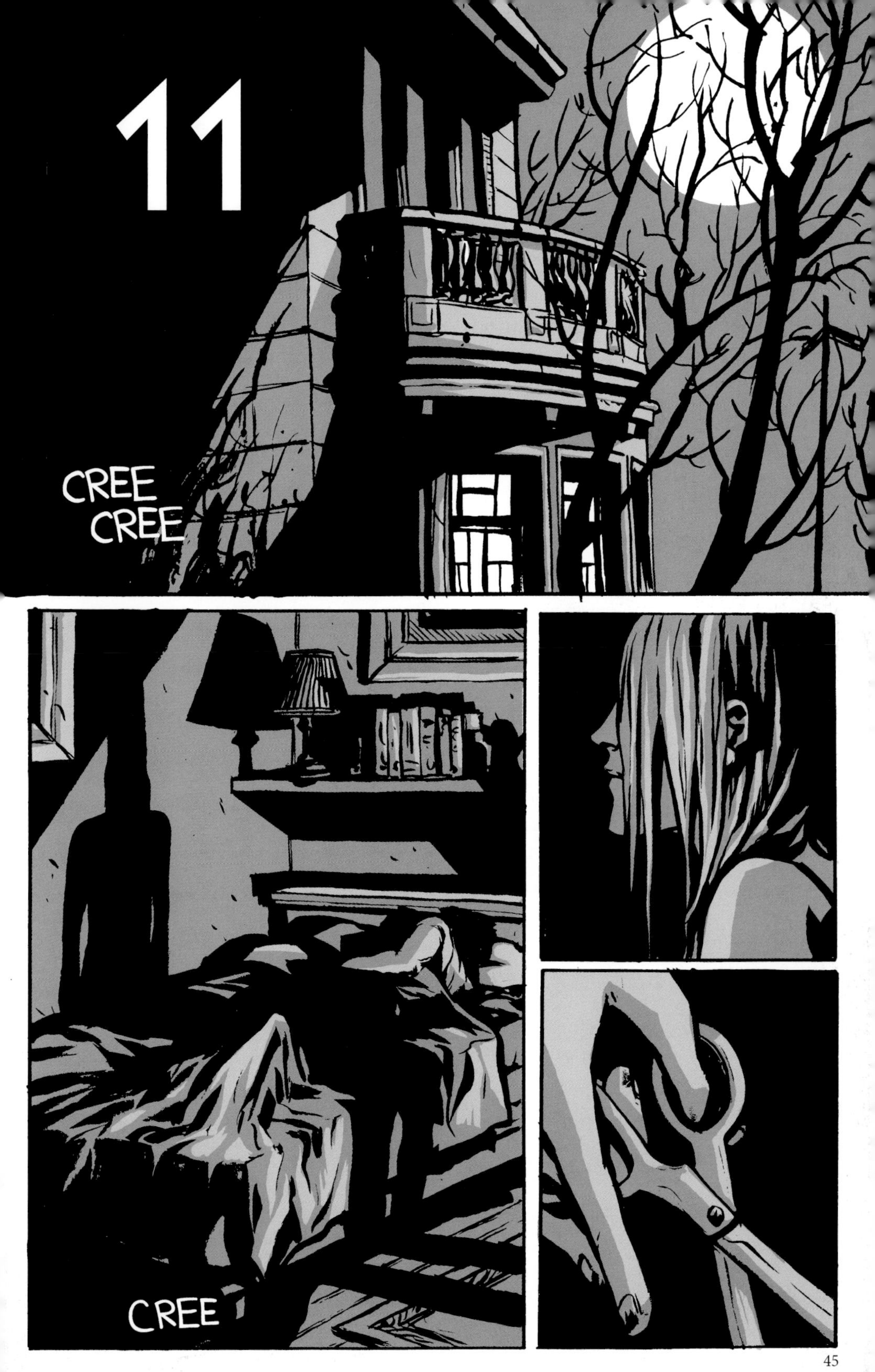
11
CREE
CREE
CREE

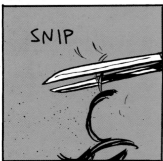

SNIP

SNIP

SNIP

SNIP
SNIPP
SNIP

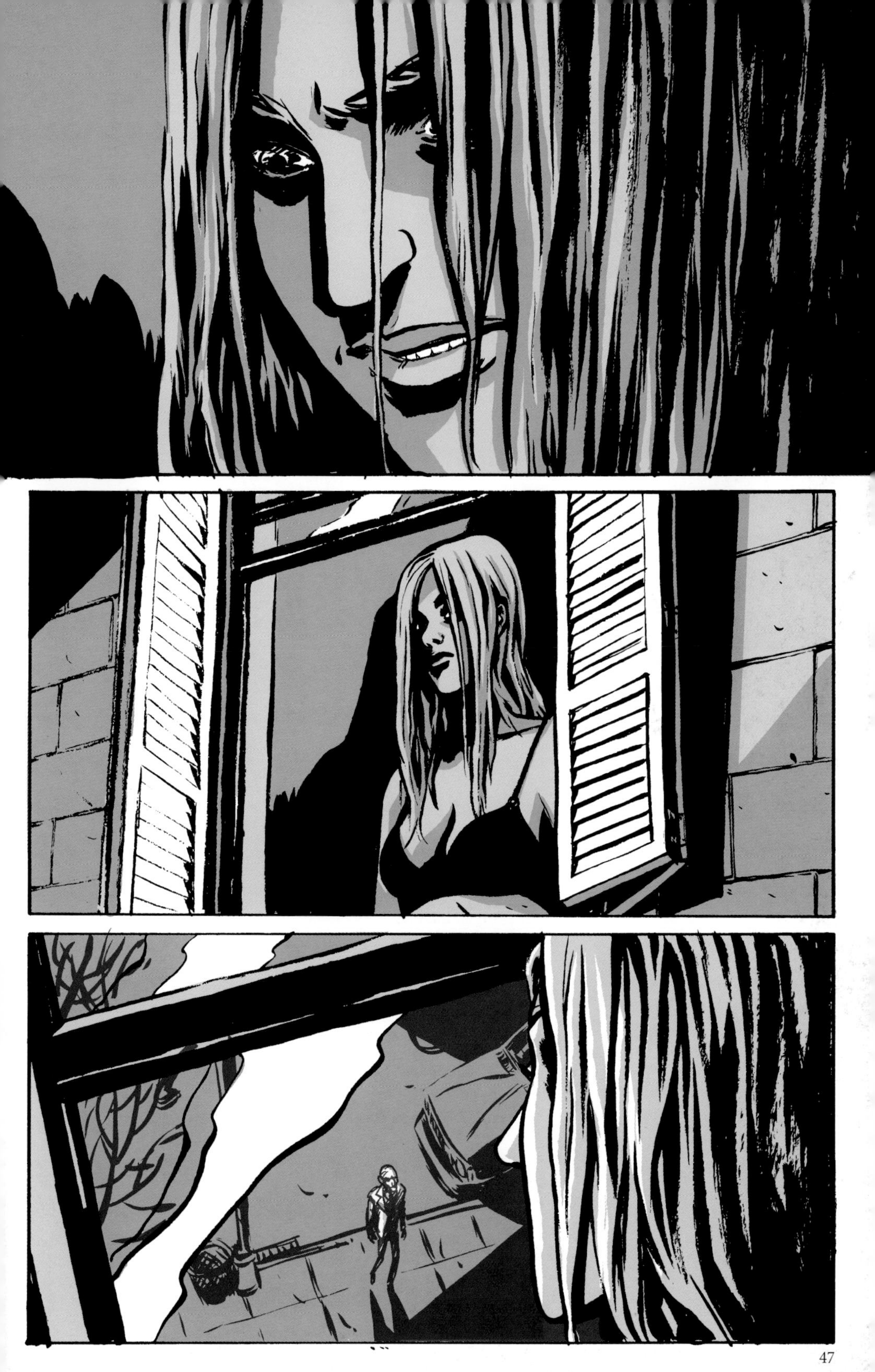

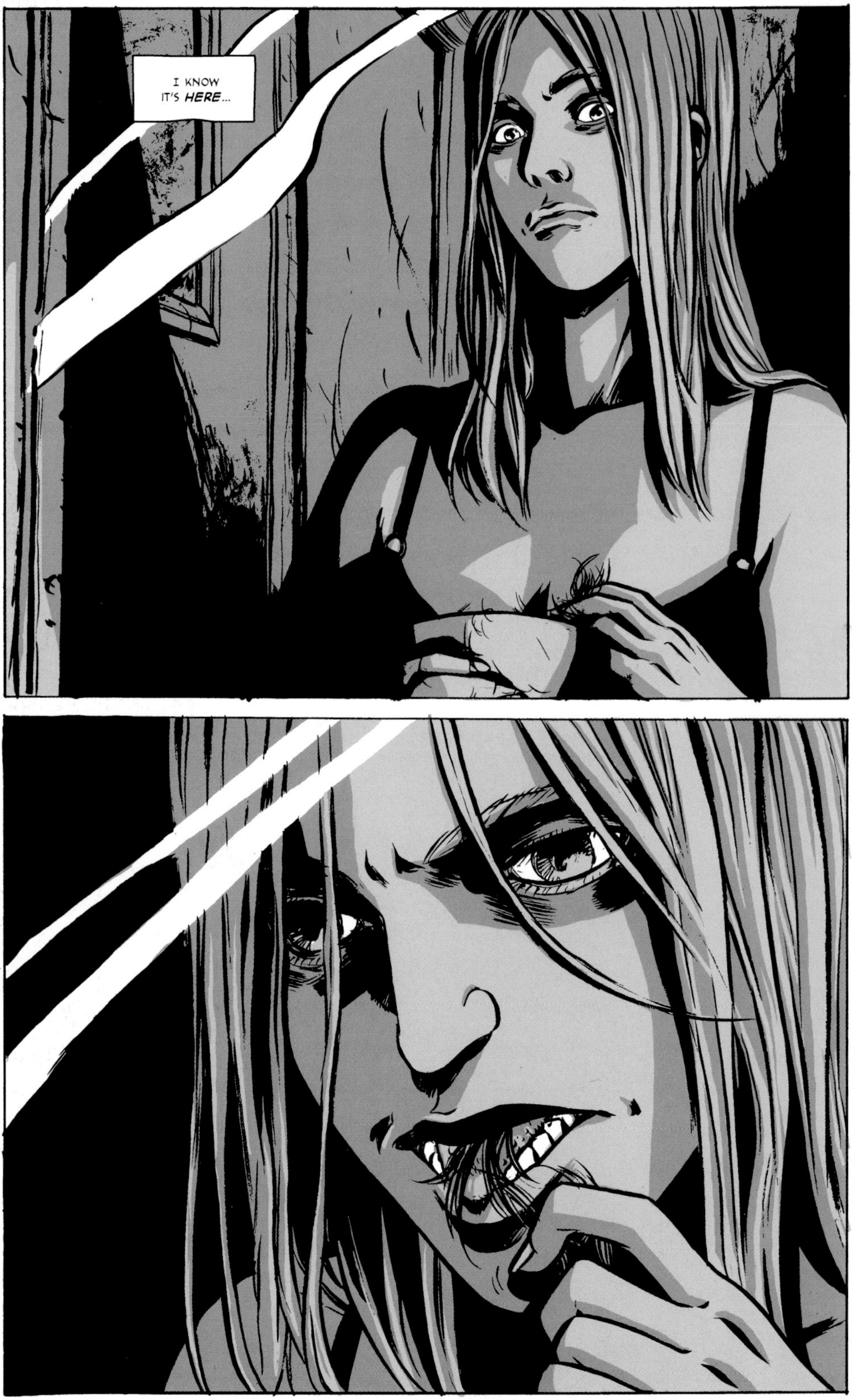
I KNOW IT'S *HERE*...

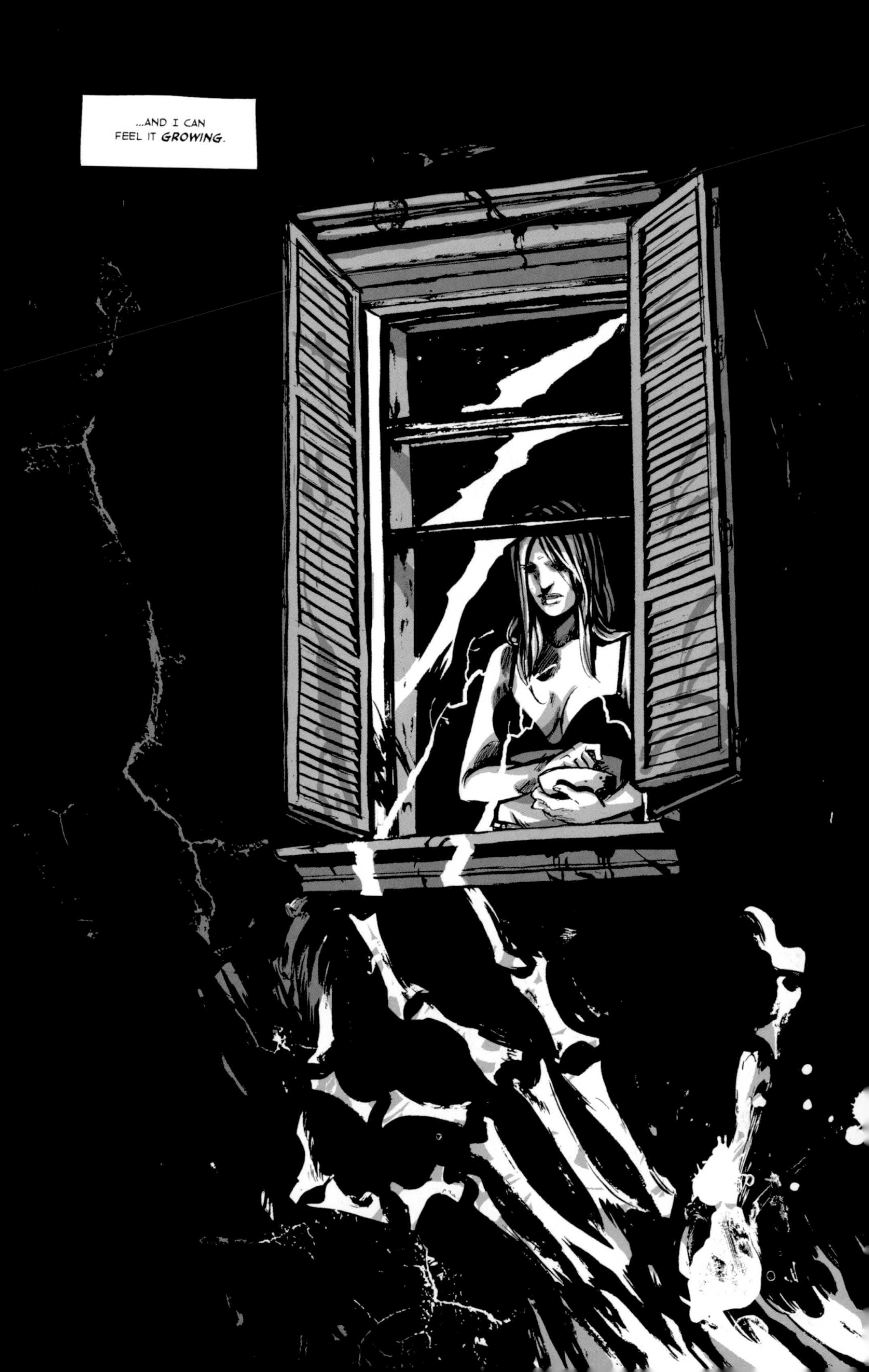
...AND I CAN FEEL IT GROWING.

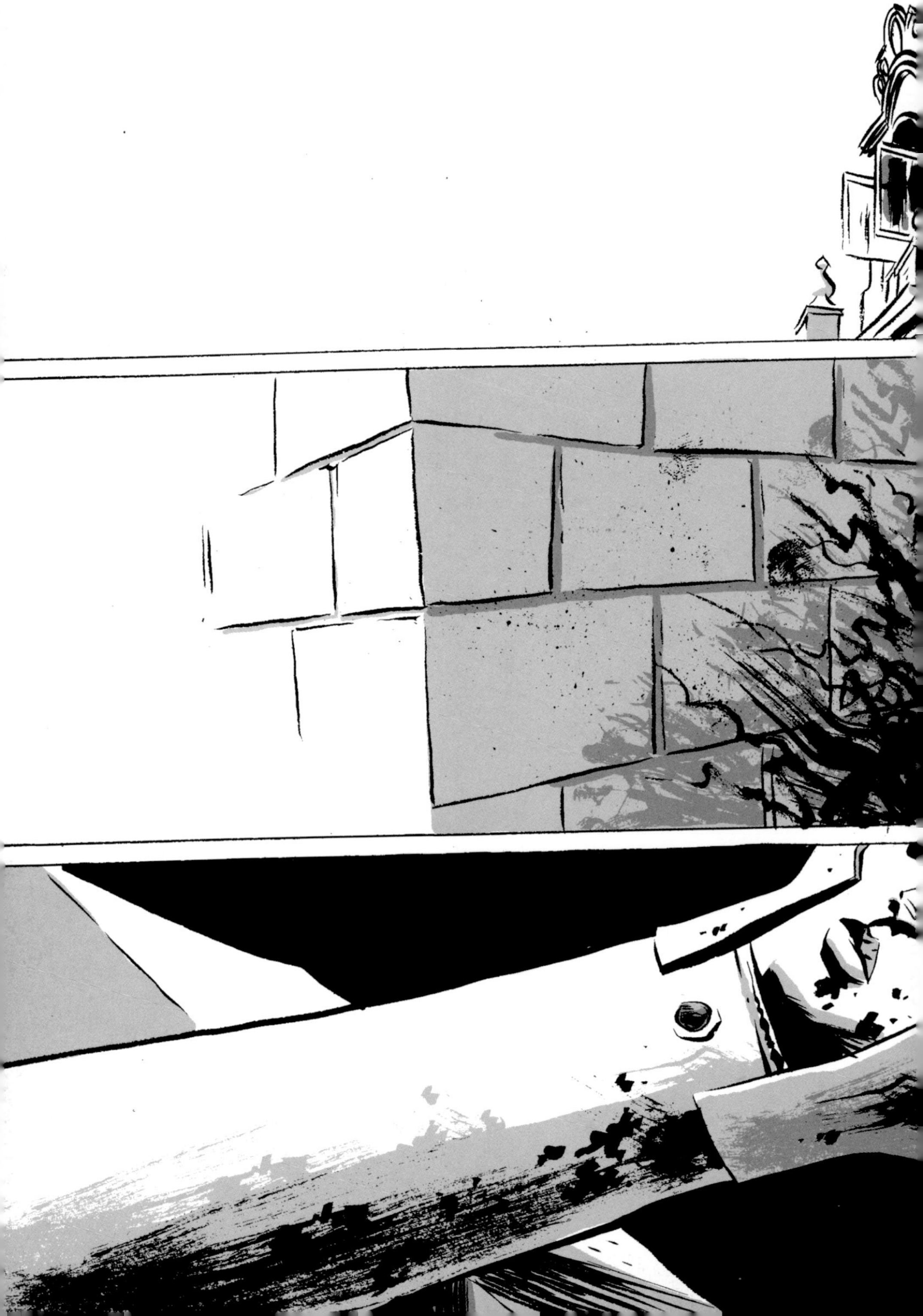

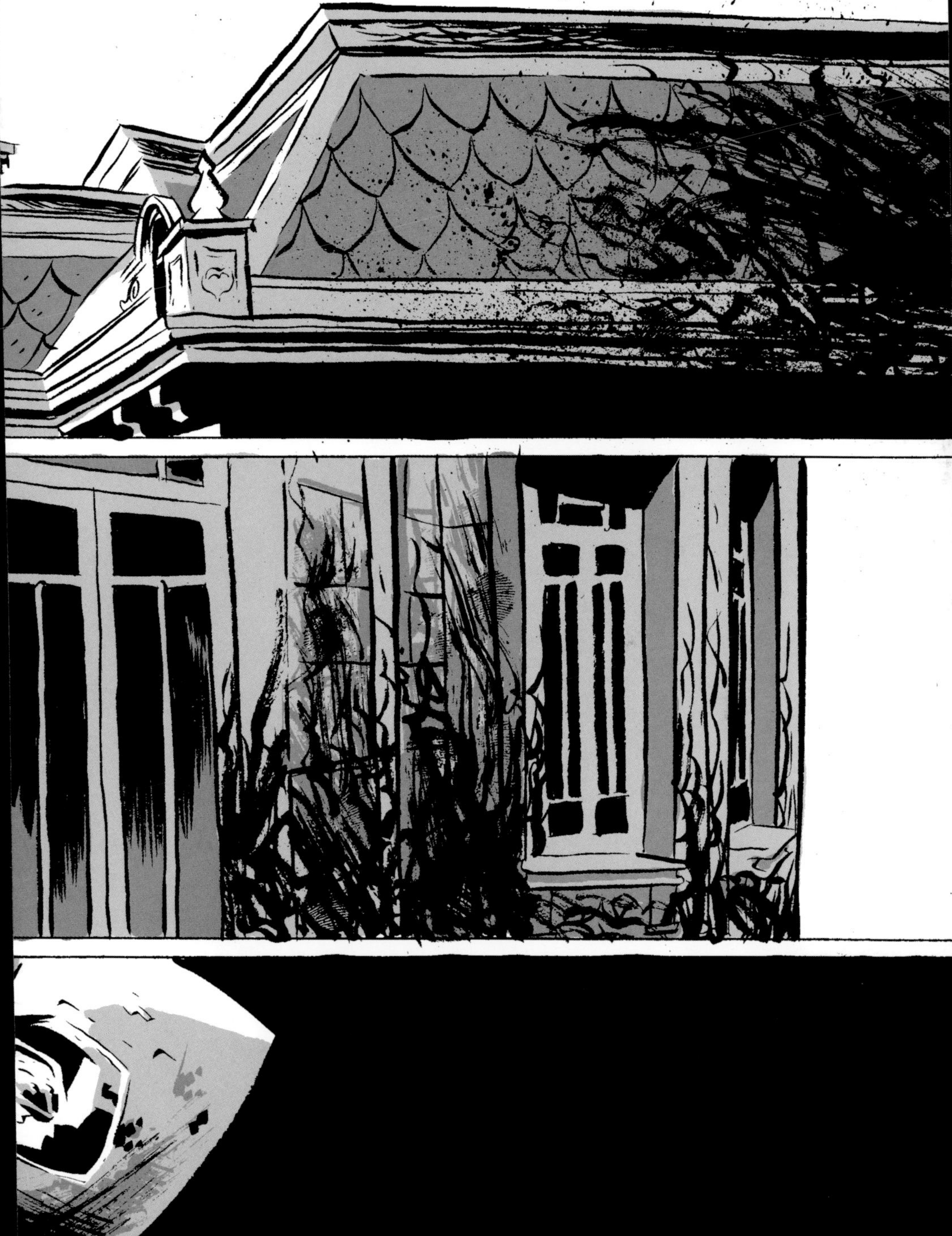

12

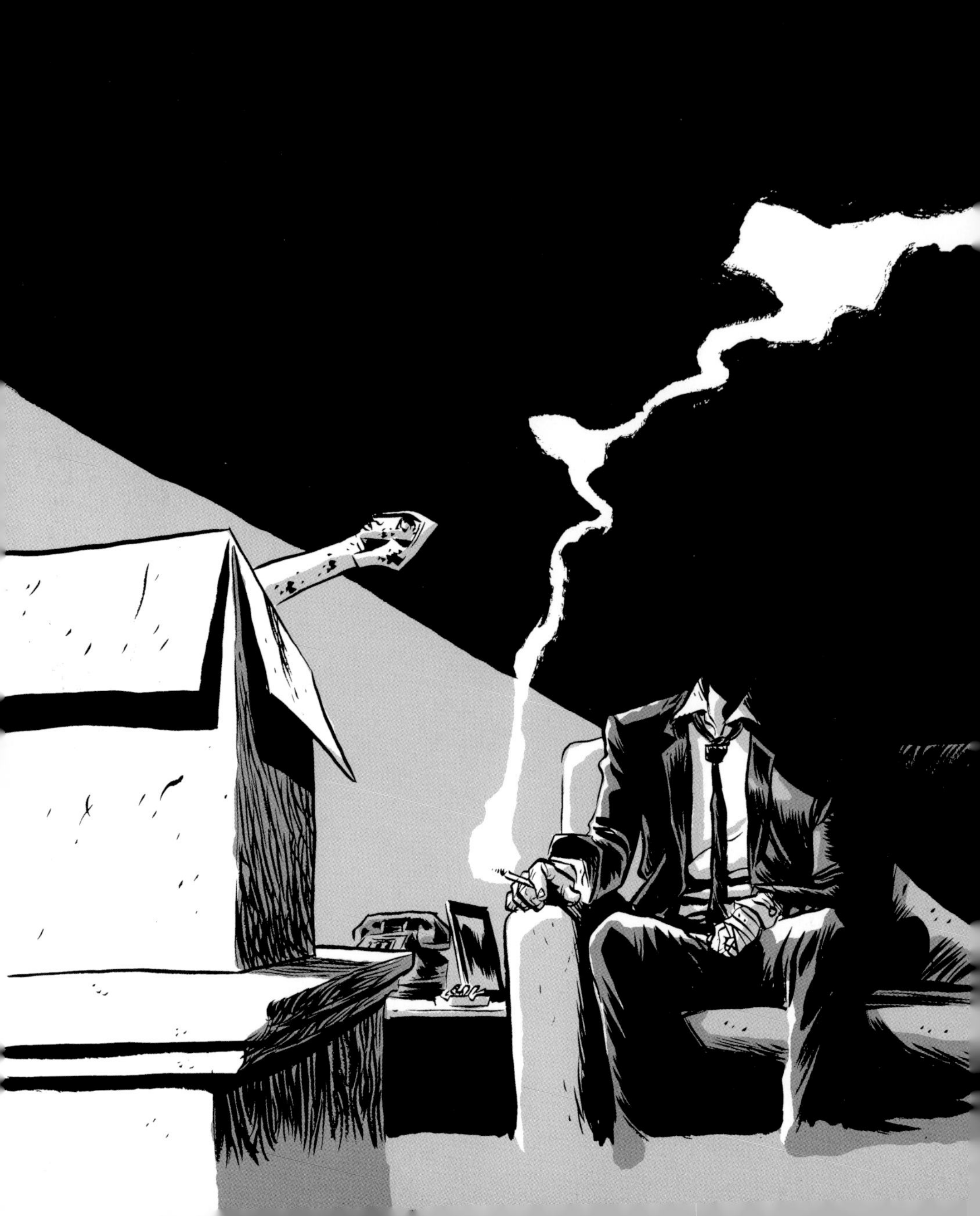

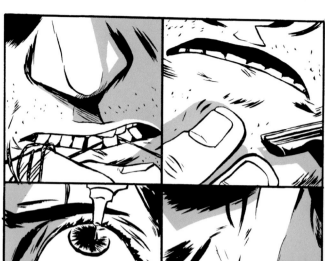

EVERYTHING IS SET.

I MADE ALL PREPARATIONS.

I'VE HAD THE CANDLES BURNING FOR ALMOST A WEEK NOW.

AND THIS...

THIS SHOULD DO THE TRICK.

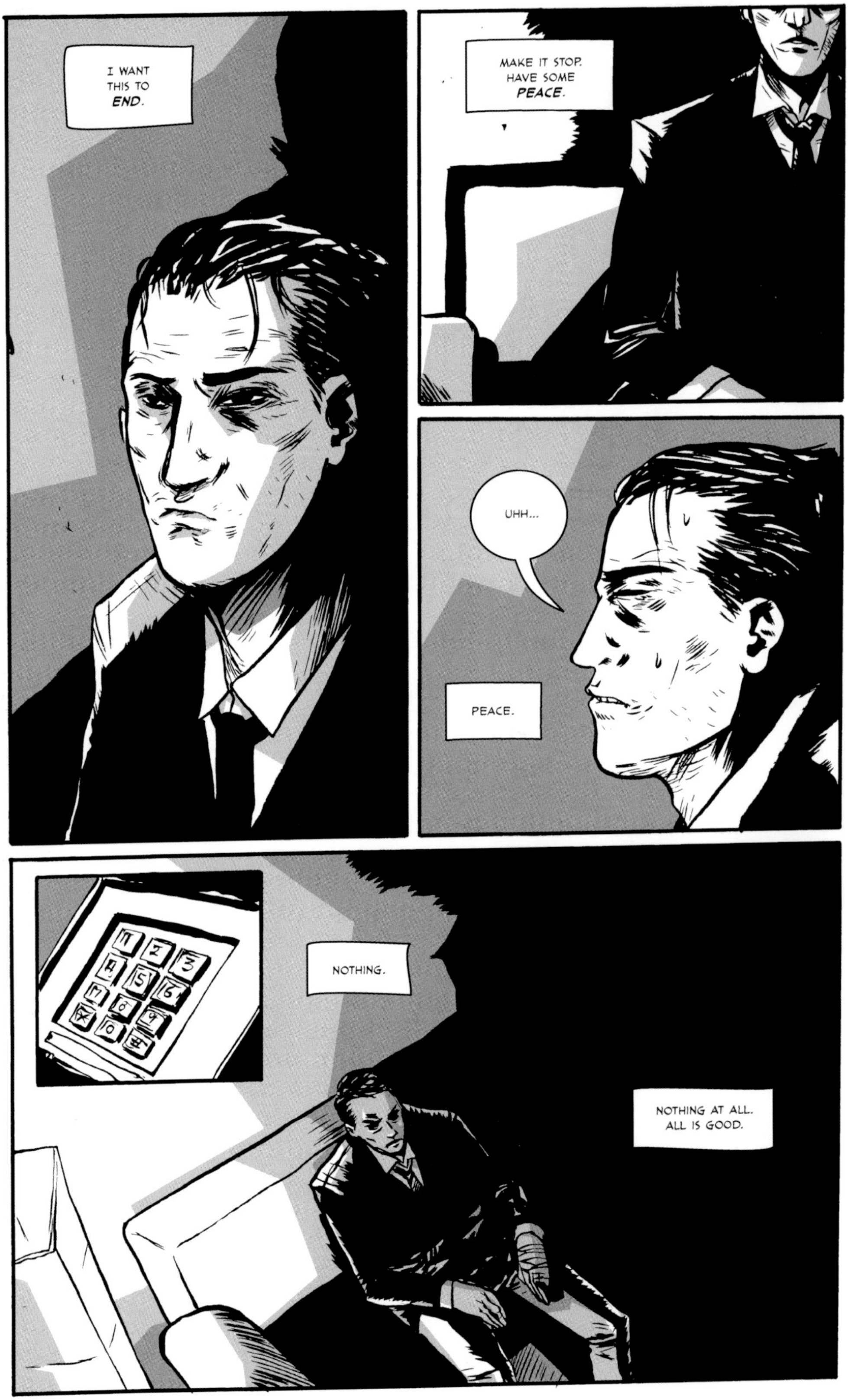
I WANT THIS TO END.
MAKE IT STOP. HAVE SOME PEACE.
UHH...
PEACE.
NOTHING.
NOTHING AT ALL. ALL IS GOOD.

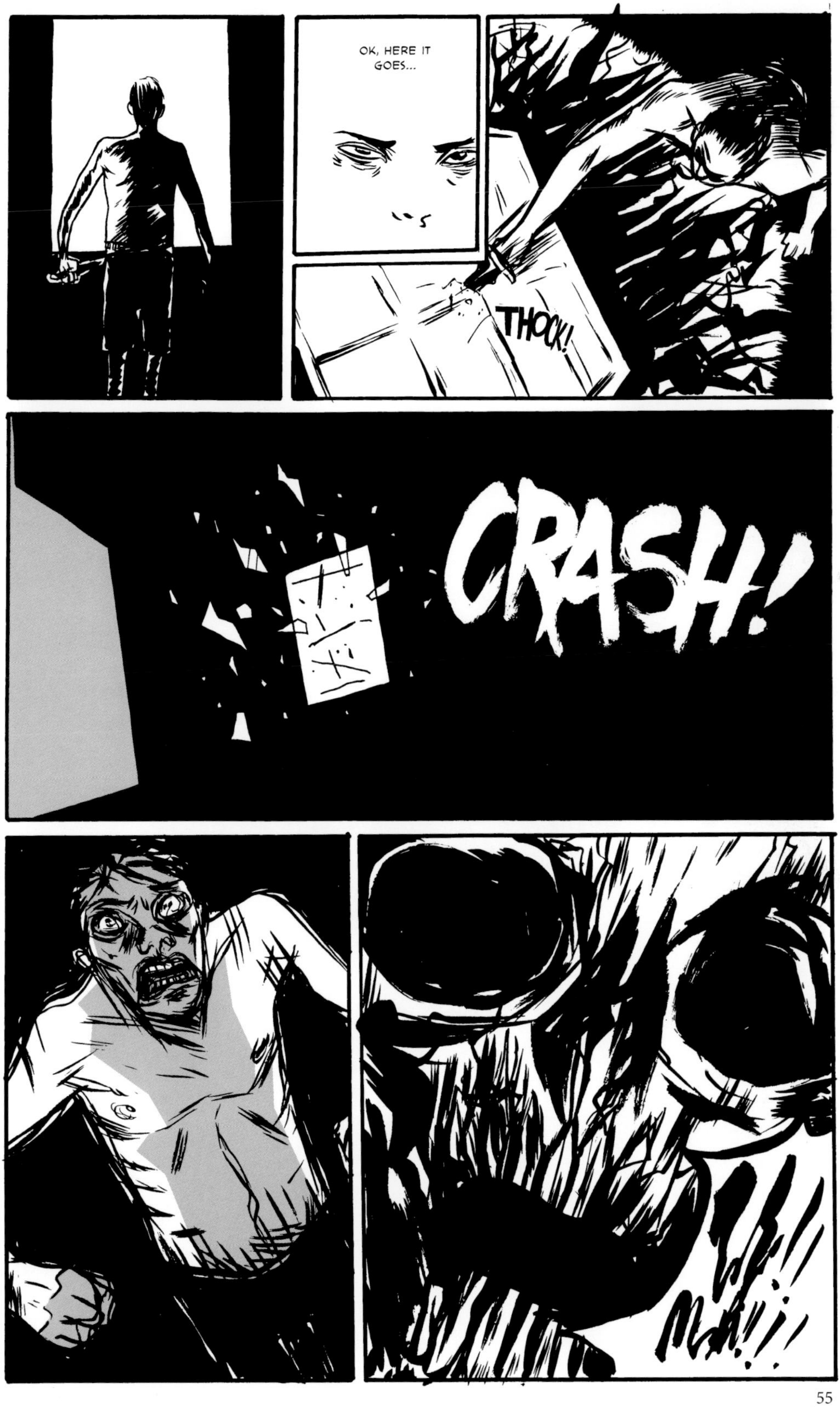
OK, HERE IT GOES...
THOCK!
CRASH!

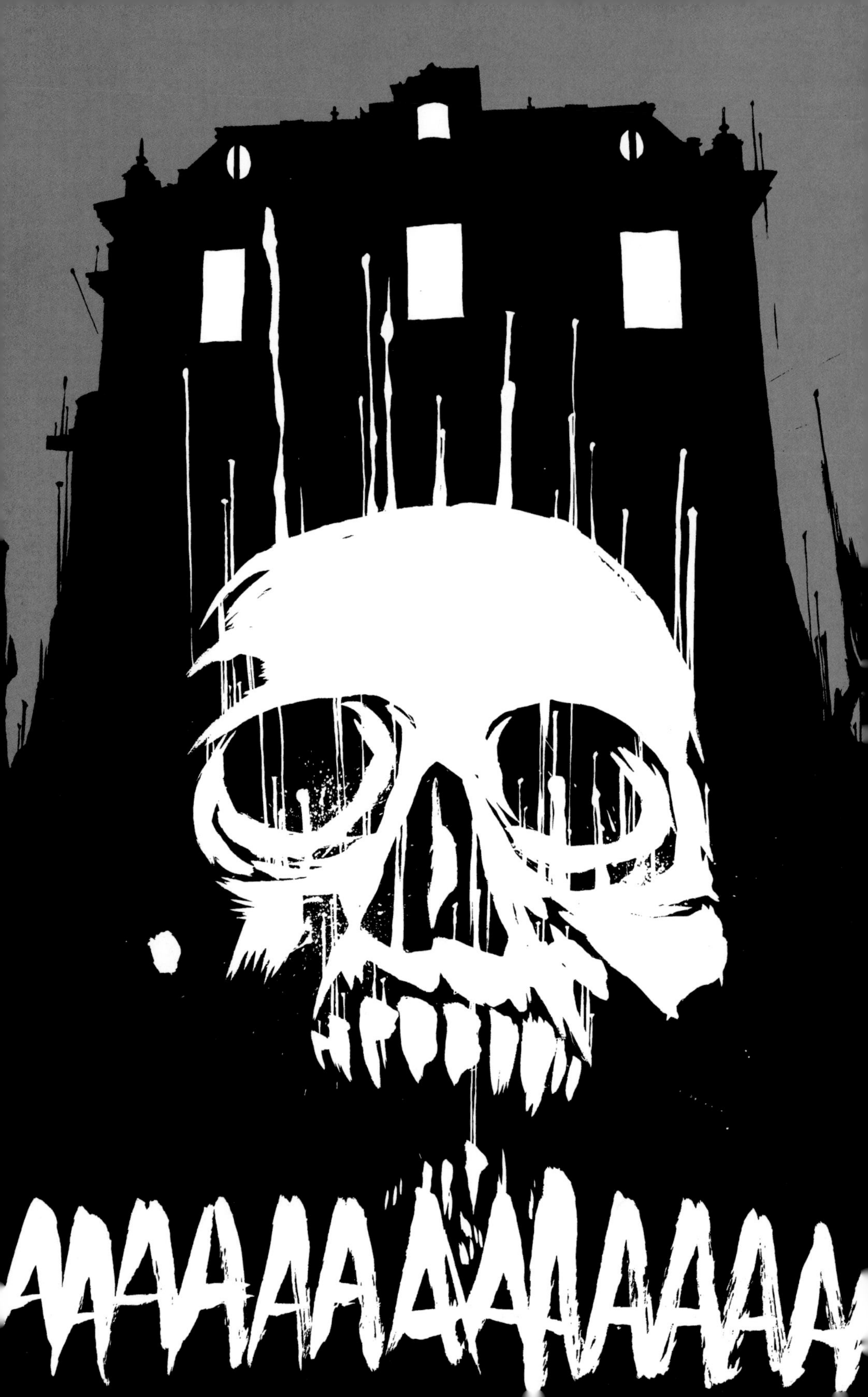
AAAAAAAAAAAAA

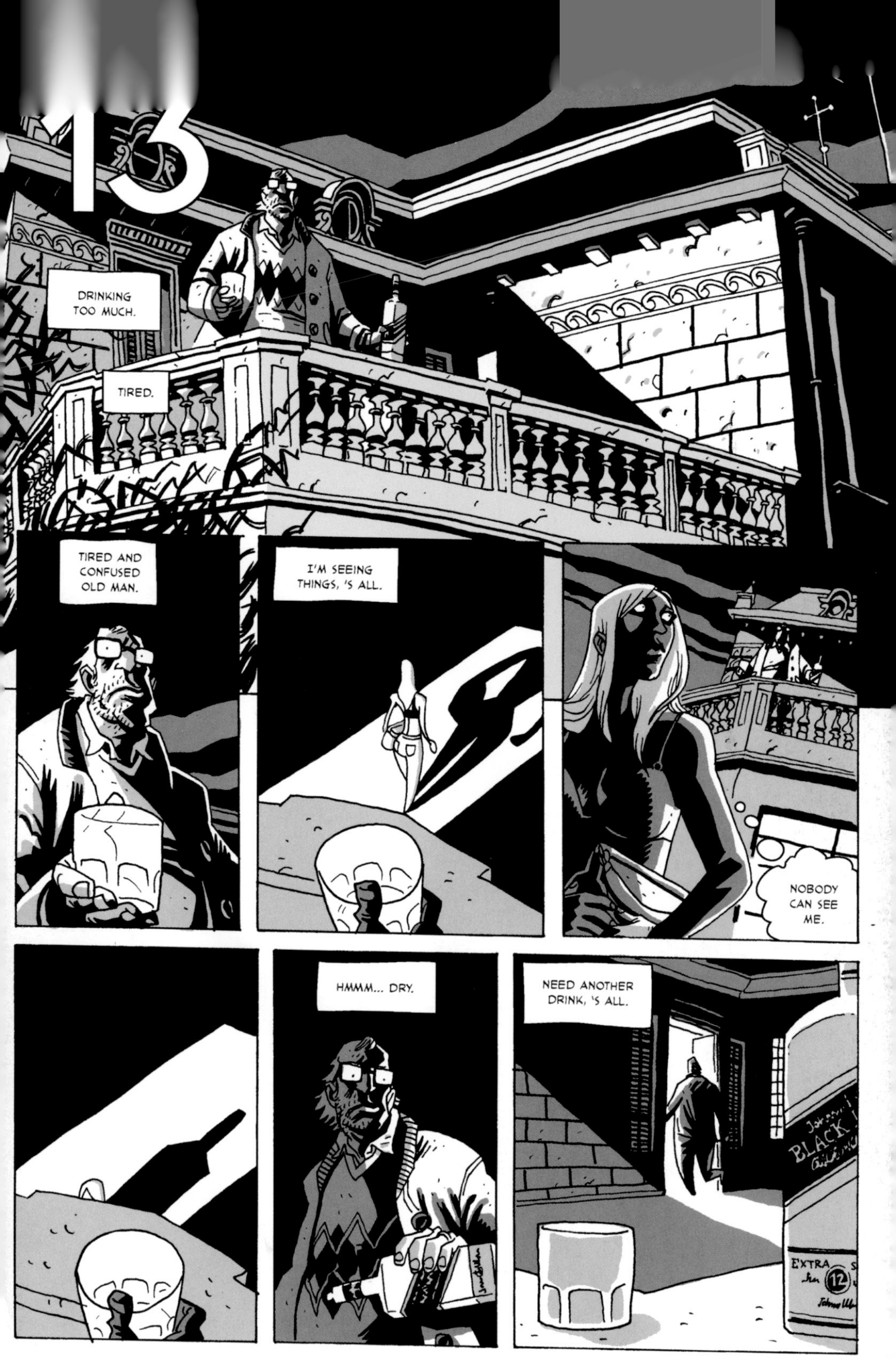
13
DRINKING TOO MUCH.
TIRED.
TIRED AND CONFUSED OLD MAN.
I'M SEEING THINGS, 'S ALL.
NOBODY CAN SEE ME.
HMMM... DRY.
NEED ANOTHER DRINK, 'S ALL.
EXTRA
12

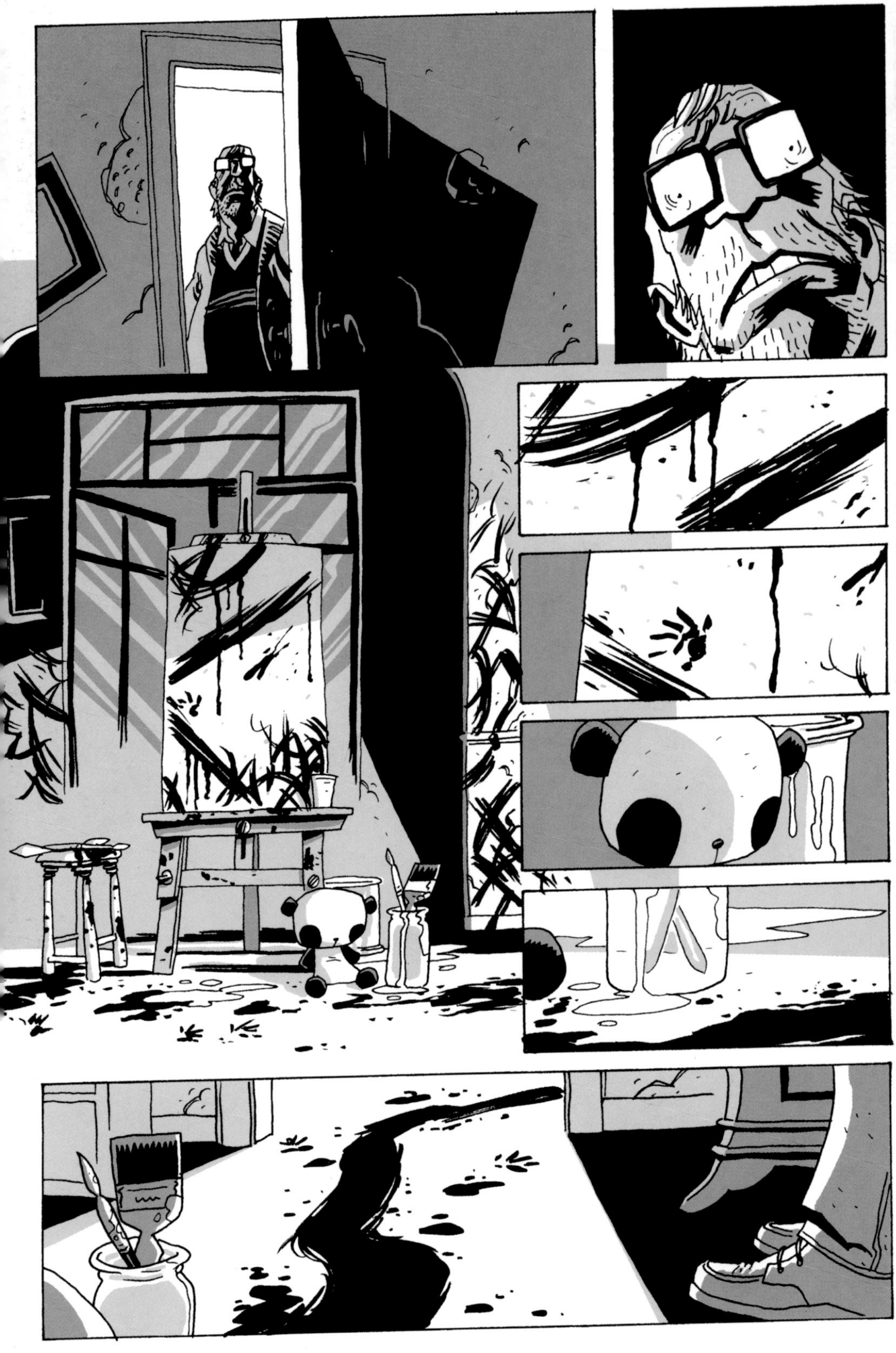

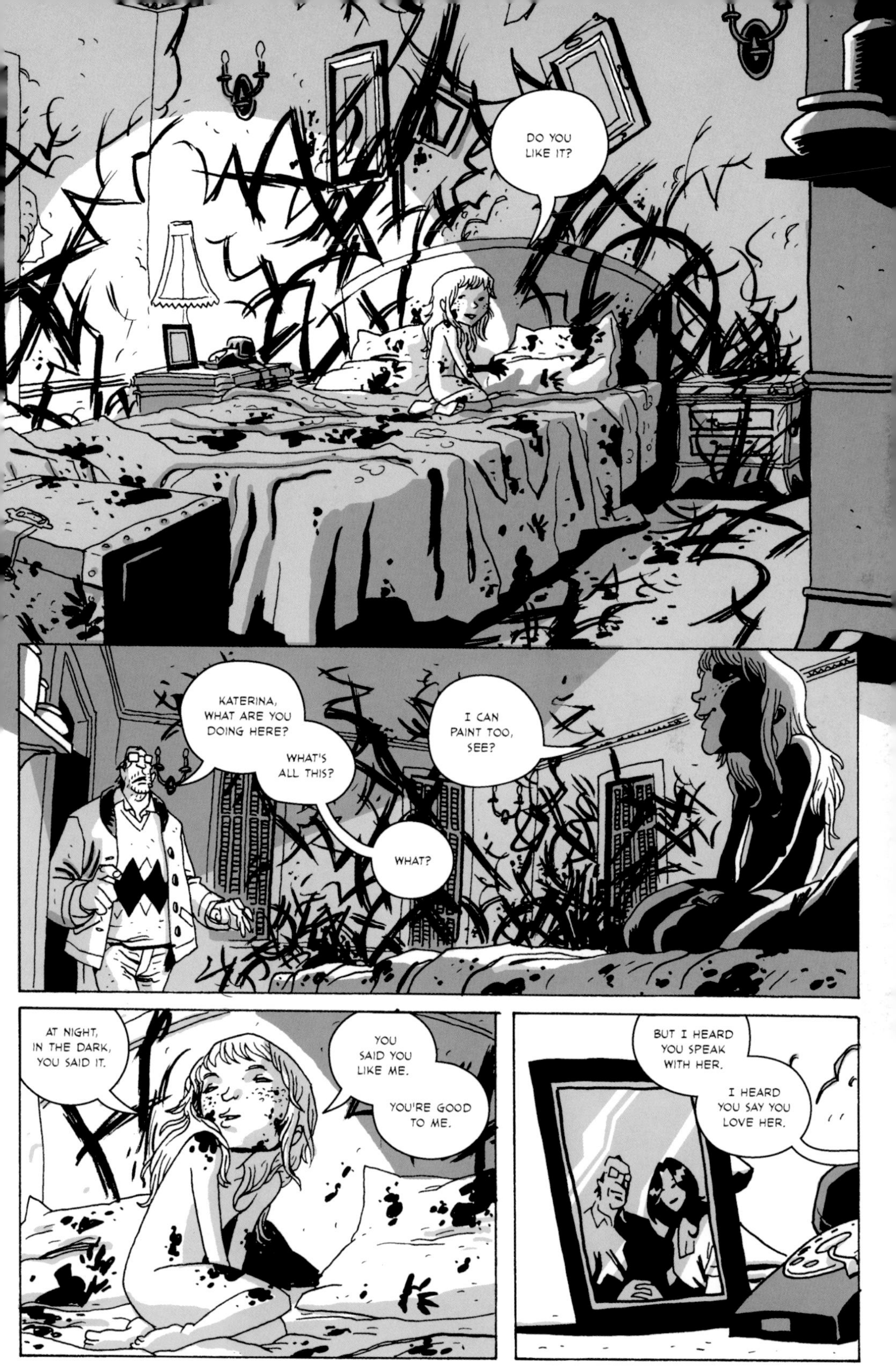

DO YOU LIKE IT?
KATERINA, WHAT ARE YOU DOING HERE?
WHAT'S ALL THIS?
WHAT?
I CAN PAINT TOO, SEE?
AT NIGHT, IN THE DARK, YOU SAID IT.
YOU SAID YOU LIKE ME.
YOU'RE GOOD TO ME.
BUT I HEARD YOU SPEAK WITH HER.
I HEARD YOU SAY YOU LOVE HER.

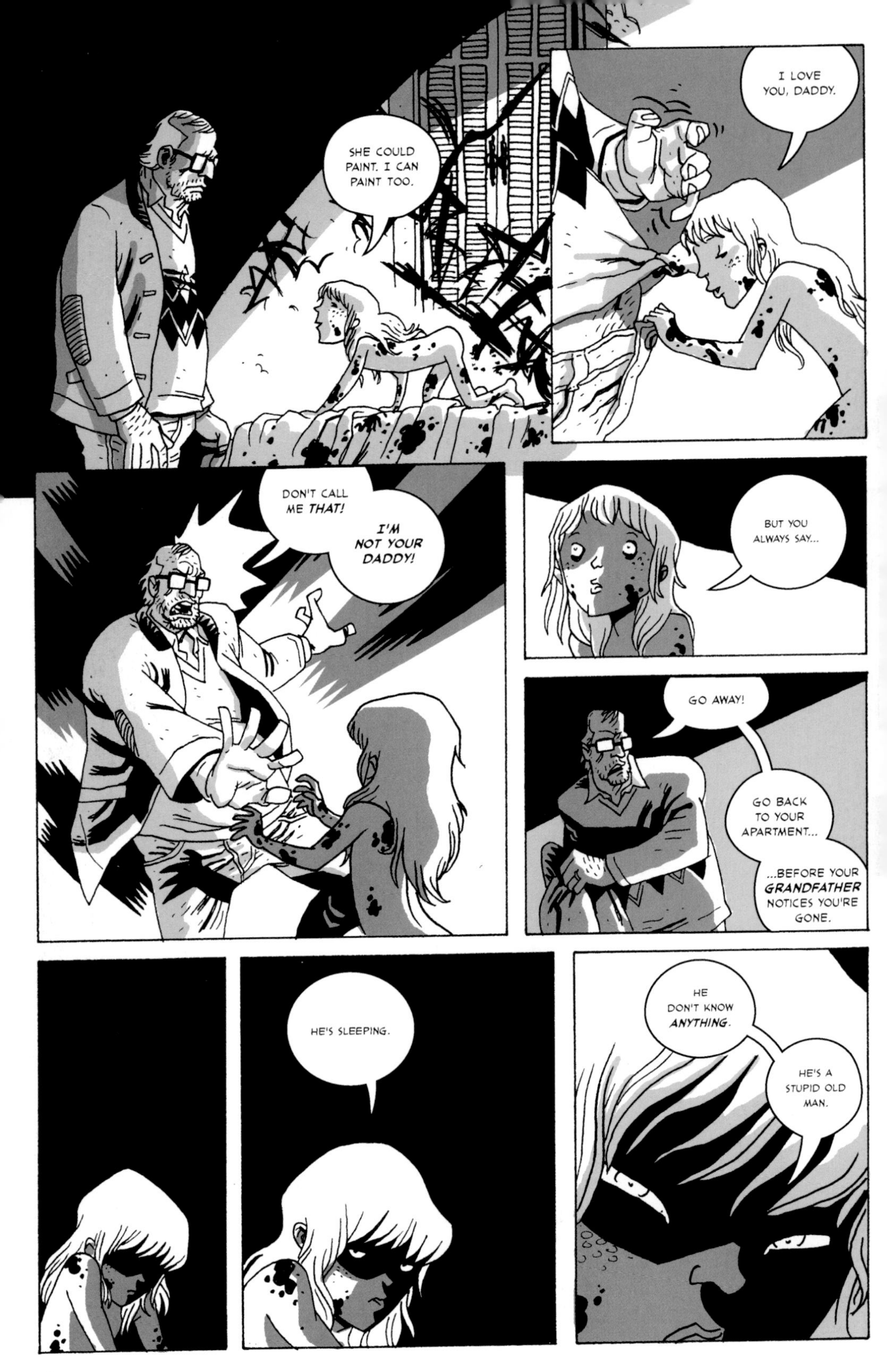
SHE COULD PAINT. I CAN PAINT TOO.
I LOVE YOU, DADDY.
DON'T CALL ME THAT!
I'M NOT YOUR DADDY!
BUT YOU ALWAYS SAY...
GO AWAY!
GO BACK TO YOUR APARTMENT...
...BEFORE YOUR GRANDFATHER NOTICES YOU'RE GONE.
HE'S SLEEPING.
HE DON'T KNOW ANYTHING.
HE'S A STUPID OLD MAN.

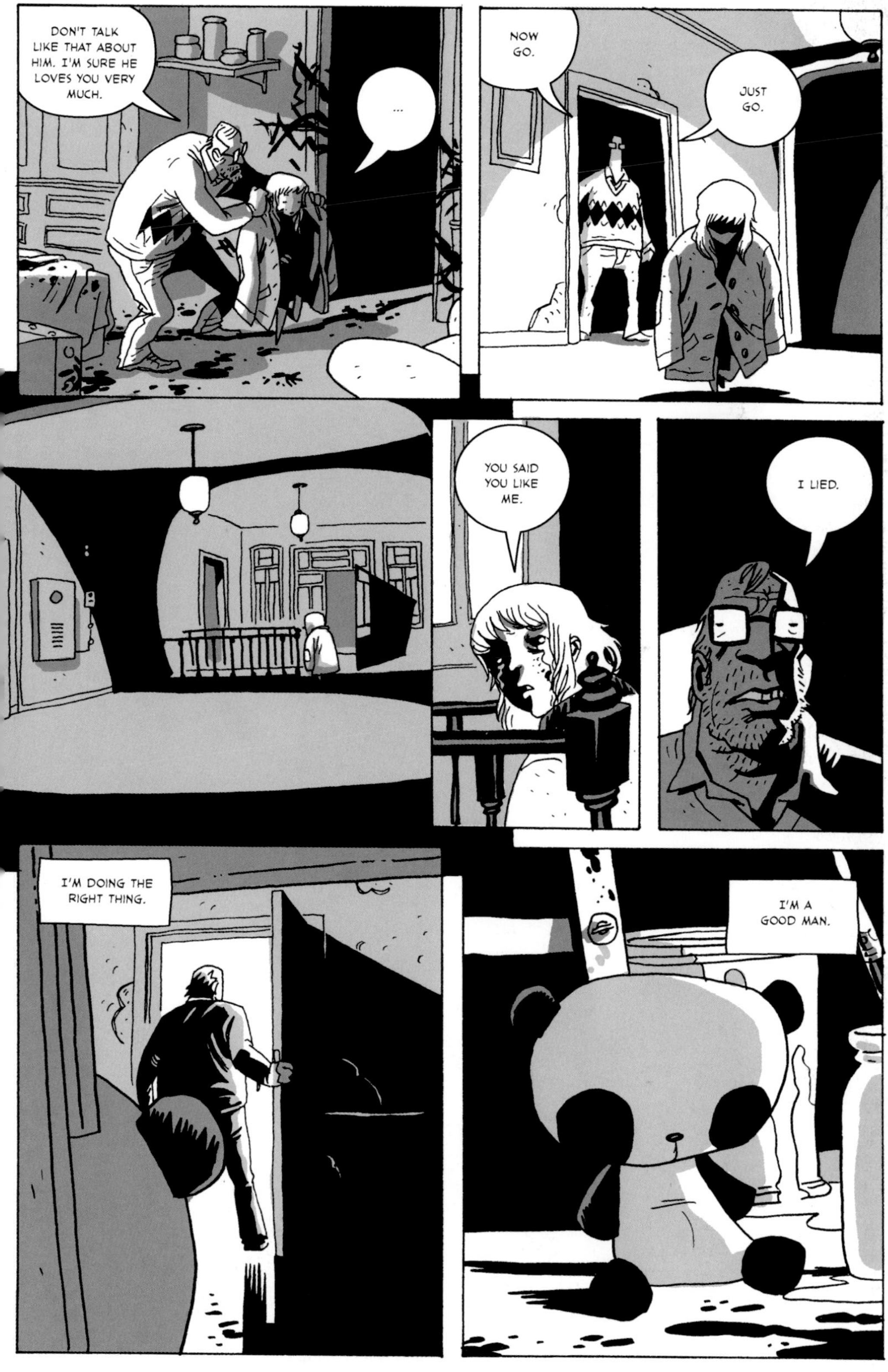
DON'T TALK LIKE THAT ABOUT HIM. I'M SURE HE LOVES YOU VERY MUCH.
...
NOW GO.
JUST GO.
YOU SAID YOU LIKE ME.
I LIED.
I'M DOING THE RIGHT THING.
I'M A GOOD MAN.

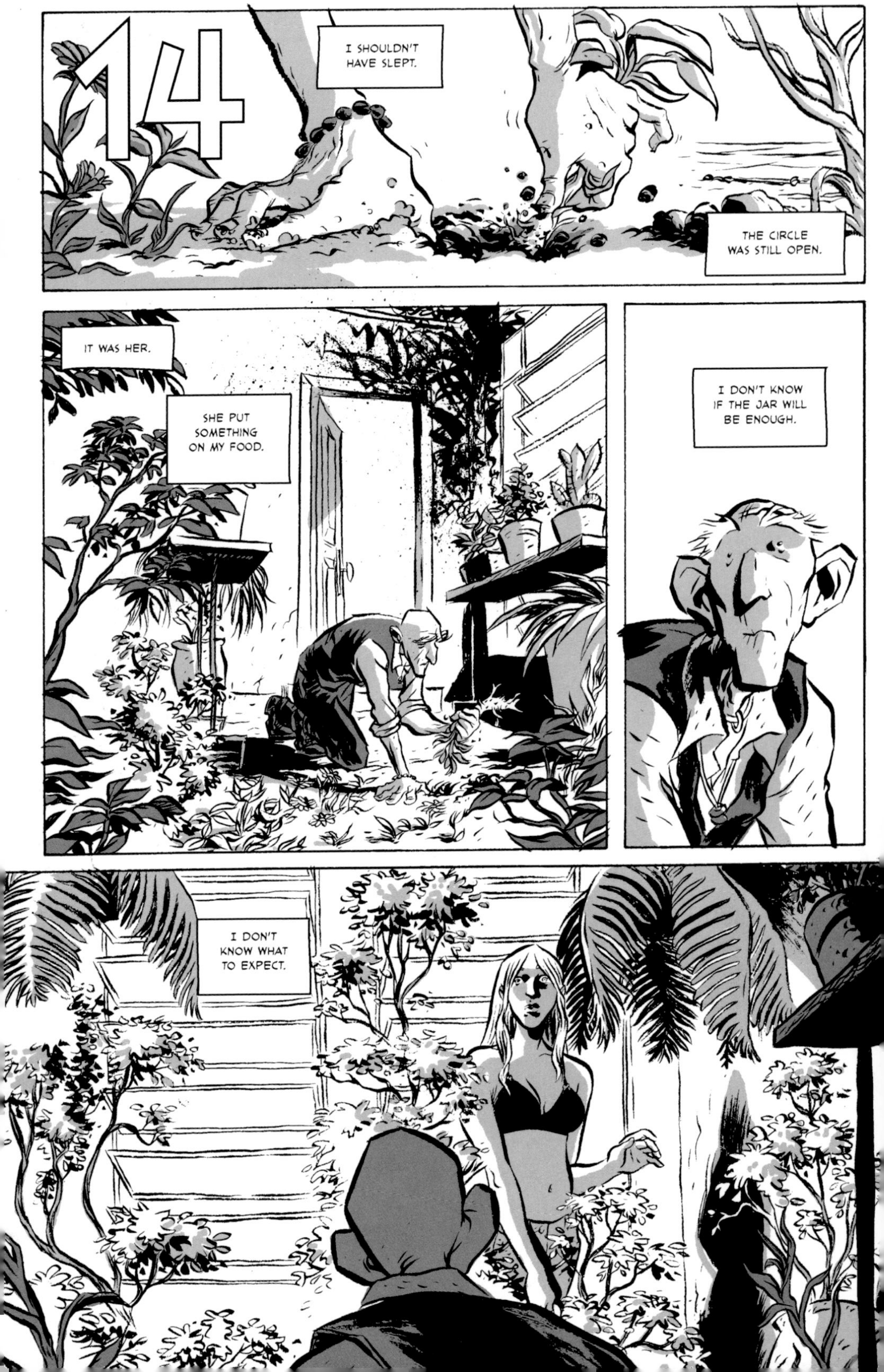
14
I SHOULDN'T HAVE SLEPT.
THE CIRCLE WAS STILL OPEN.
IT WAS HER.
SHE PUT SOMETHING ON MY FOOD.
I DON'T KNOW IF THE JAR WILL BE ENOUGH.
I DON'T KNOW WHAT TO EXPECT.

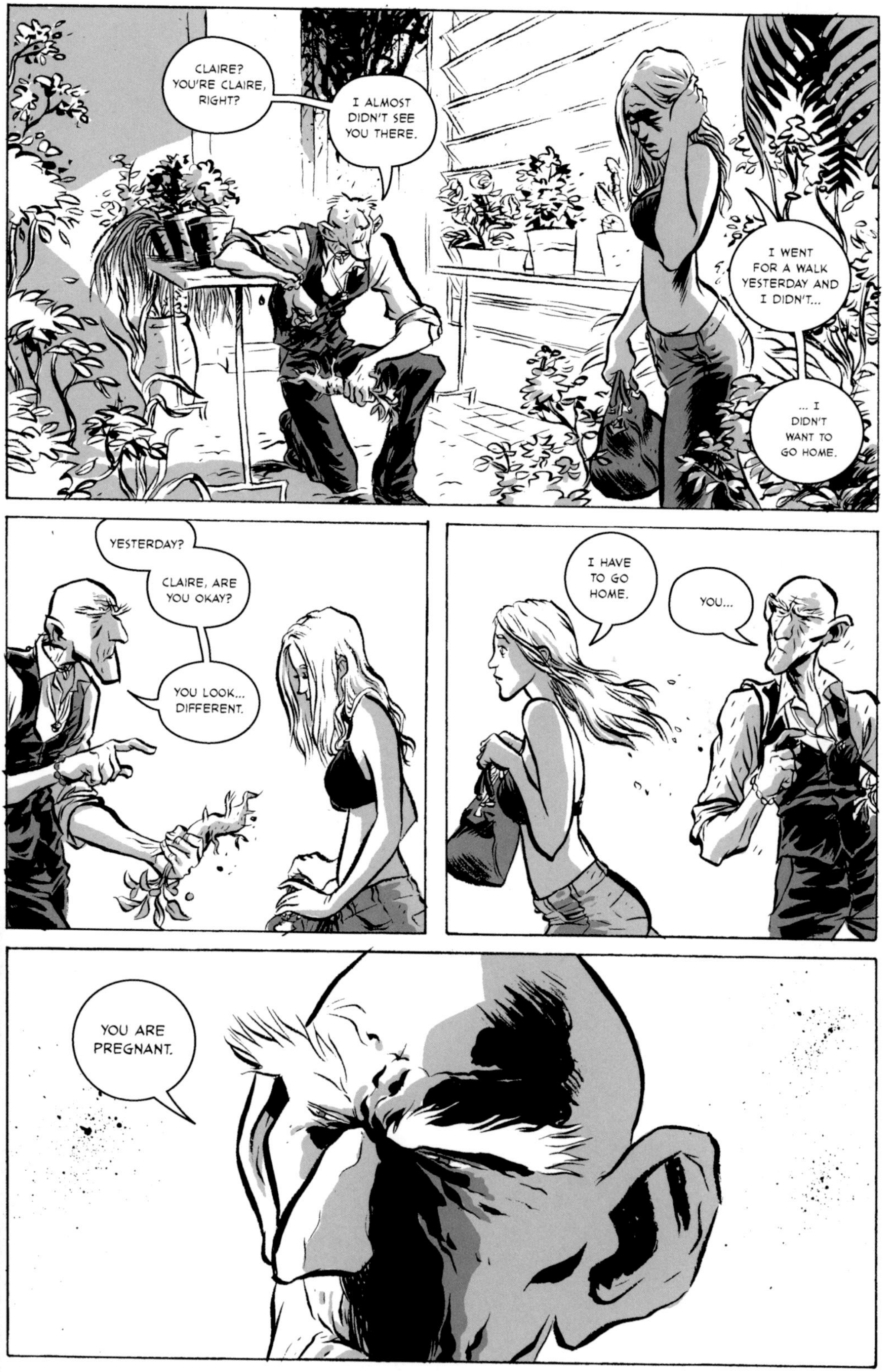

CLAIRE? YOU'RE CLAIRE, RIGHT?
I ALMOST DIDN'T SEE YOU THERE.
I WENT FOR A WALK YESTERDAY AND I DIDN'T...
... I DIDN'T WANT TO GO HOME.
YESTERDAY?
CLAIRE, ARE YOU OKAY?
YOU LOOK... DIFFERENT.
I HAVE TO GO HOME.
YOU...
YOU ARE PREGNANT.

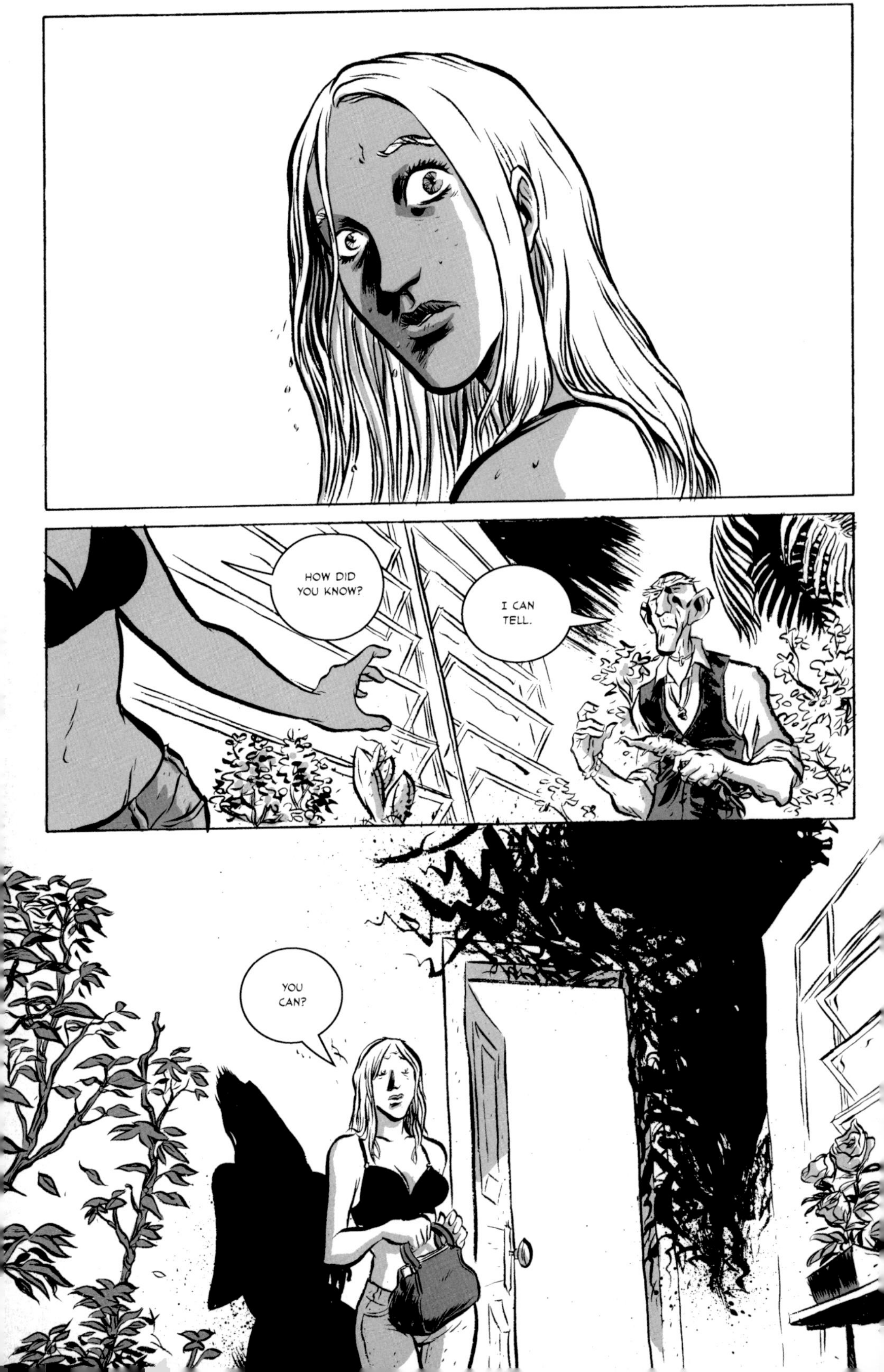
HOW DID YOU KNOW?
I CAN TELL.
YOU CAN?

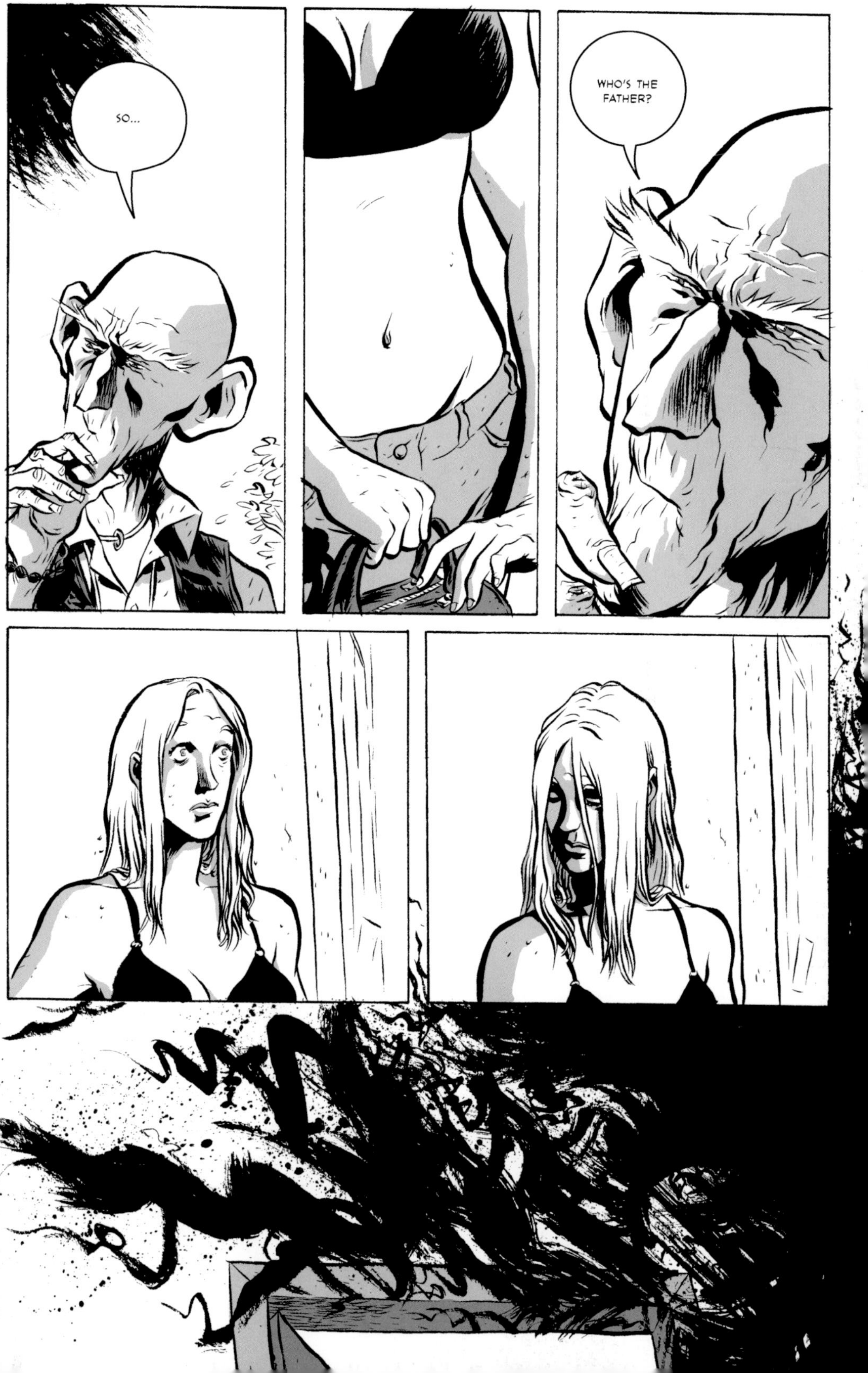
SO...
WHO'S THE FATHER?

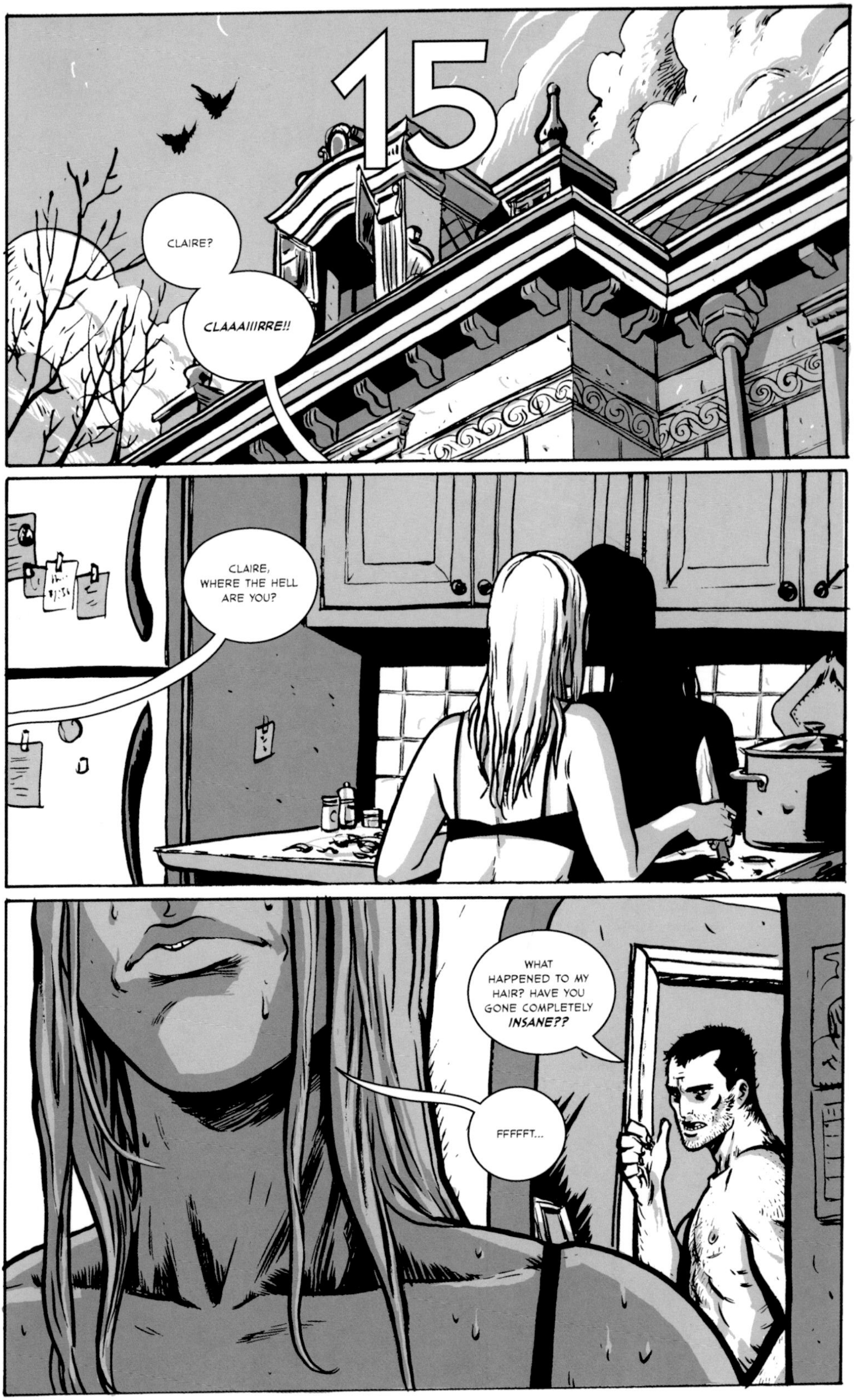
15
CLAIRE?
CLAAAIIIRRE!!
CLAIRE, WHERE THE HELL ARE YOU?
WHAT HAPPENED TO MY HAIR? HAVE YOU GONE COMPLETELY INSANE??
FFFFFT...

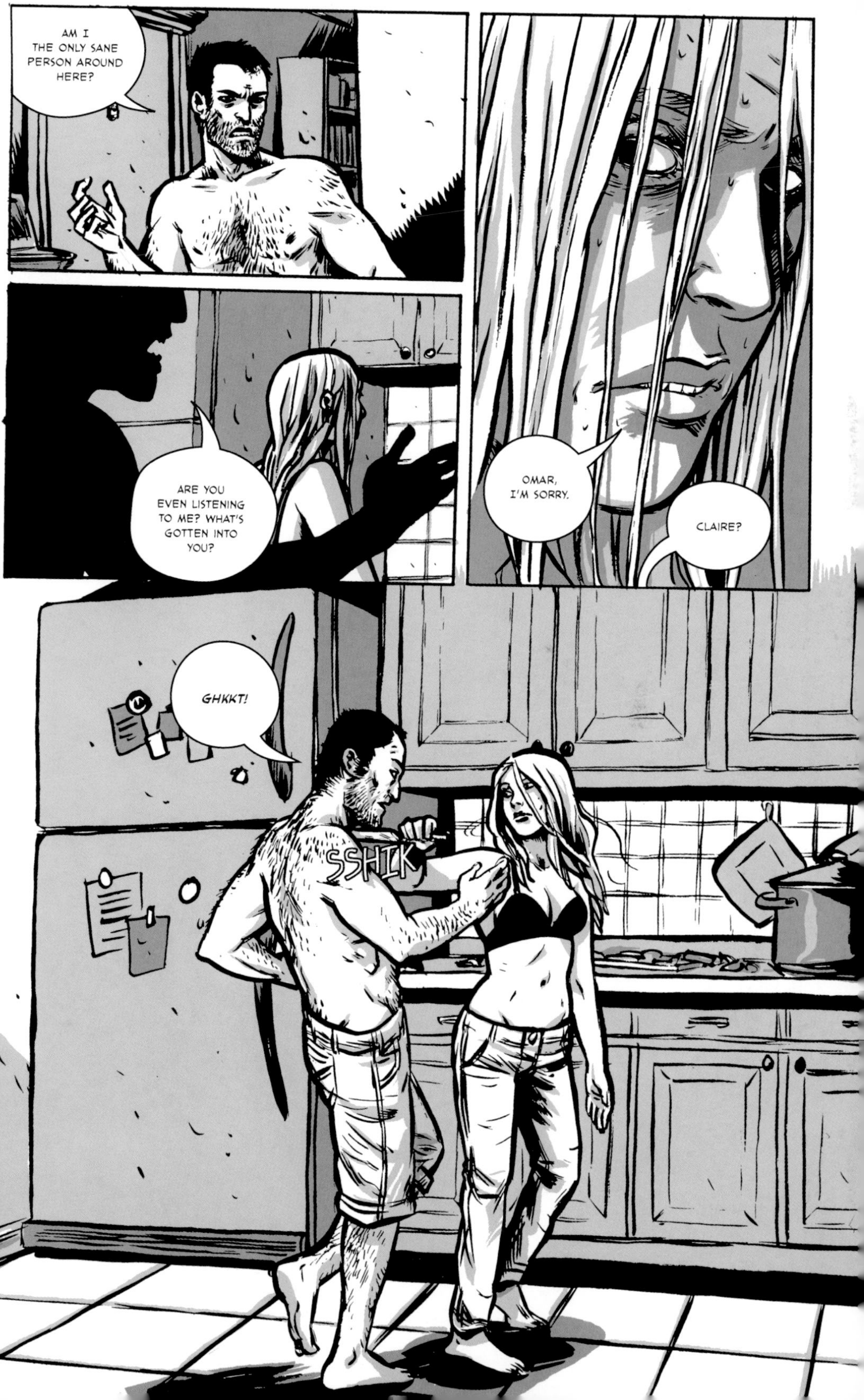
AM I THE ONLY SANE PERSON AROUND HERE?
ARE YOU EVEN LISTENING TO ME? WHAT'S GOTTEN INTO YOU?
OMAR, I'M SORRY.
CLAIRE?
GHKKT!
SSHIK

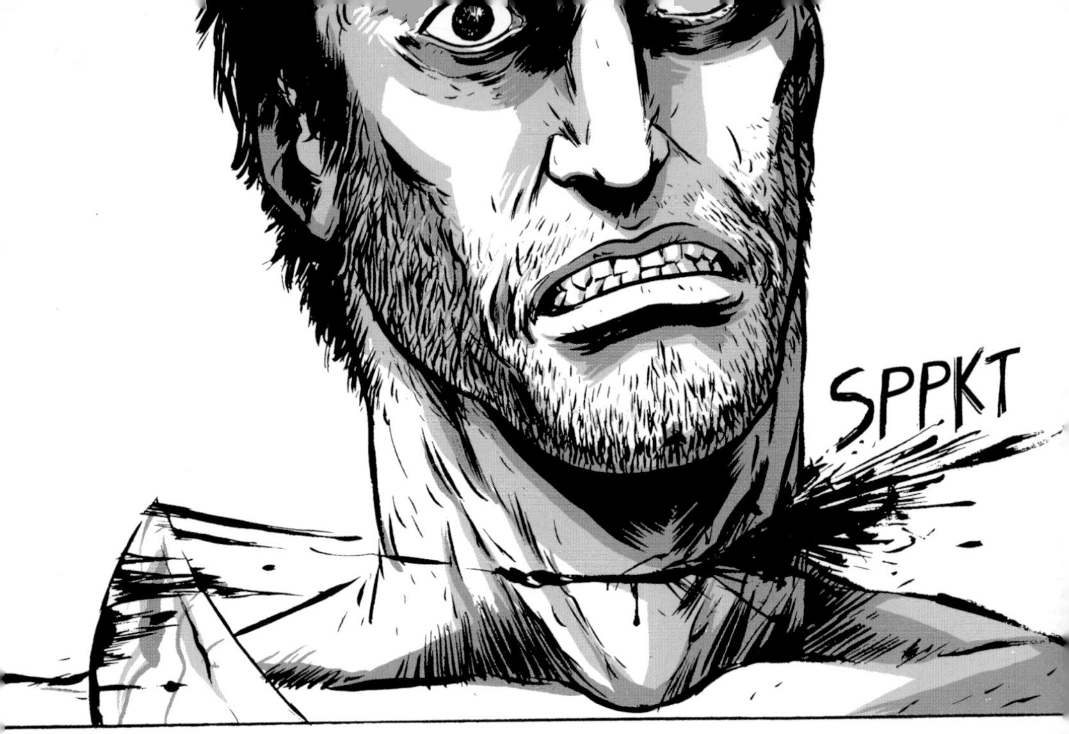
SPPKT

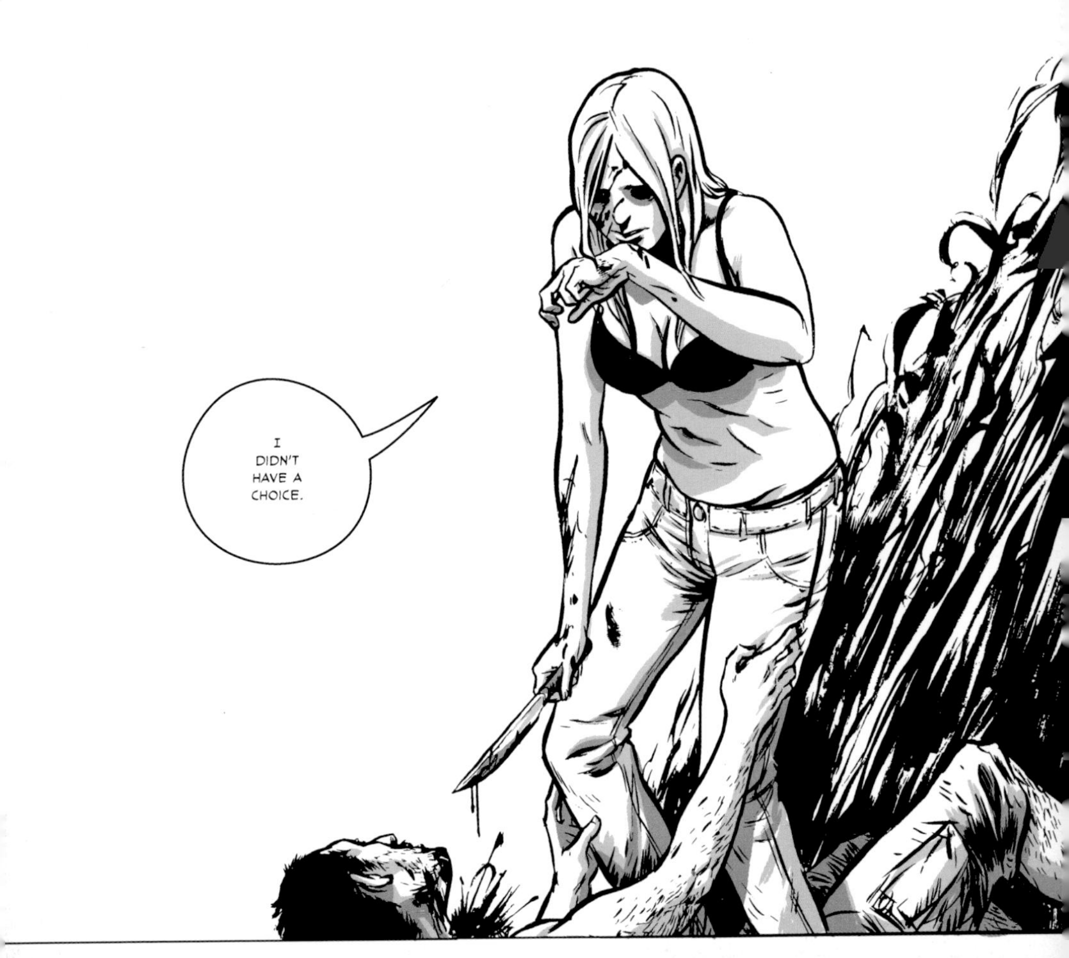
I DIDN'T HAVE A CHOICE.

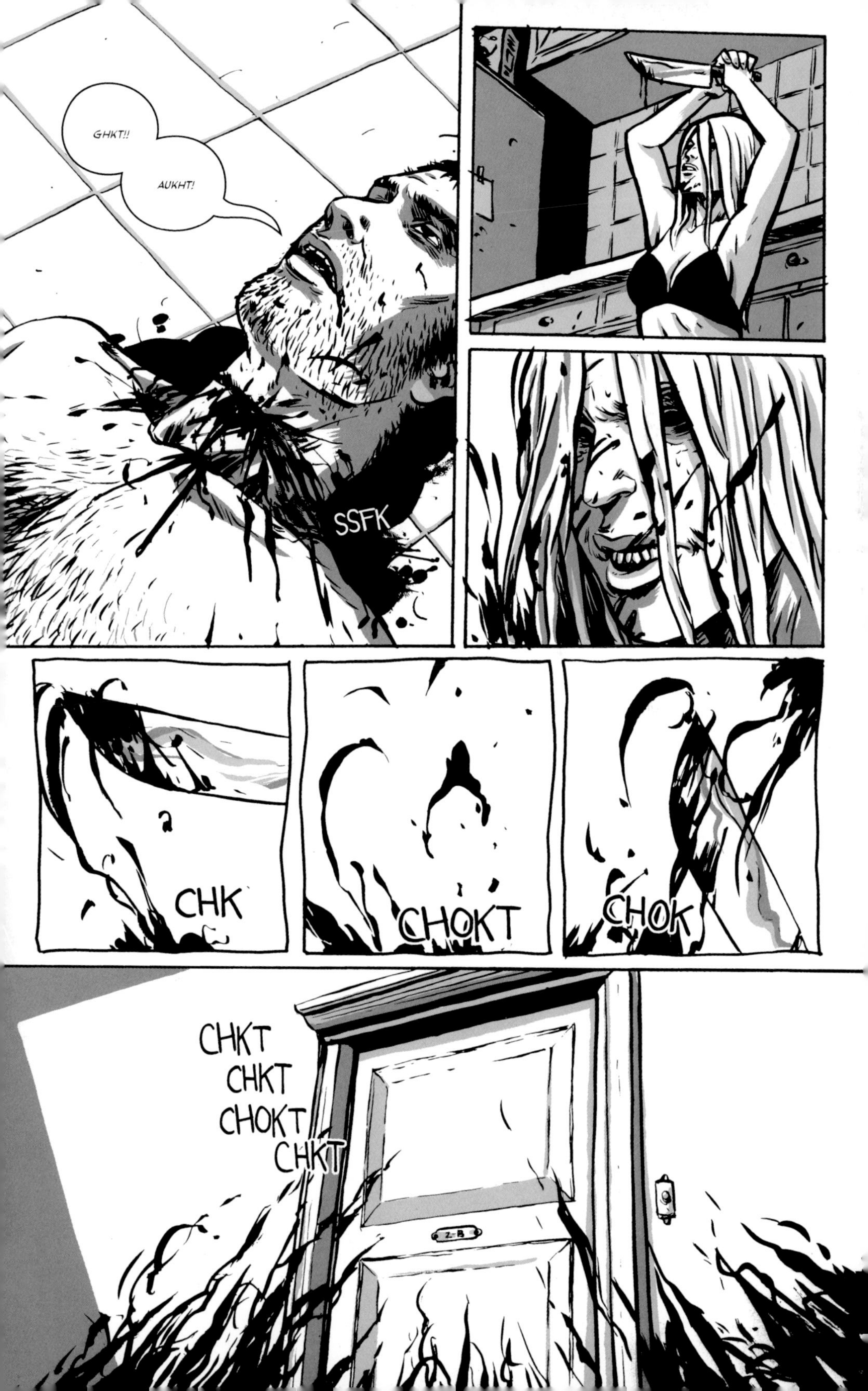
GHKT!!
AUKHT!
SSFK
CHK
CHOKT
CHOK
CHKT
CHKT
CHOKT
CHKT

NOW WE WAIT.

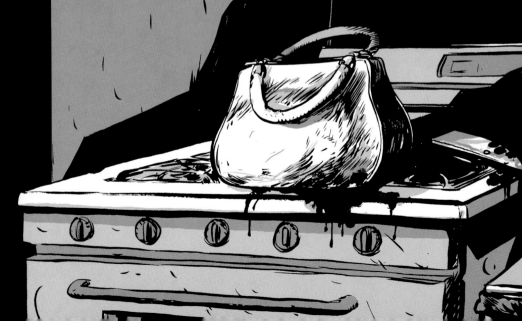

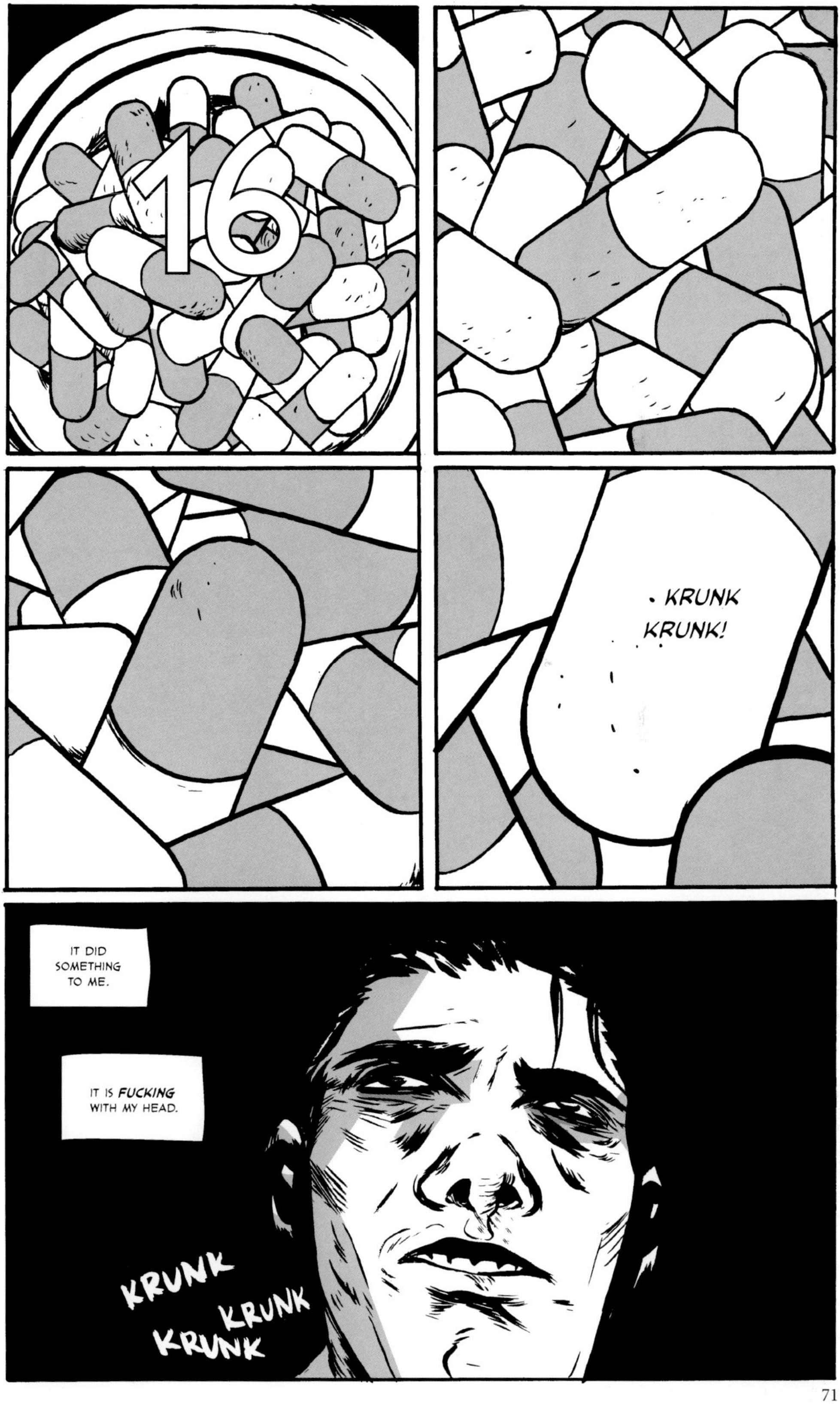
16
• KRUNK
KRUNK!
IT DID SOMETHING TO ME.
IT IS *FUCKING* WITH MY HEAD.
KRUNK
KRUNK
KRUNK

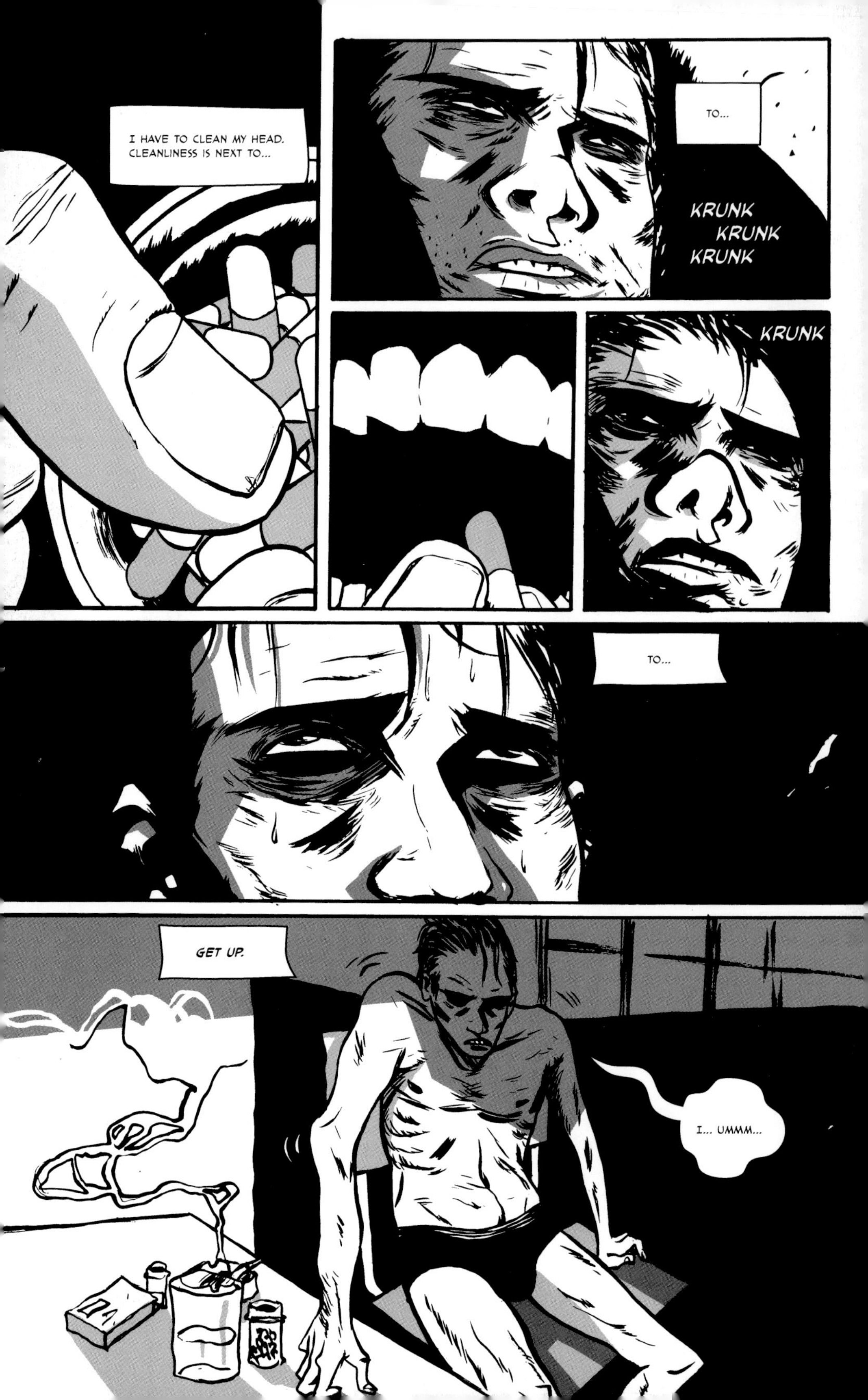
I HAVE TO CLEAN MY HEAD.
CLEANLINESS IS NEXT TO...
TO...
KRUNK
KRUNK
KRUNK
KRUNK
TO...
GET UP.
I... UMMM...

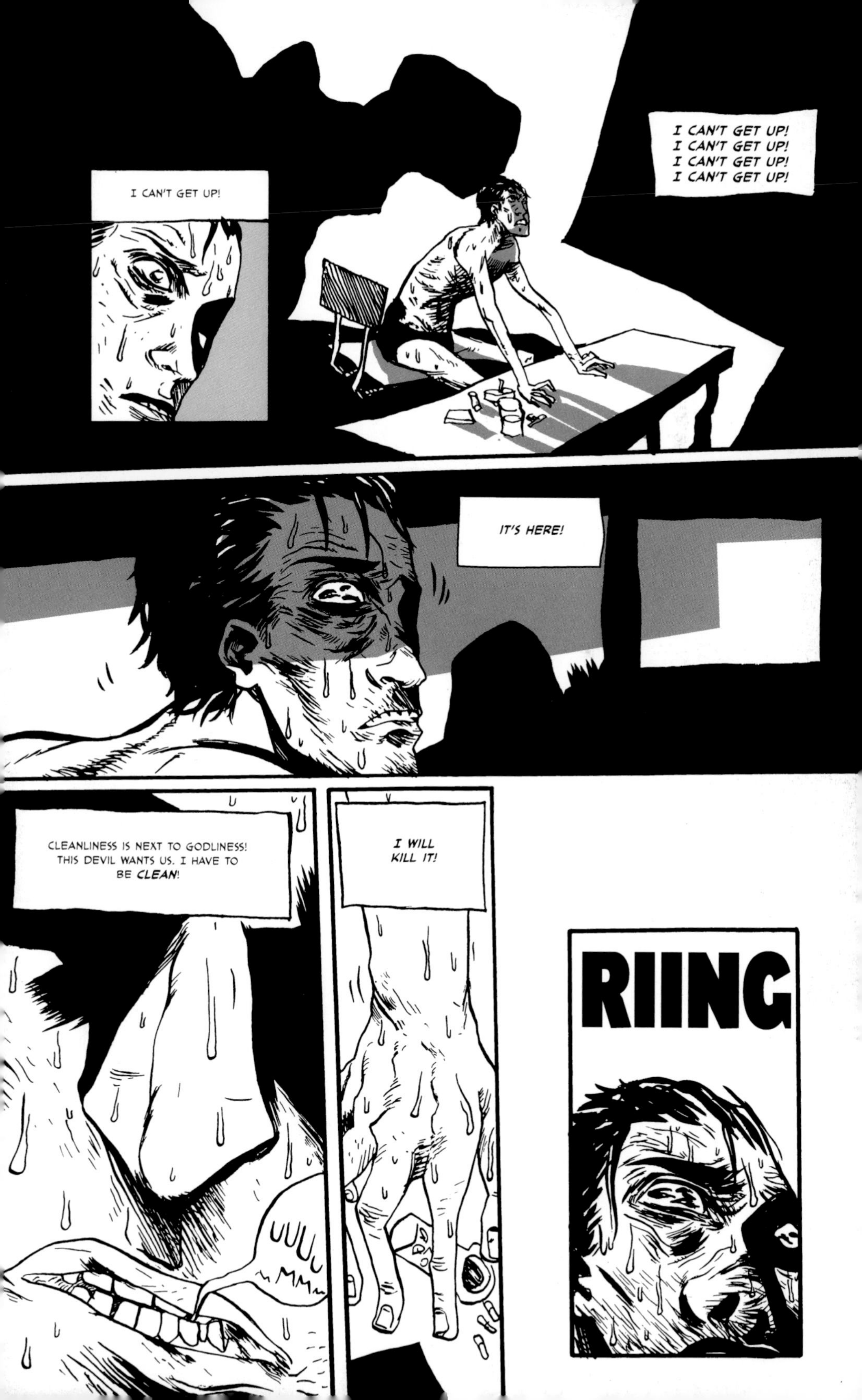
I CAN'T GET UP!
I CAN'T GET UP!
I CAN'T GET UP!
I CAN'T GET UP!
I CAN'T GET UP!
IT'S HERE!
CLEANLINESS IS NEXT TO GODLINESS! THIS DEVIL WANTS US. I HAVE TO BE CLEAN!
I WILL KILL IT!
RIING

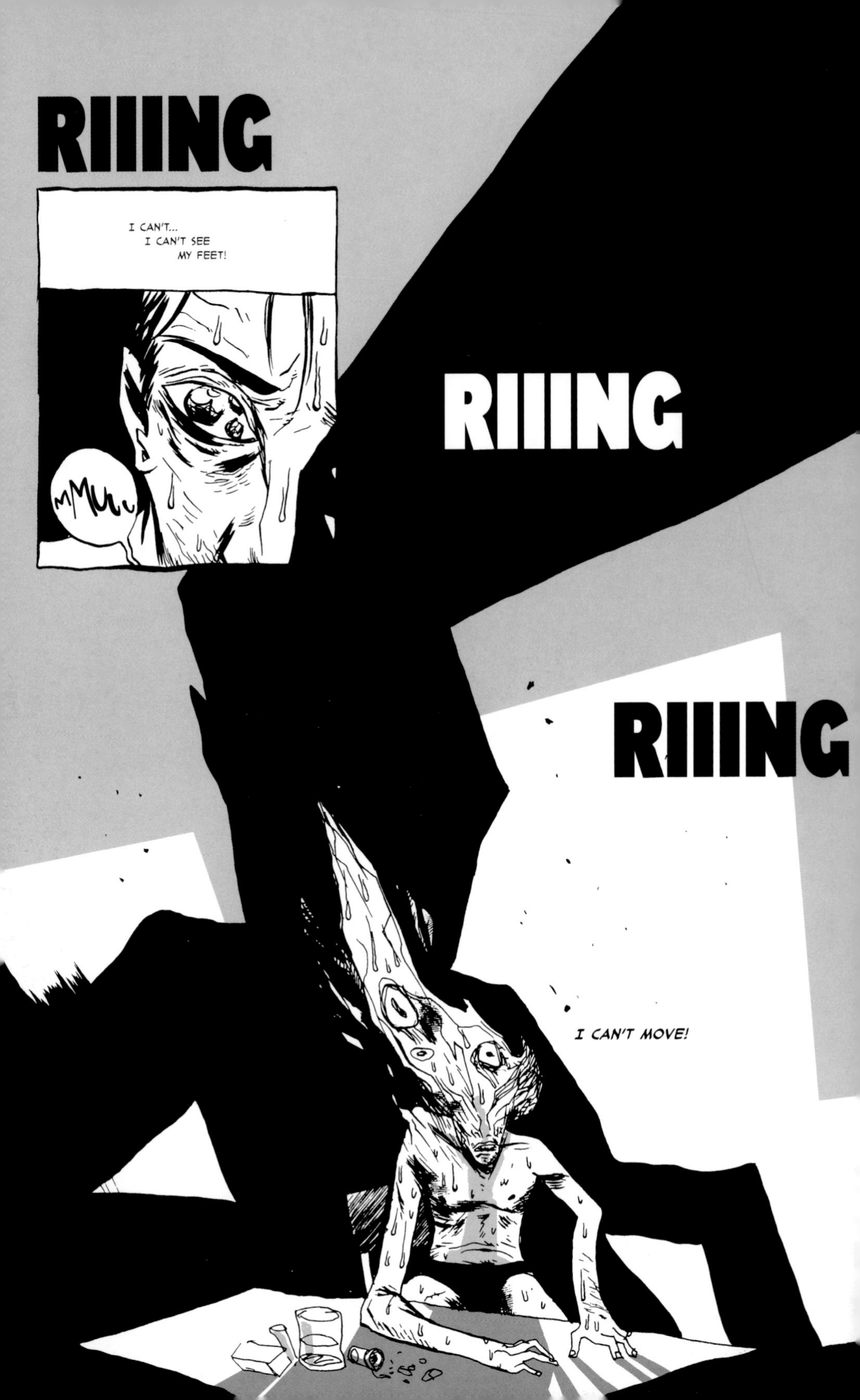
RIIING
I CAN'T... I CAN'T SEE MY FEET!
MMU..
RIIING
RIIING
I CAN'T MOVE!

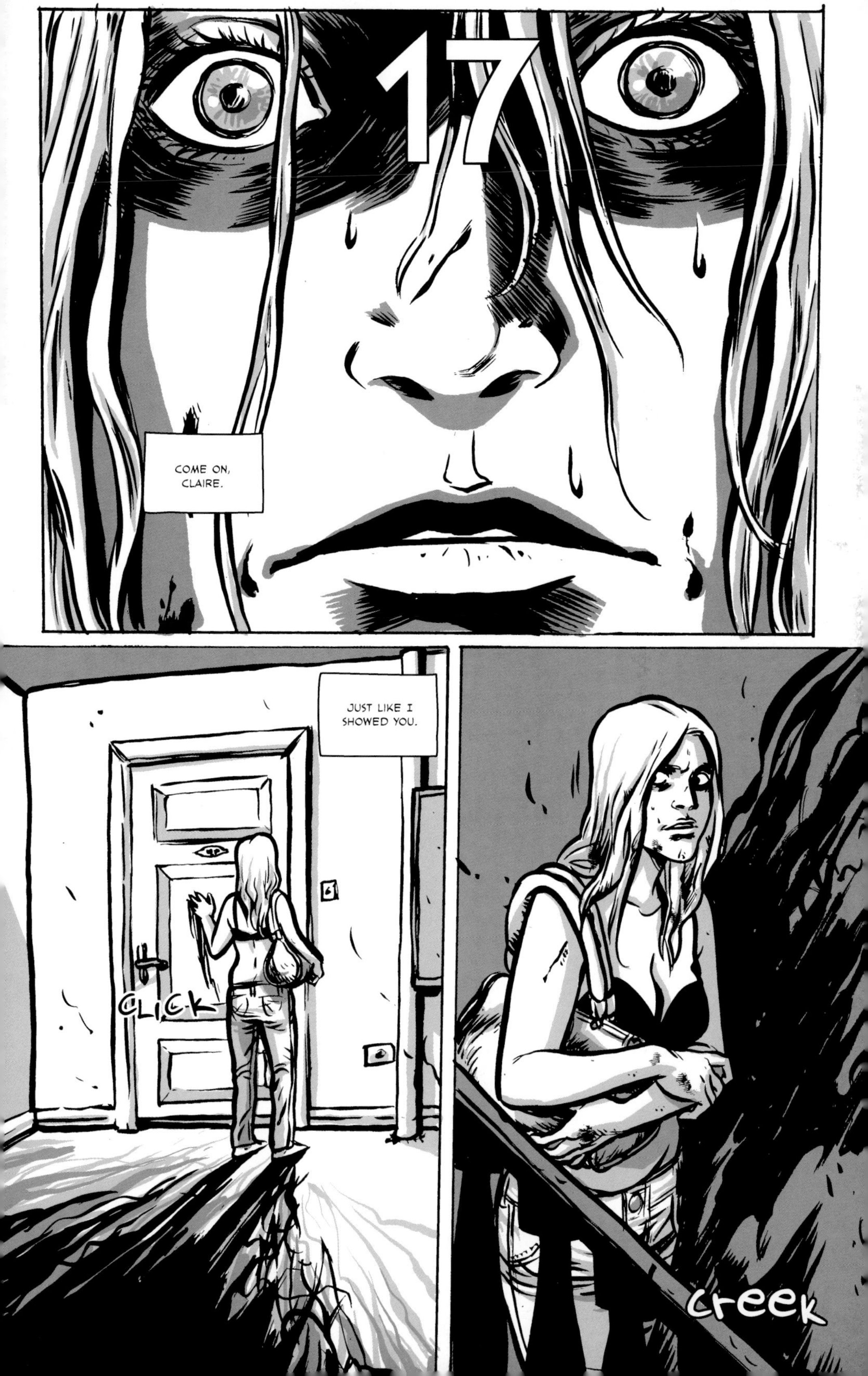
17
COME ON, CLAIRE.
JUST LIKE I SHOWED YOU.
CLICK
creek

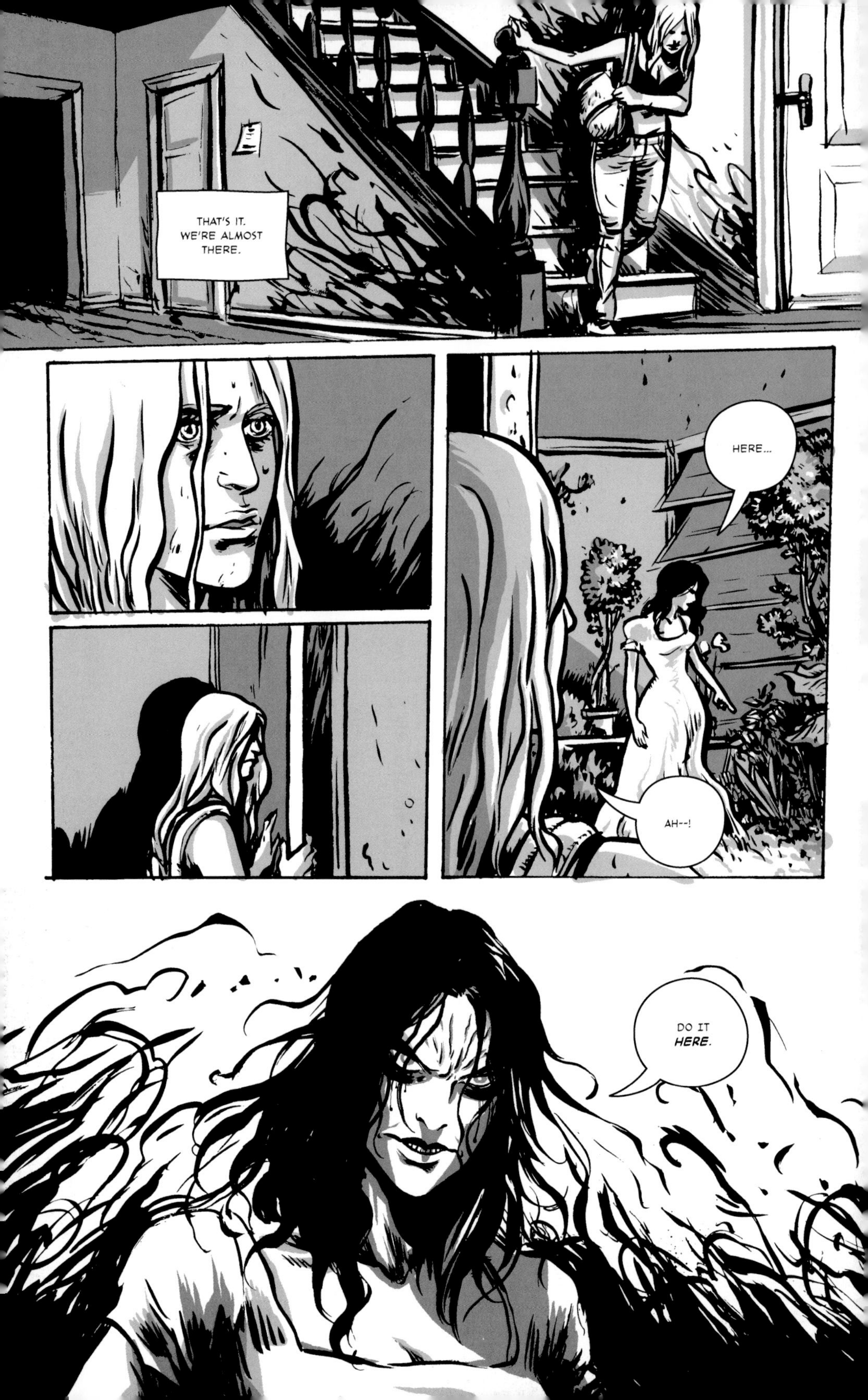
THAT'S IT. WE'RE ALMOST THERE.
HERE...
AH--!
DO IT HERE.

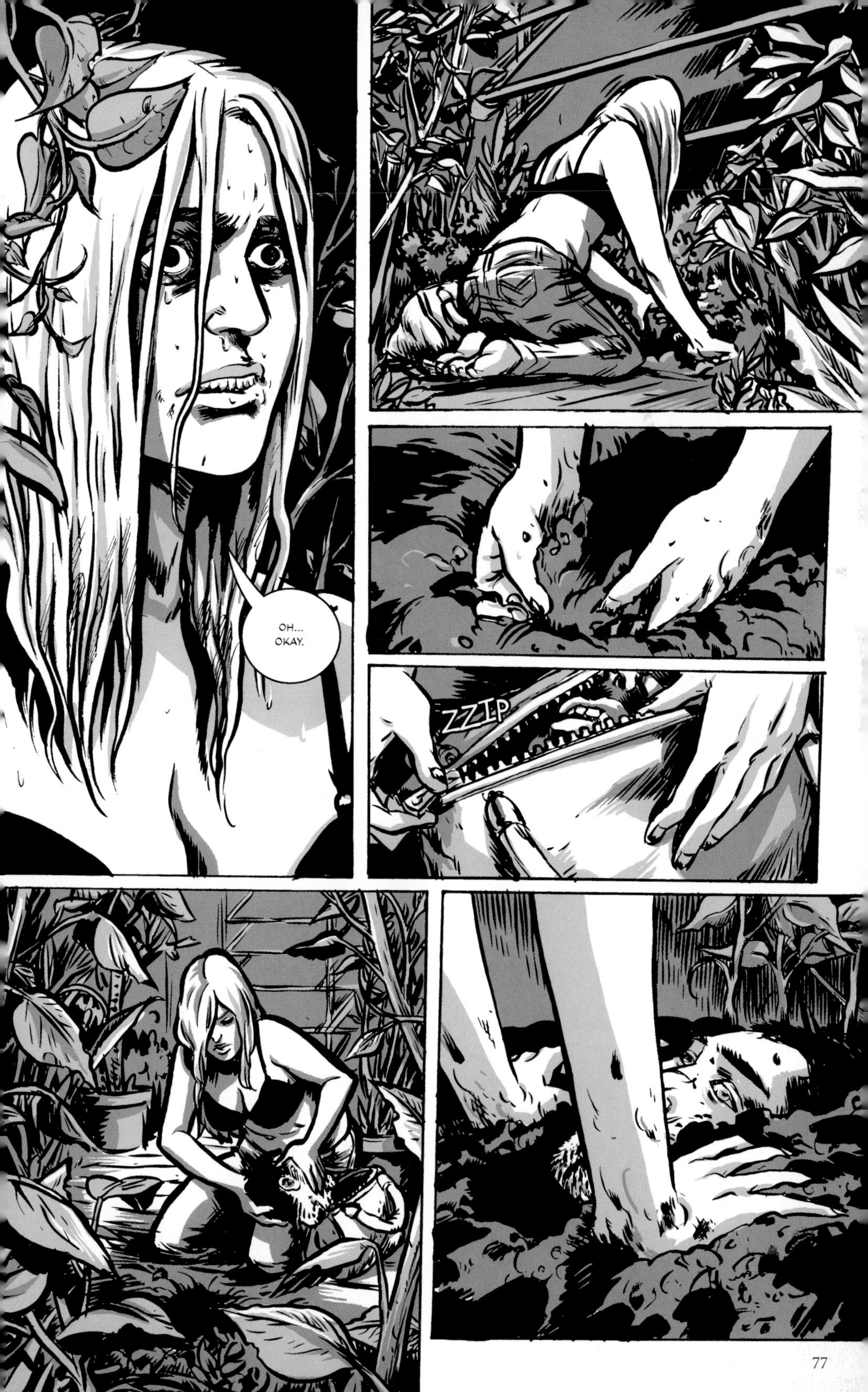
OH... OKAY.
ZZIP

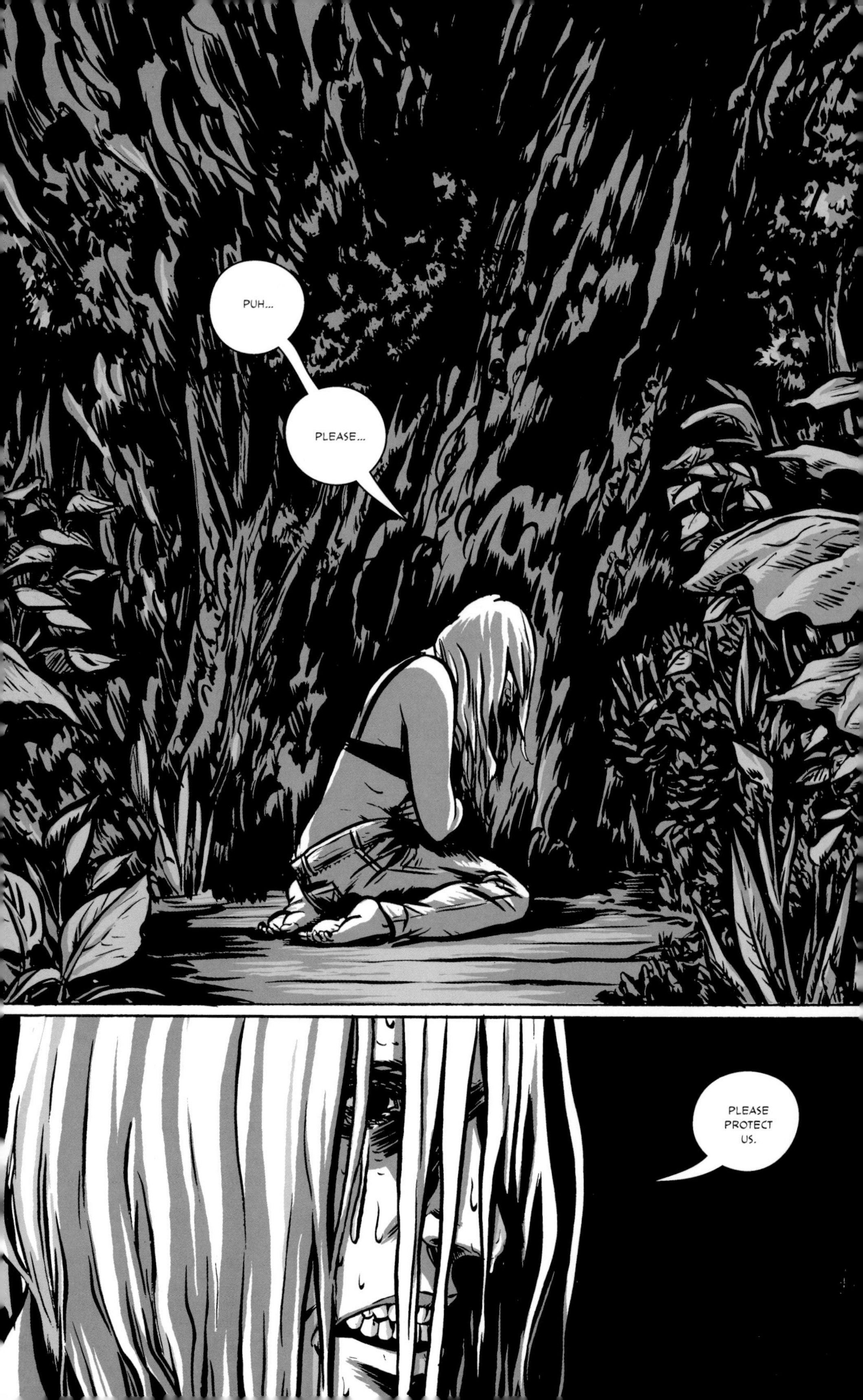
PUH...
PLEASE...
PLEASE PROTECT US.

I'M A
GOOD MAN.

I'M DOING
THE RIGHT
THING.

YOU'D BE
PROUD OF ME.

RIIIING

RIIIIIING

I'M DOING
THE RIGHT
THING.

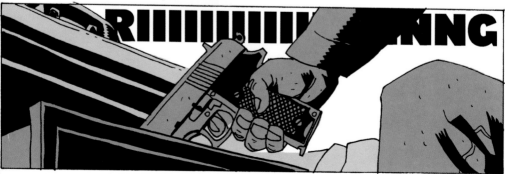

RIIIIIIIIIIIING

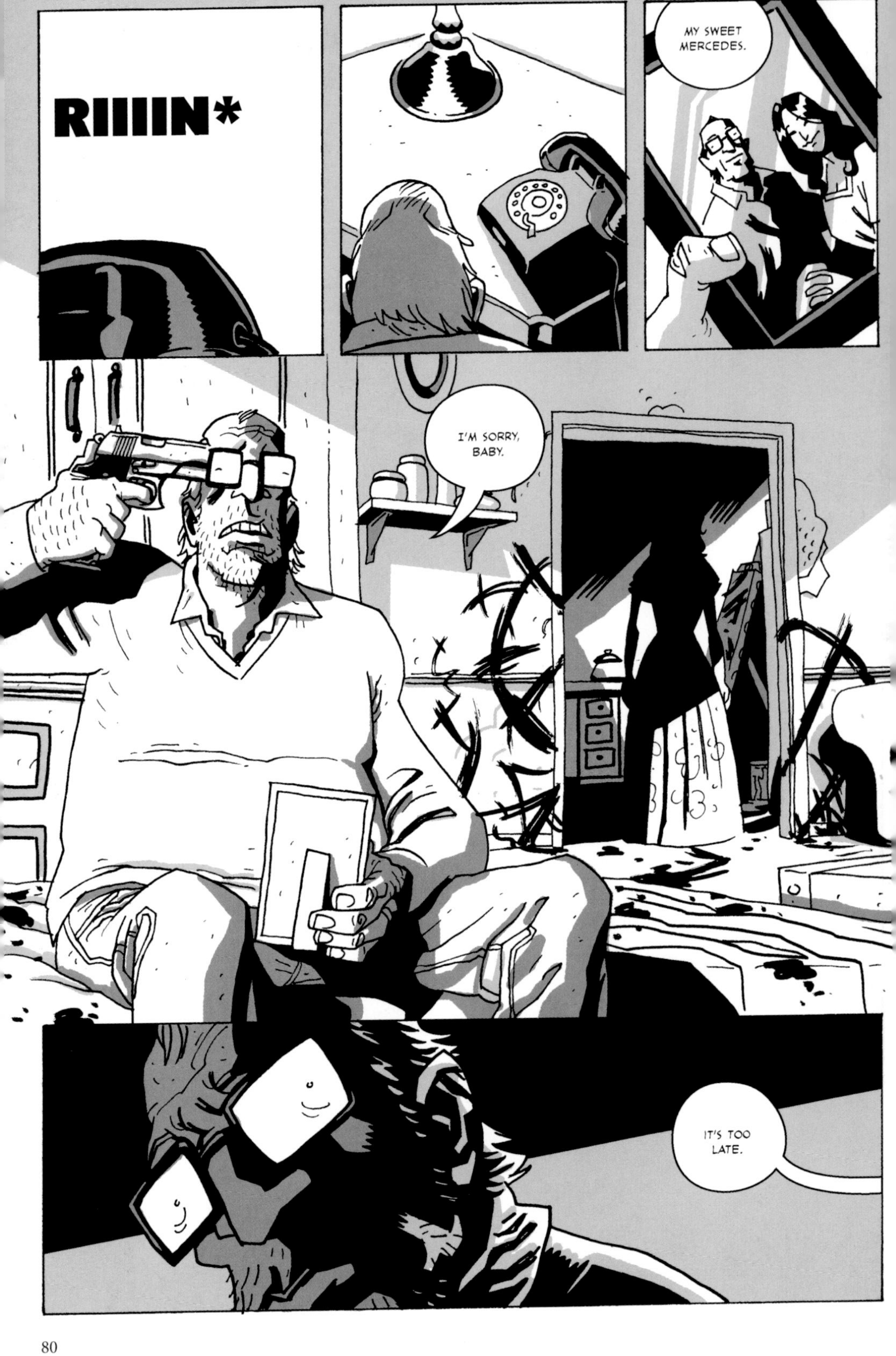
RIIIIN*
MY SWEET MERCEDES.
I'M SORRY, BABY.
IT'S TOO LATE.

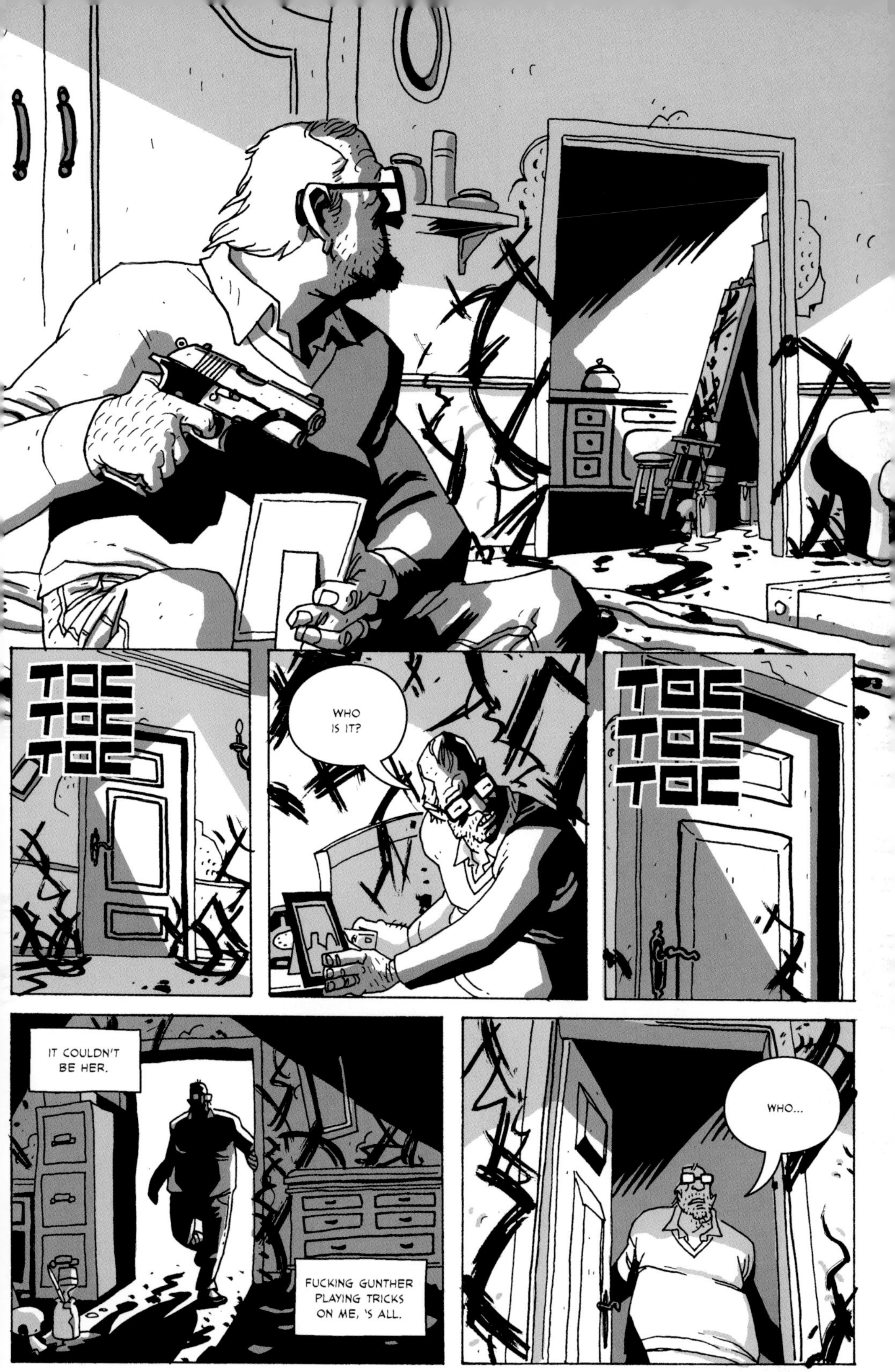
TOC
TOC
TOC
WHO
IS IT?
TOC
TOC
TOC
IT COULDN'T
BE HER.
FUCKING GUNTHER
PLAYING TRICKS
ON ME, 'S ALL.
WHO...

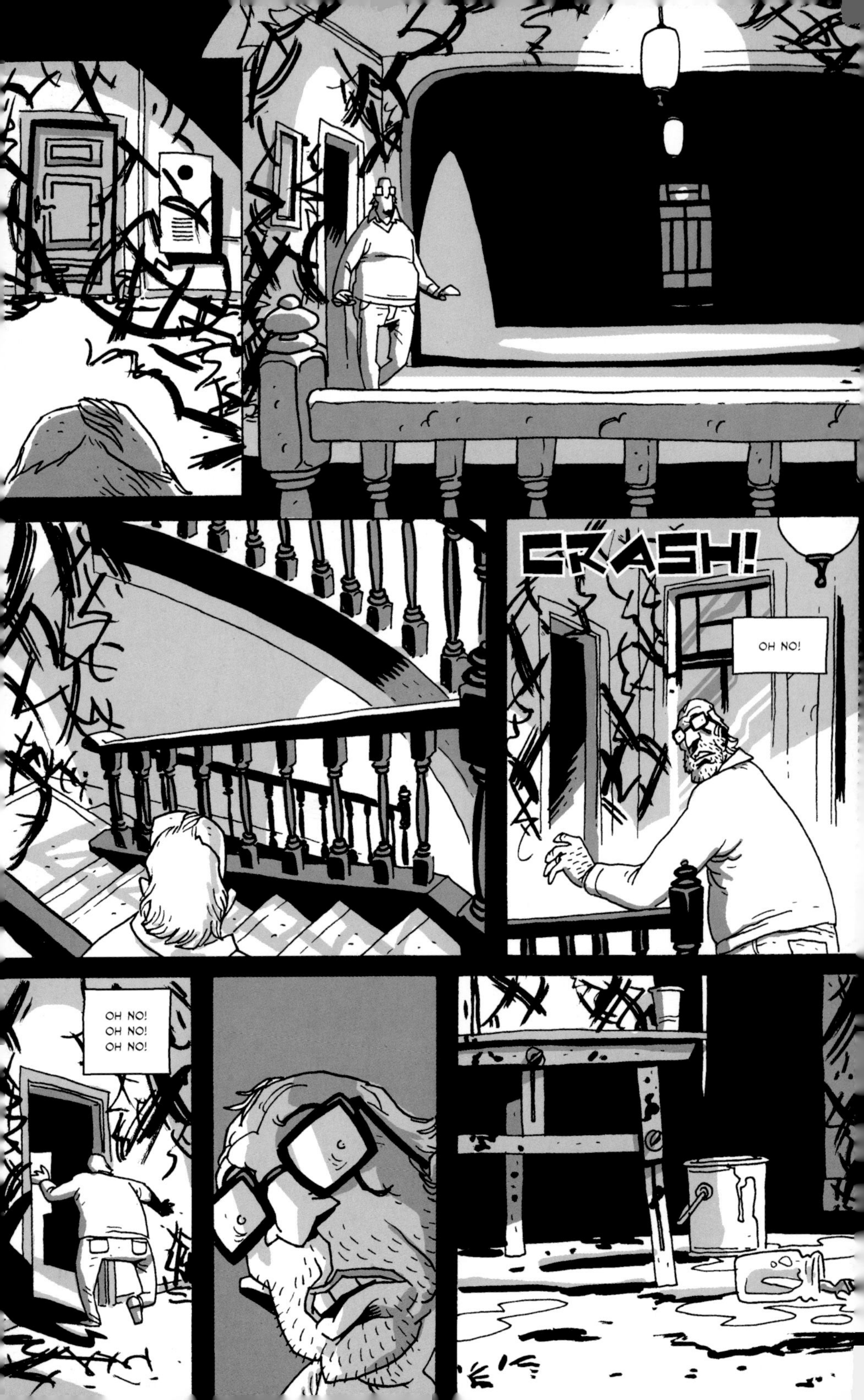
CRASH!
OH NO!
OH NO!
OH NO!
OH NO!

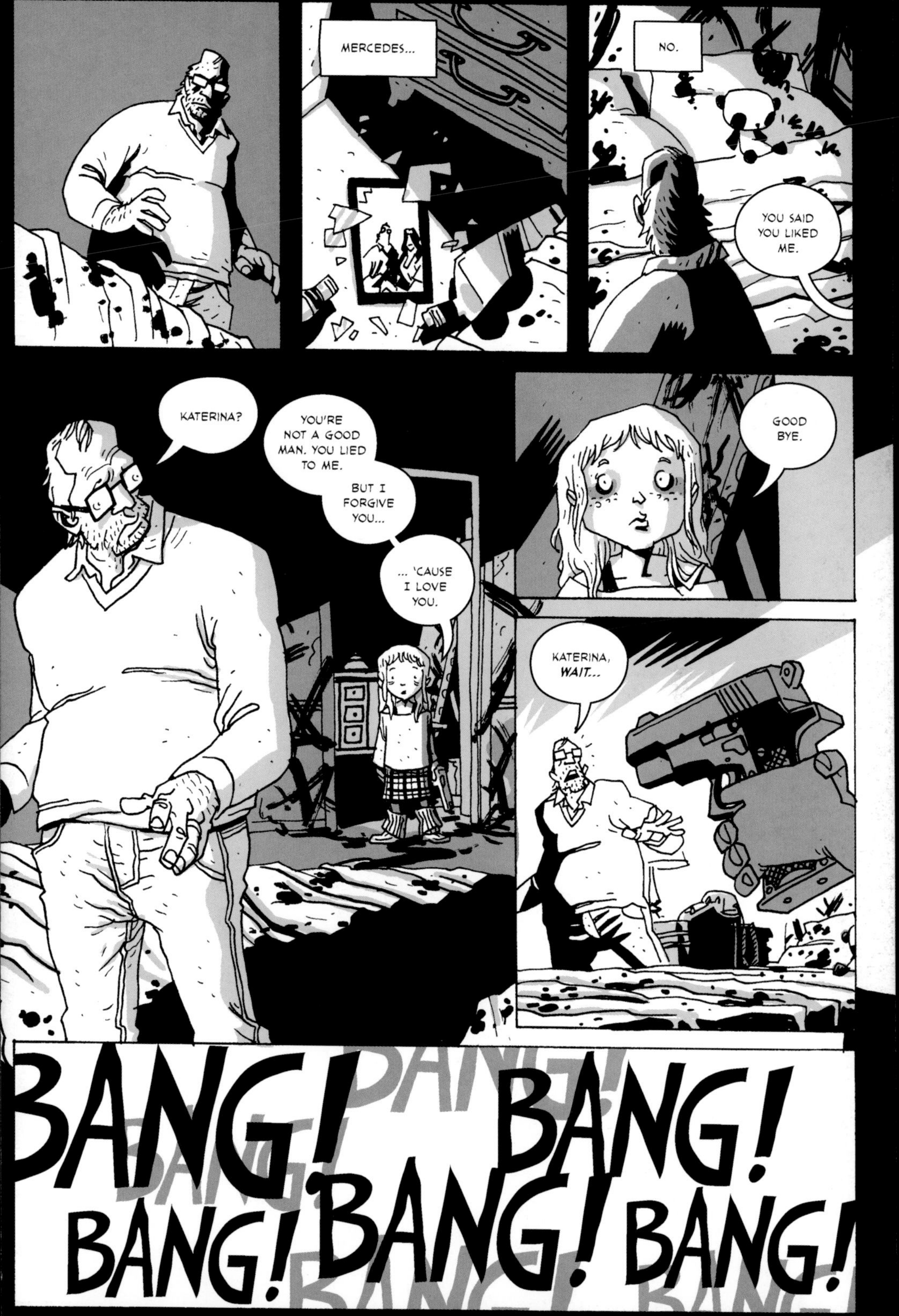
MERCEDES...
NO.
YOU SAID YOU LIKED ME.
KATERINA?
YOU'RE NOT A GOOD MAN. YOU LIED TO ME.
BUT I FORGIVE YOU...
... 'CAUSE I LOVE YOU.
GOOD BYE.
KATERINA, *WAIT...*
BANG! BANG!
BANG! BANG! BANG!

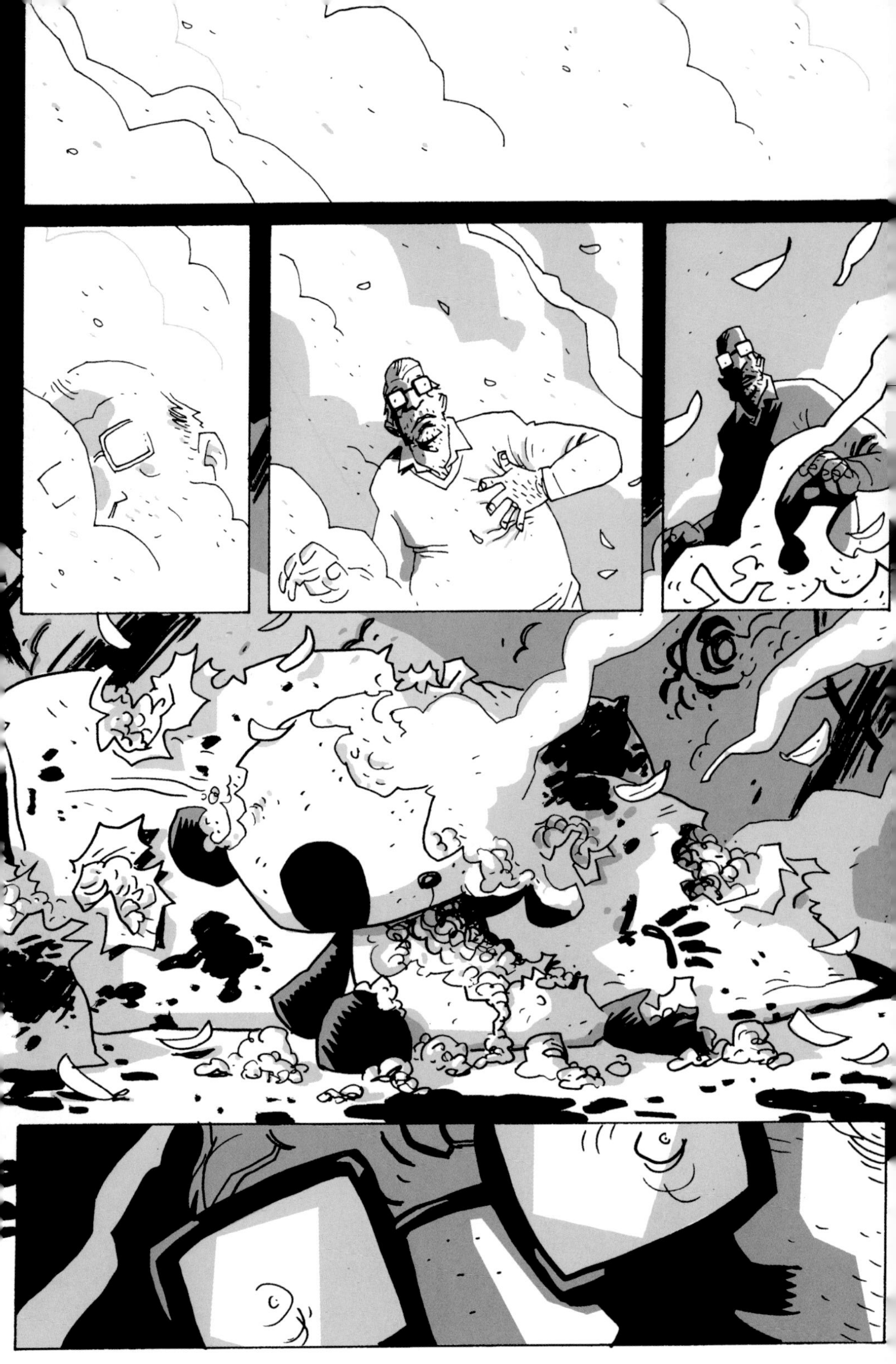

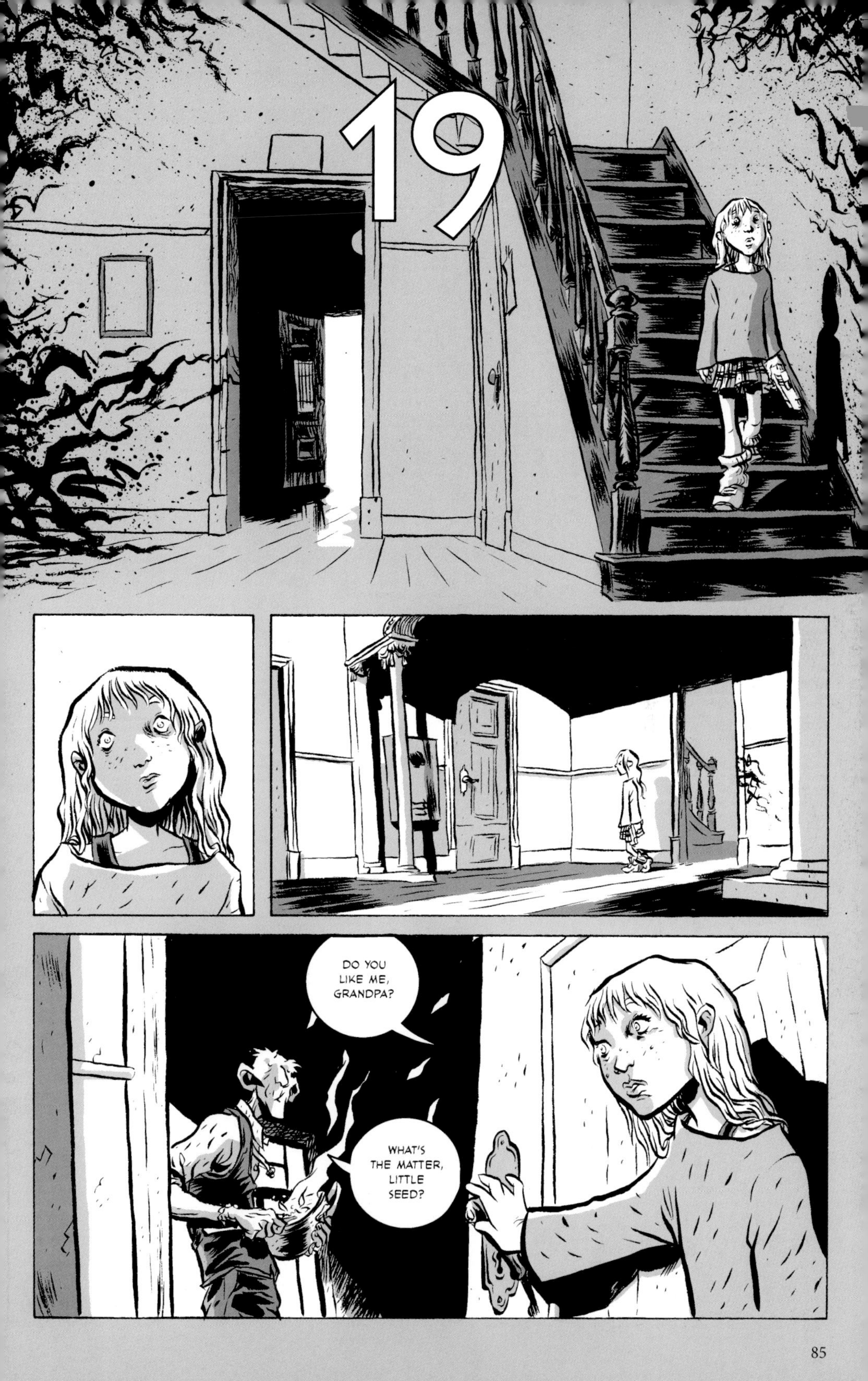
19
DO YOU LIKE ME, GRANDPA?
WHAT'S THE MATTER, LITTLE SEED?

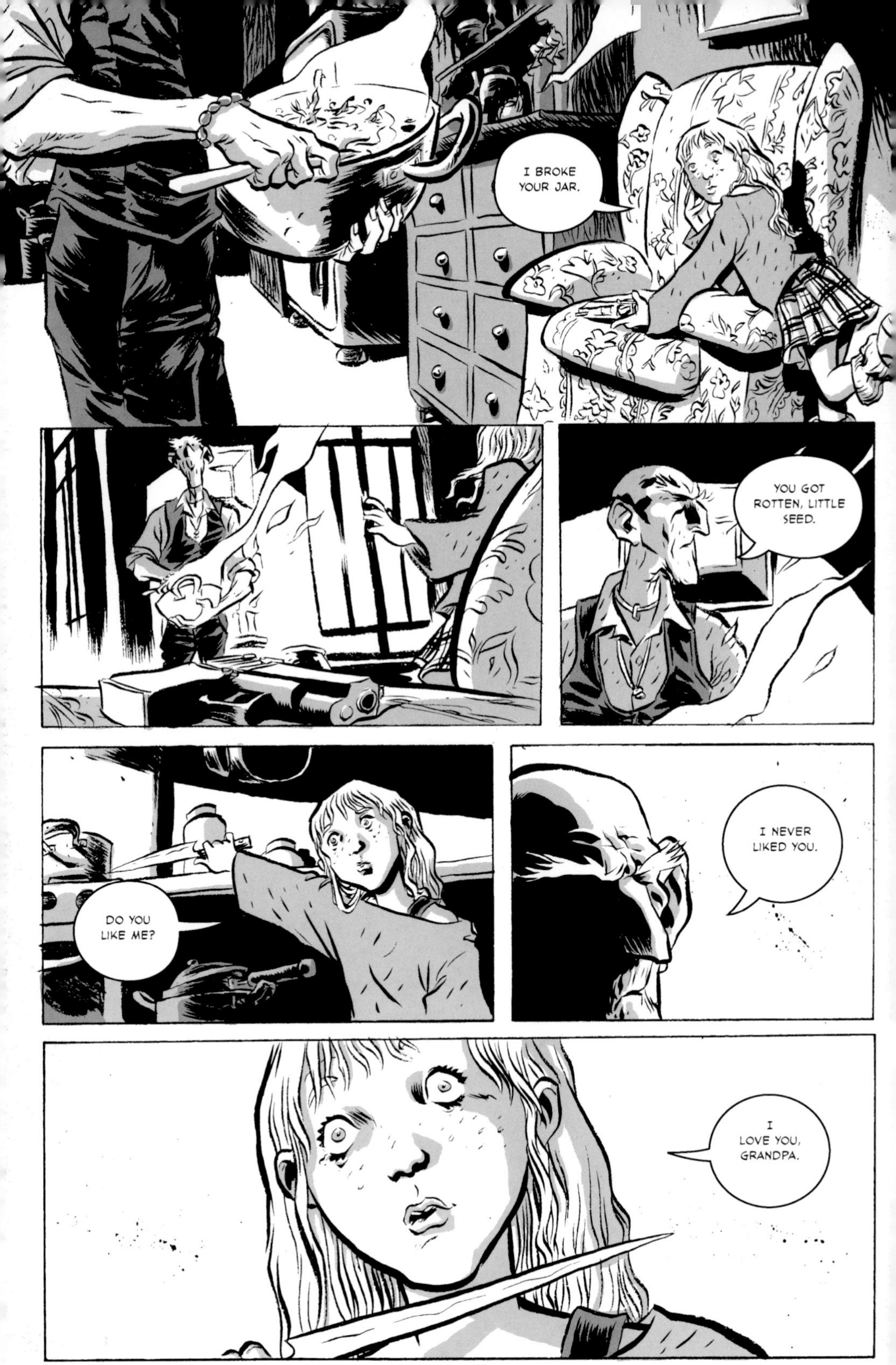
I BROKE YOUR JAR.
YOU GOT ROTTEN, LITTLE SEED.
DO YOU LIKE ME?
I NEVER LIKED YOU.
I LOVE YOU, GRANDPA.

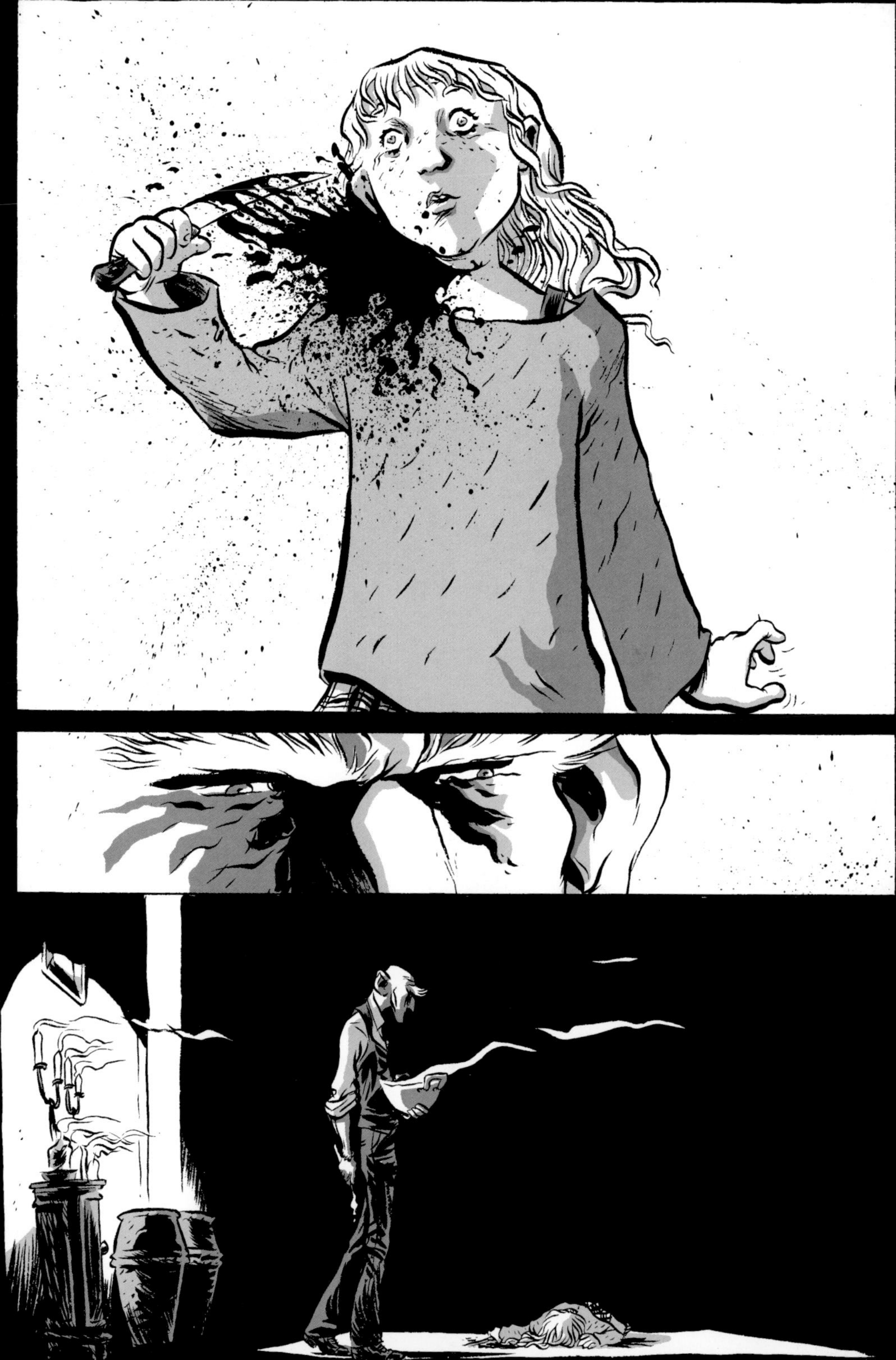

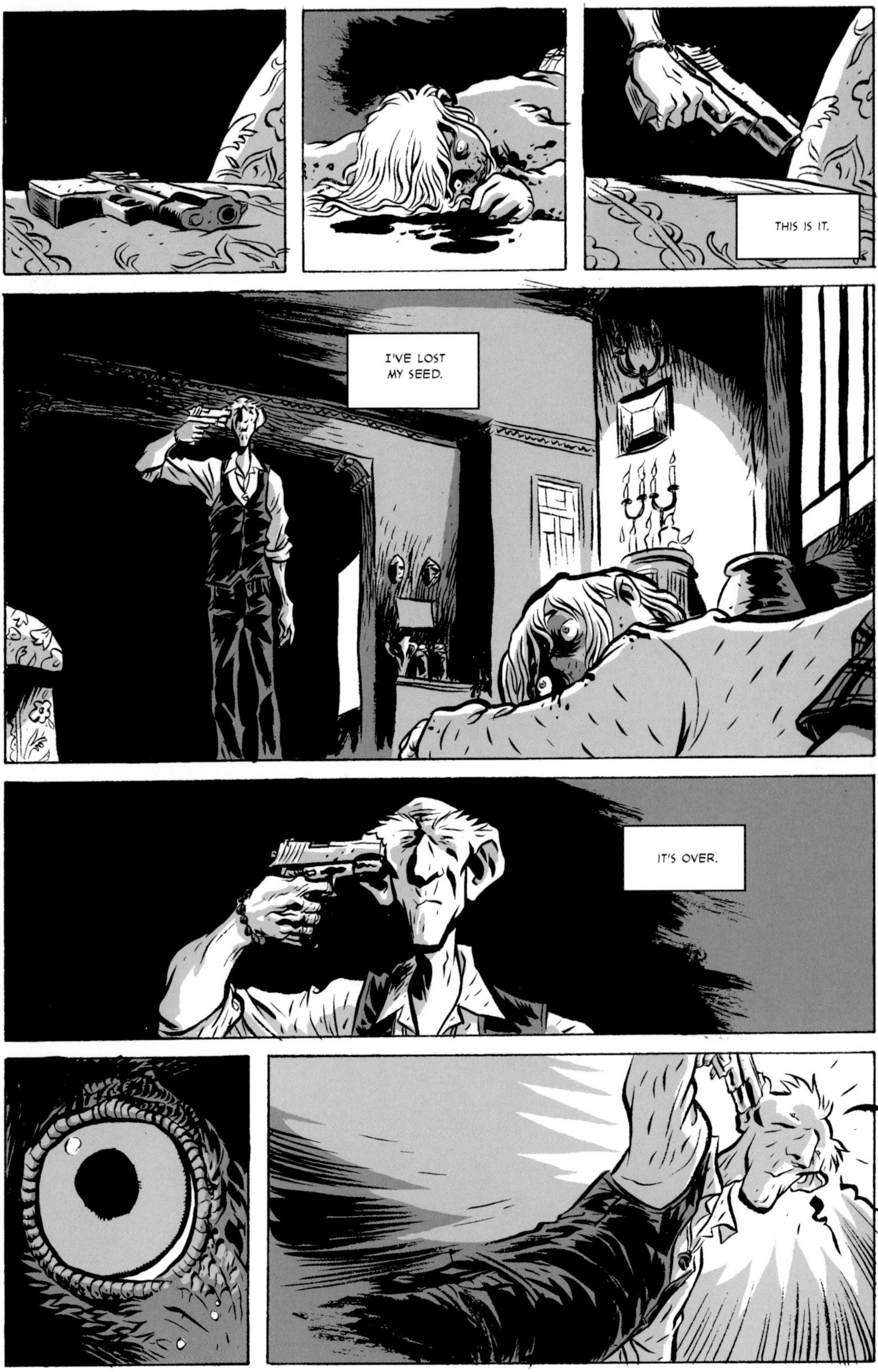
THIS IS IT.
I'VE LOST MY SEED.
IT'S OVER.

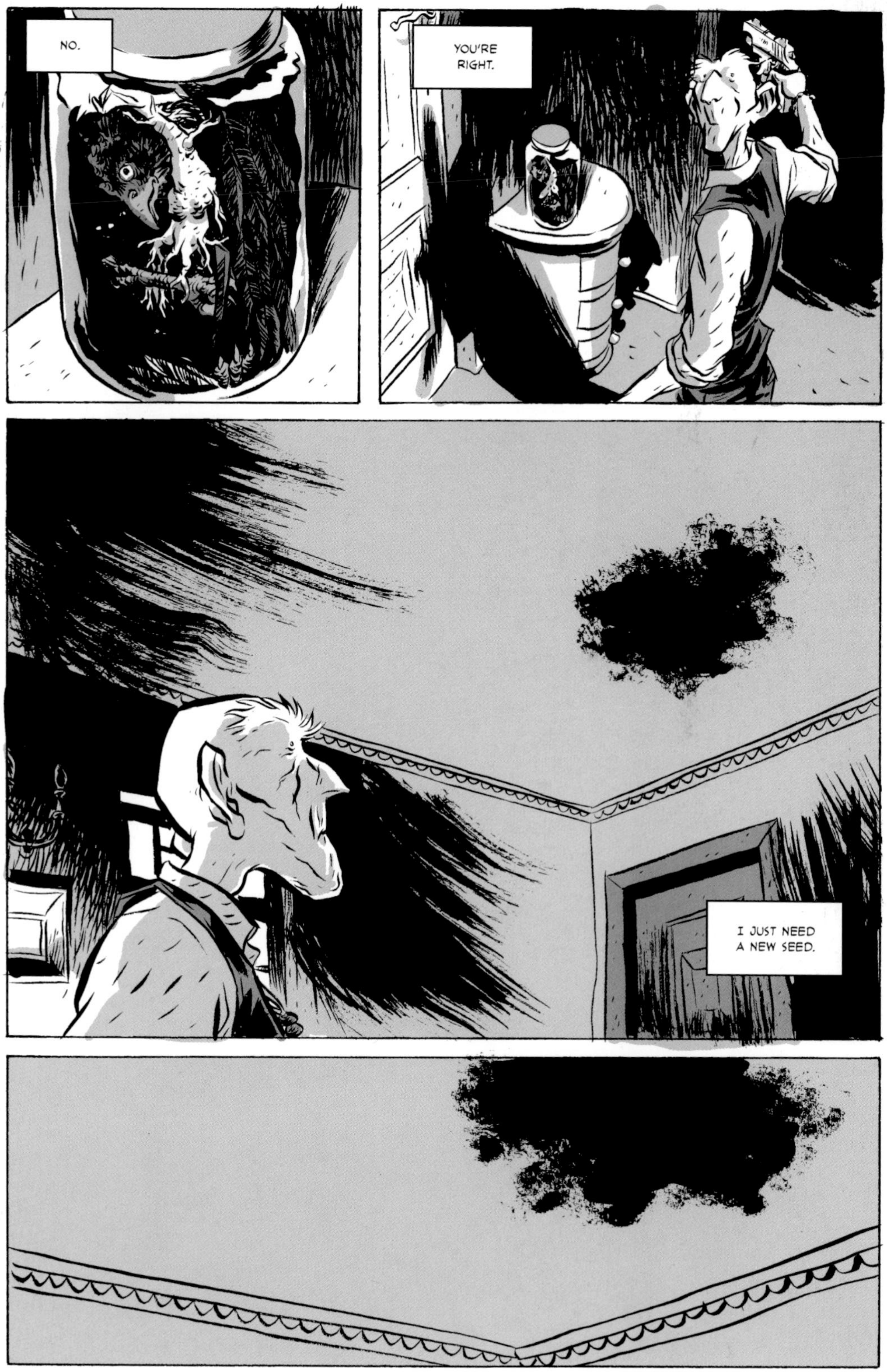
NO.
YOU'RE RIGHT.
I JUST NEED A NEW SEED.

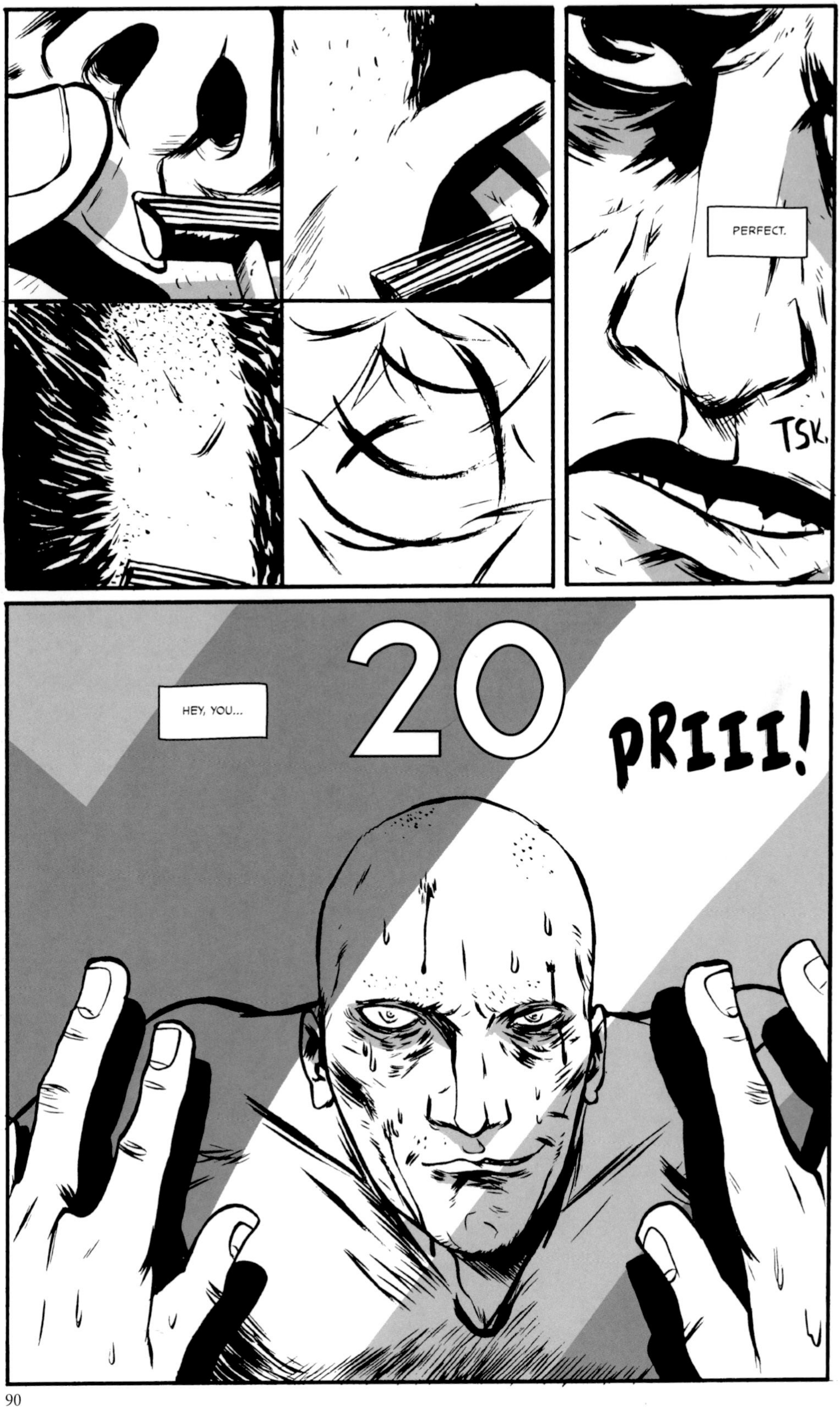
PERFECT.
TSK.
HEY, YOU...
20
PRIII!

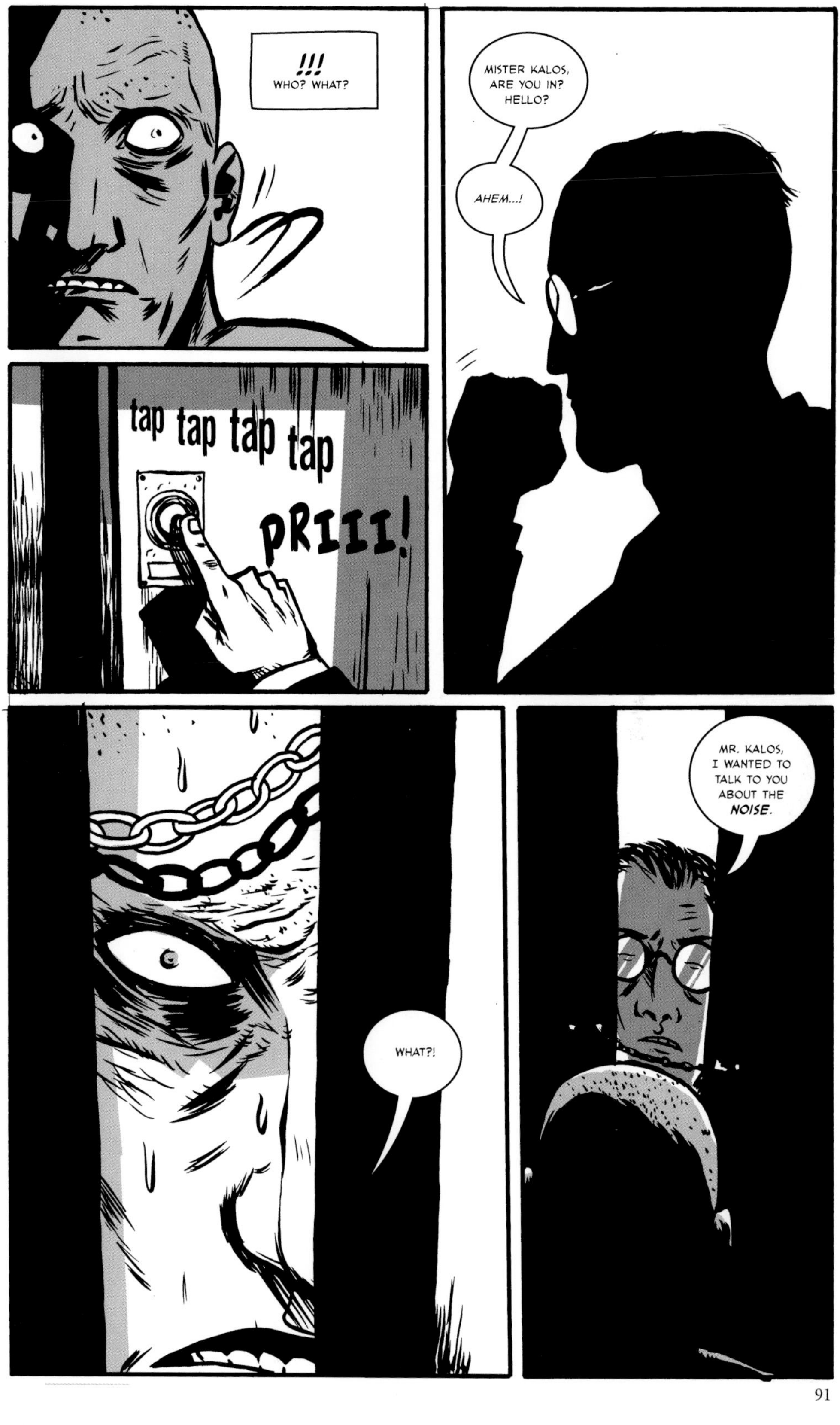
!!!
WHO? WHAT?
MISTER KALOS, ARE YOU IN? HELLO?
AHEM...!
tap tap tap tap
PRIII!
MR. KALOS, I WANTED TO TALK TO YOU ABOUT THE *NOISE*.
WHAT?!

YEAH? WHAT ABOUT I-TT...

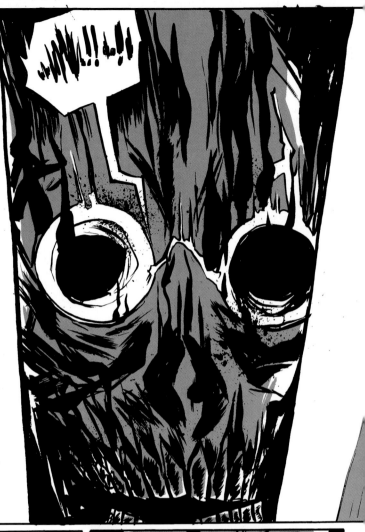

OHMYGOD OHMYGOD OHMYGOD!

IS EVERYTHING OKAY?

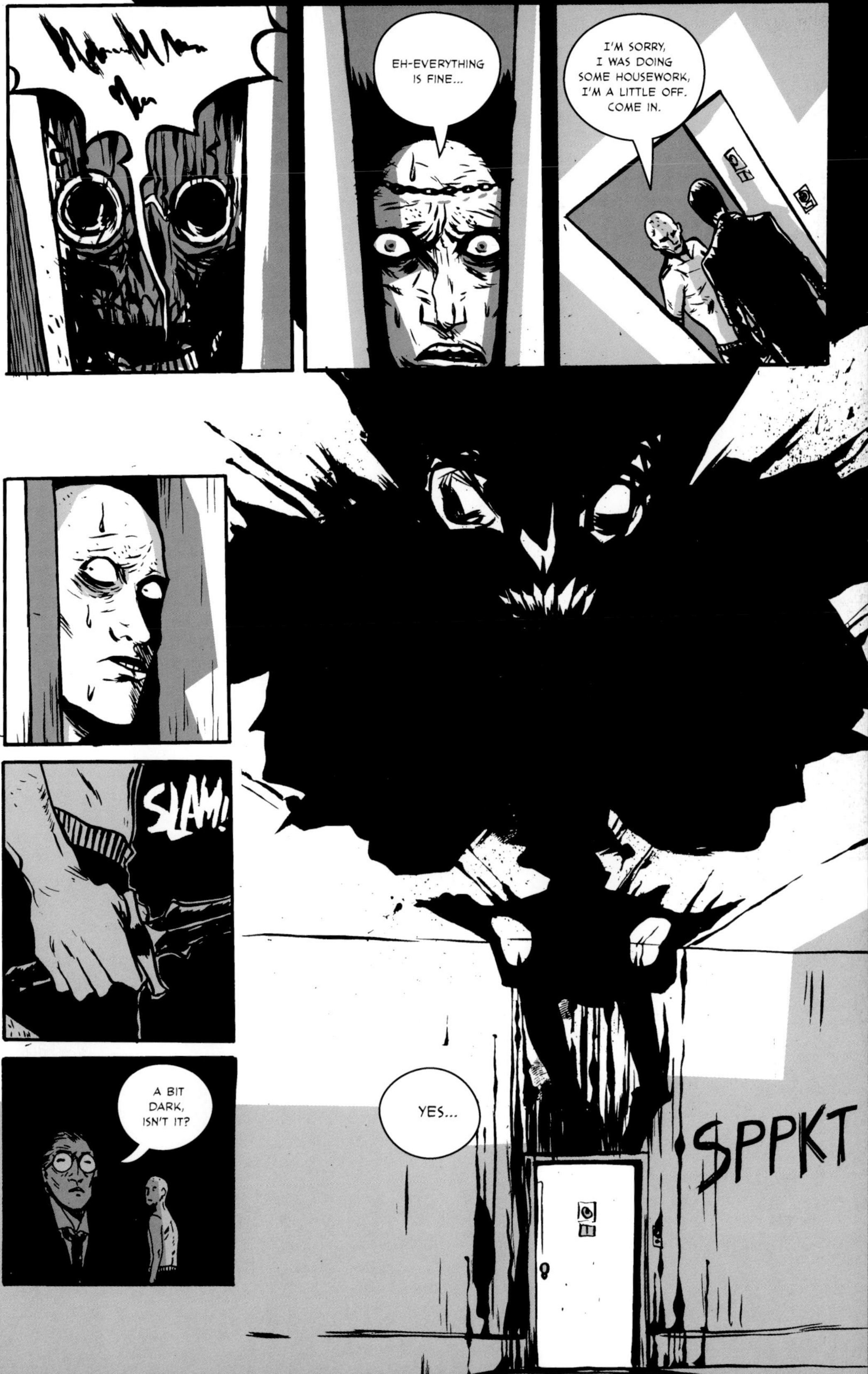
EH-EVERYTHING IS FINE...
I'M SORRY, I WAS DOING SOME HOUSEWORK, I'M A LITTLE OFF. COME IN.
SLAM!
A BIT DARK, ISN'T IT?
YES...
SPPKT

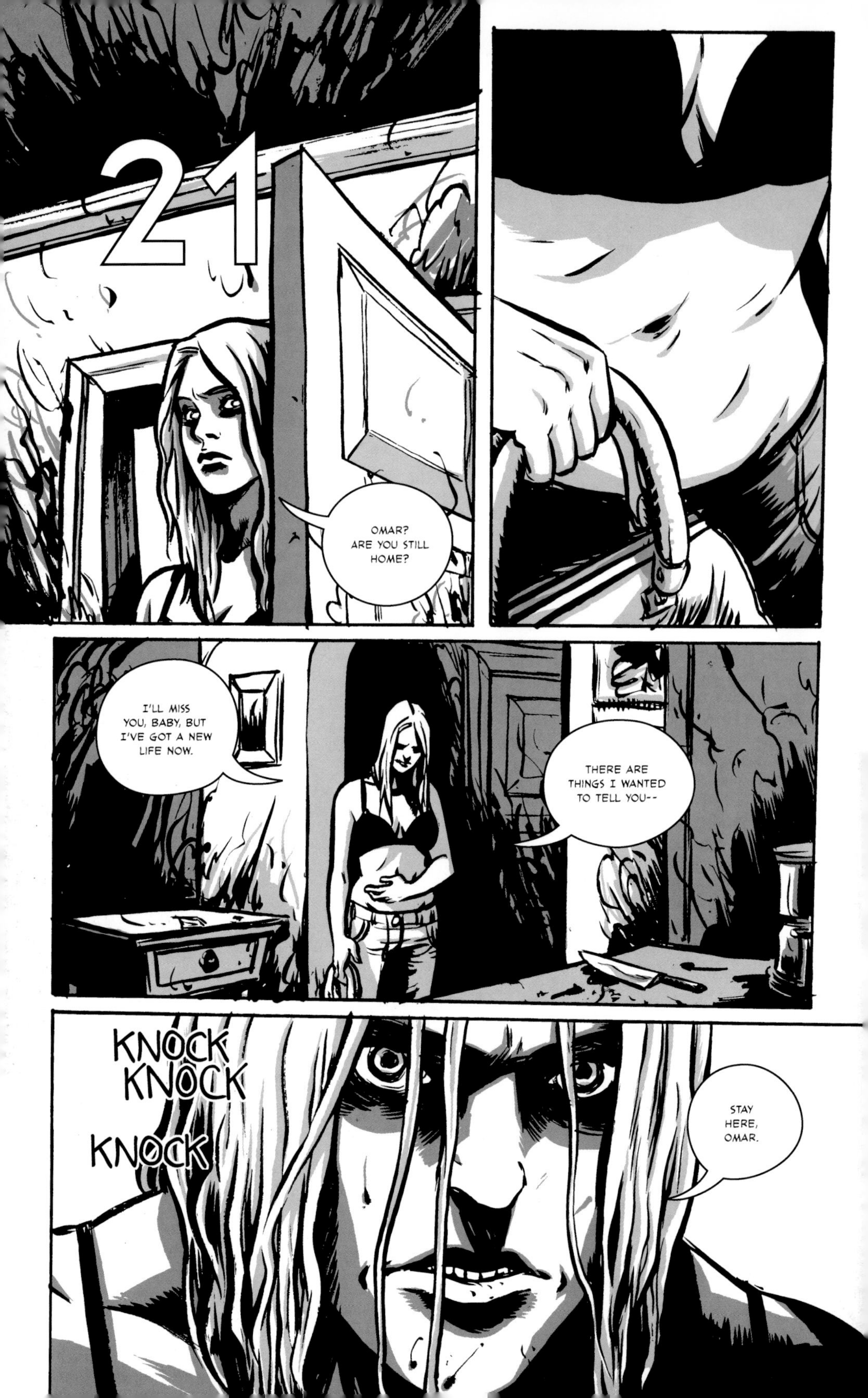
21
OMAR? ARE YOU STILL HOME?
I'LL MISS YOU, BABY, BUT I'VE GOT A NEW LIFE NOW.
THERE ARE THINGS I WANTED TO TELL YOU--
KNOCK KNOCK
KNOCK
STAY HERE, OMAR.

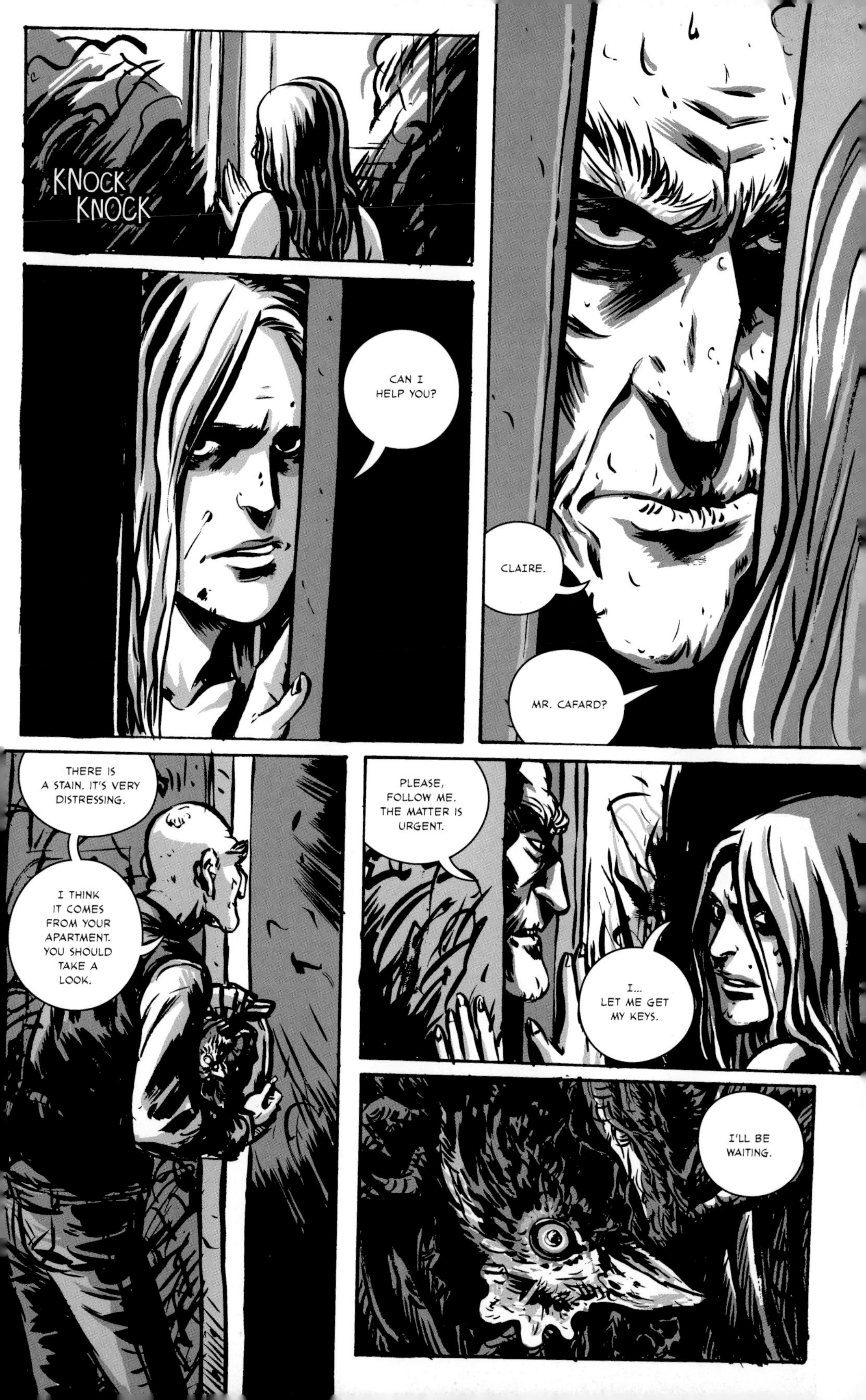
KNOCK KNOCK
CAN I HELP YOU?
CLAIRE.
MR. CAFARD?
THERE IS A STAIN. IT'S VERY DISTRESSING.
I THINK IT COMES FROM YOUR APARTMENT. YOU SHOULD TAKE A LOOK.
PLEASE, FOLLOW ME. THE MATTER IS URGENT.
I... LET ME GET MY KEYS.
I'LL BE WAITING.

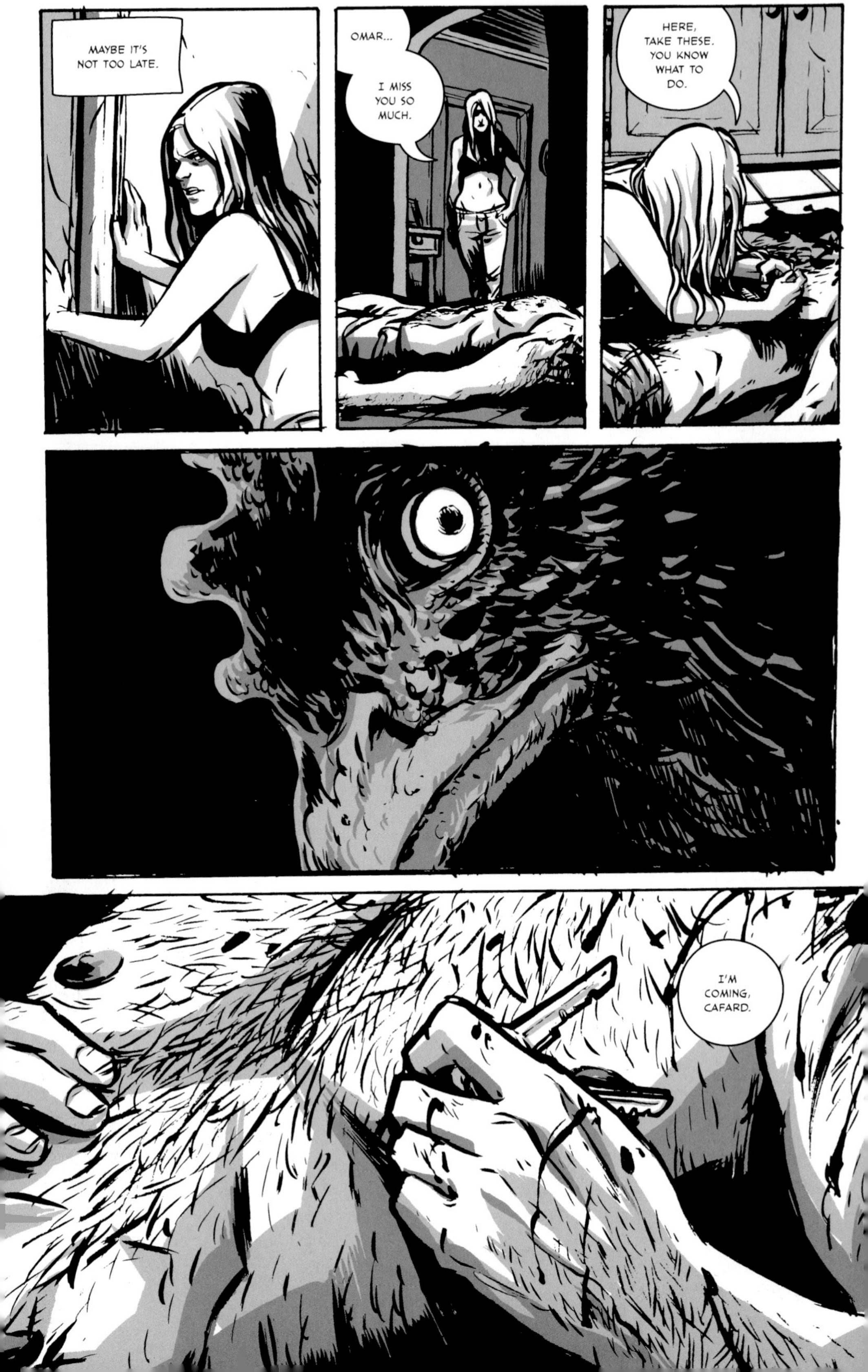
MAYBE IT'S NOT TOO LATE.
OMAR...
I MISS YOU SO MUCH.
HERE, TAKE THESE. YOU KNOW WHAT TO DO.
I'M COMING, CAFARD.

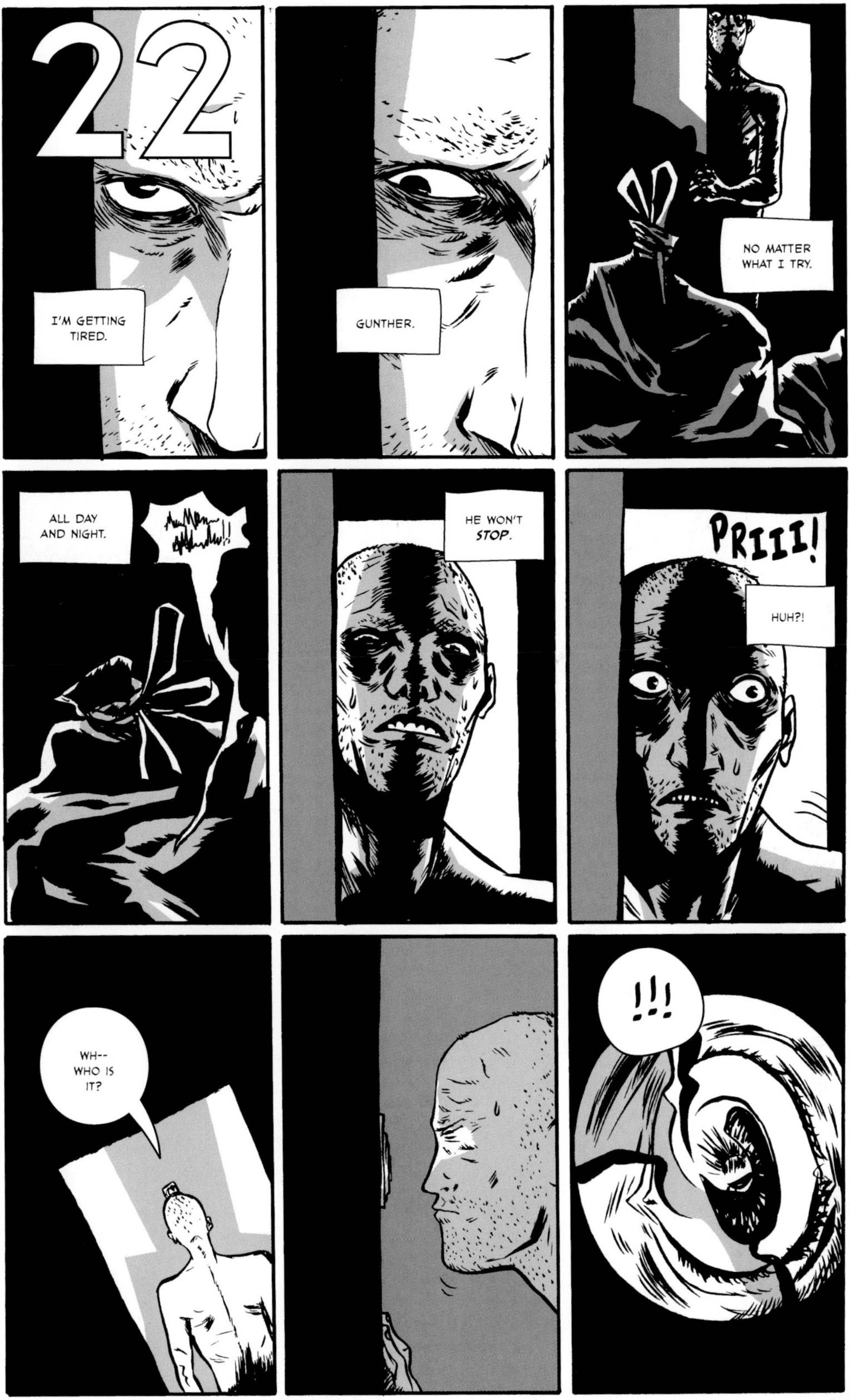
22
I'M GETTING TIRED.
GUNTHER.
NO MATTER WHAT I TRY.
ALL DAY AND NIGHT.
HE WON'T *STOP*.
PRIII!
HUH?!
WH-- WHO IS IT?
!!!

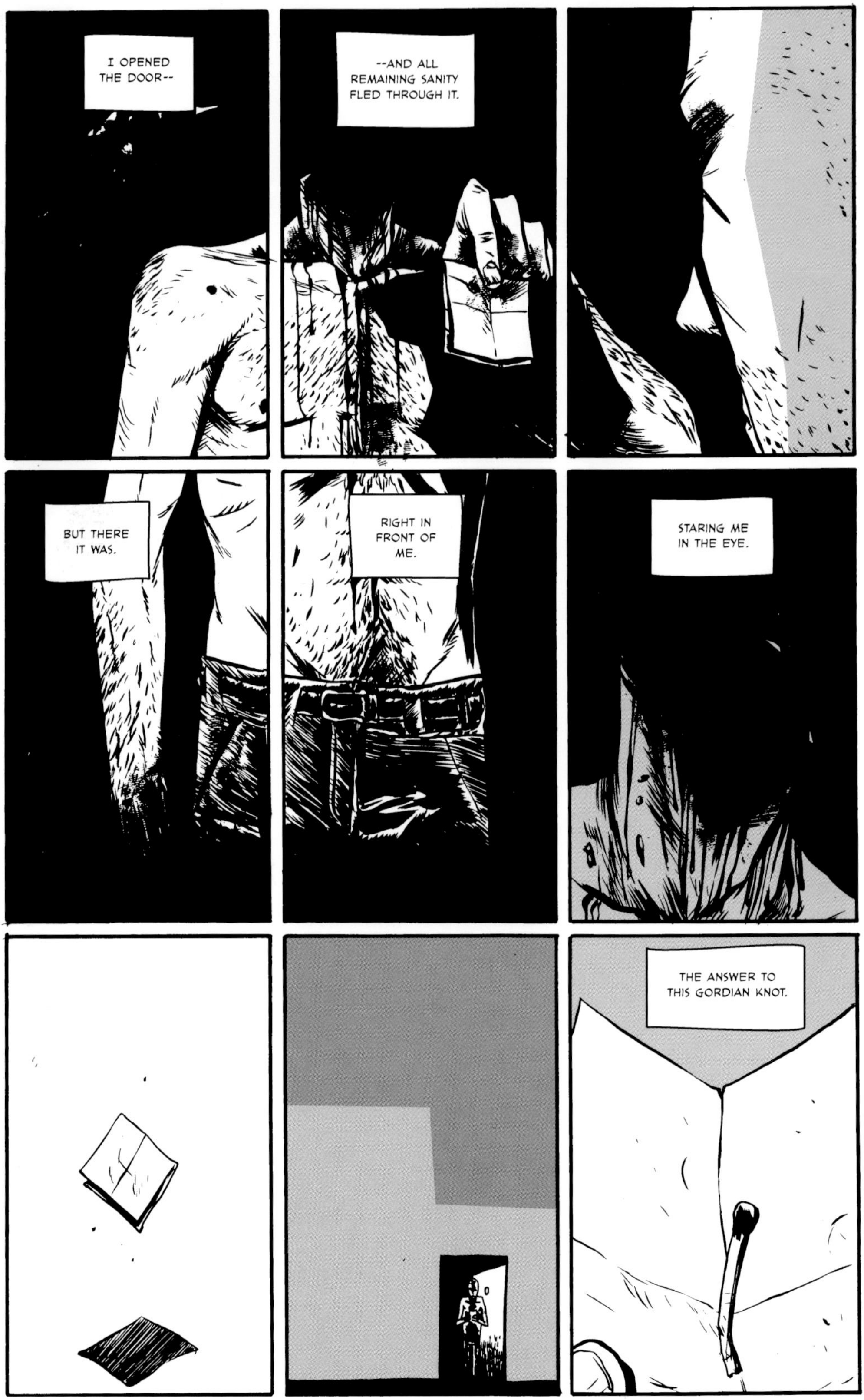
I OPENED THE DOOR--
--AND ALL REMAINING SANITY FLED THROUGH IT.
BUT THERE IT WAS.
RIGHT IN FRONT OF ME.
STARING ME IN THE EYE.
THE ANSWER TO THIS GORDIAN KNOT.

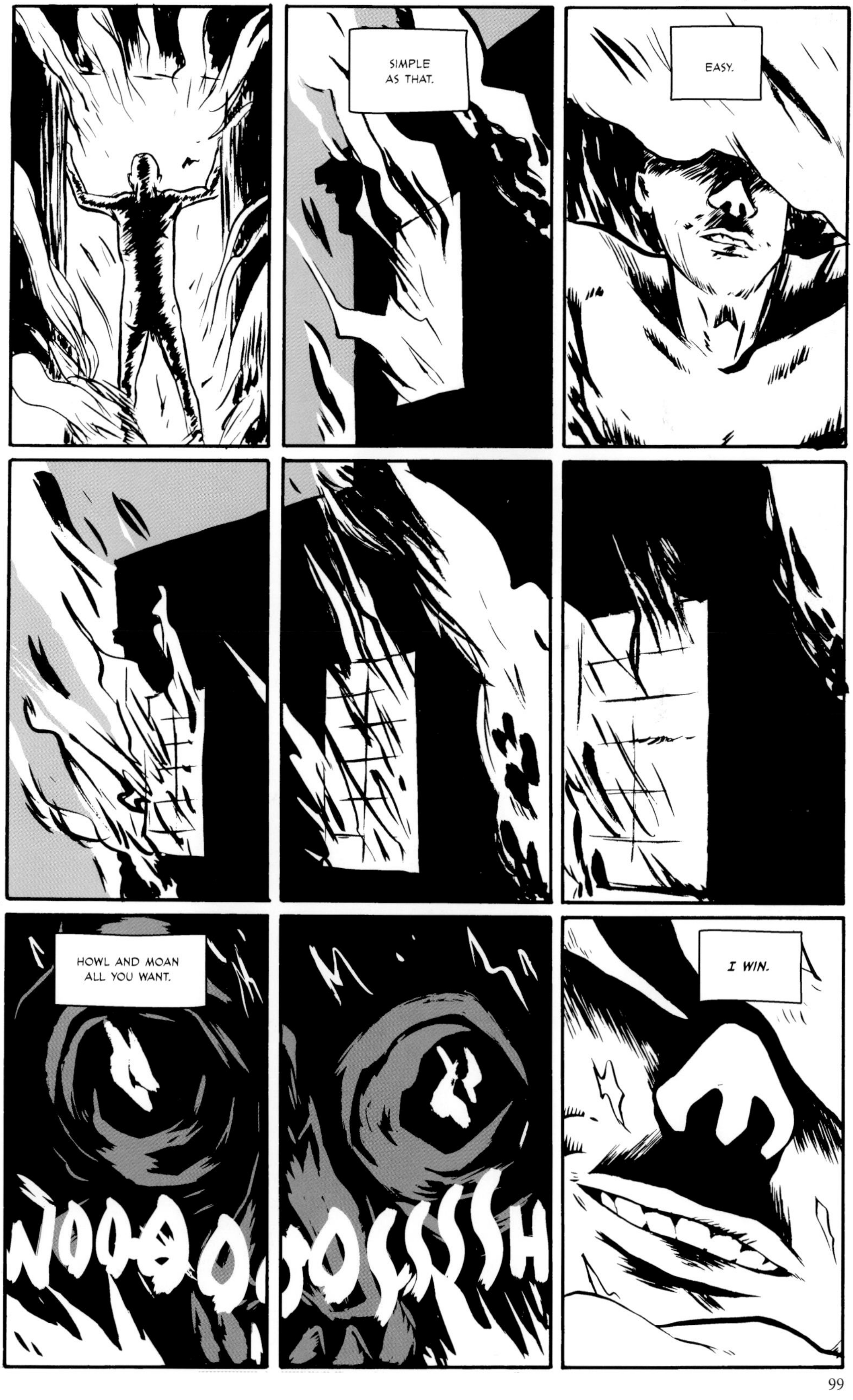
SIMPLE AS THAT.
EASY.
HOWL AND MOAN ALL YOU WANT.
WOOOOOOSSSSH
I WIN.

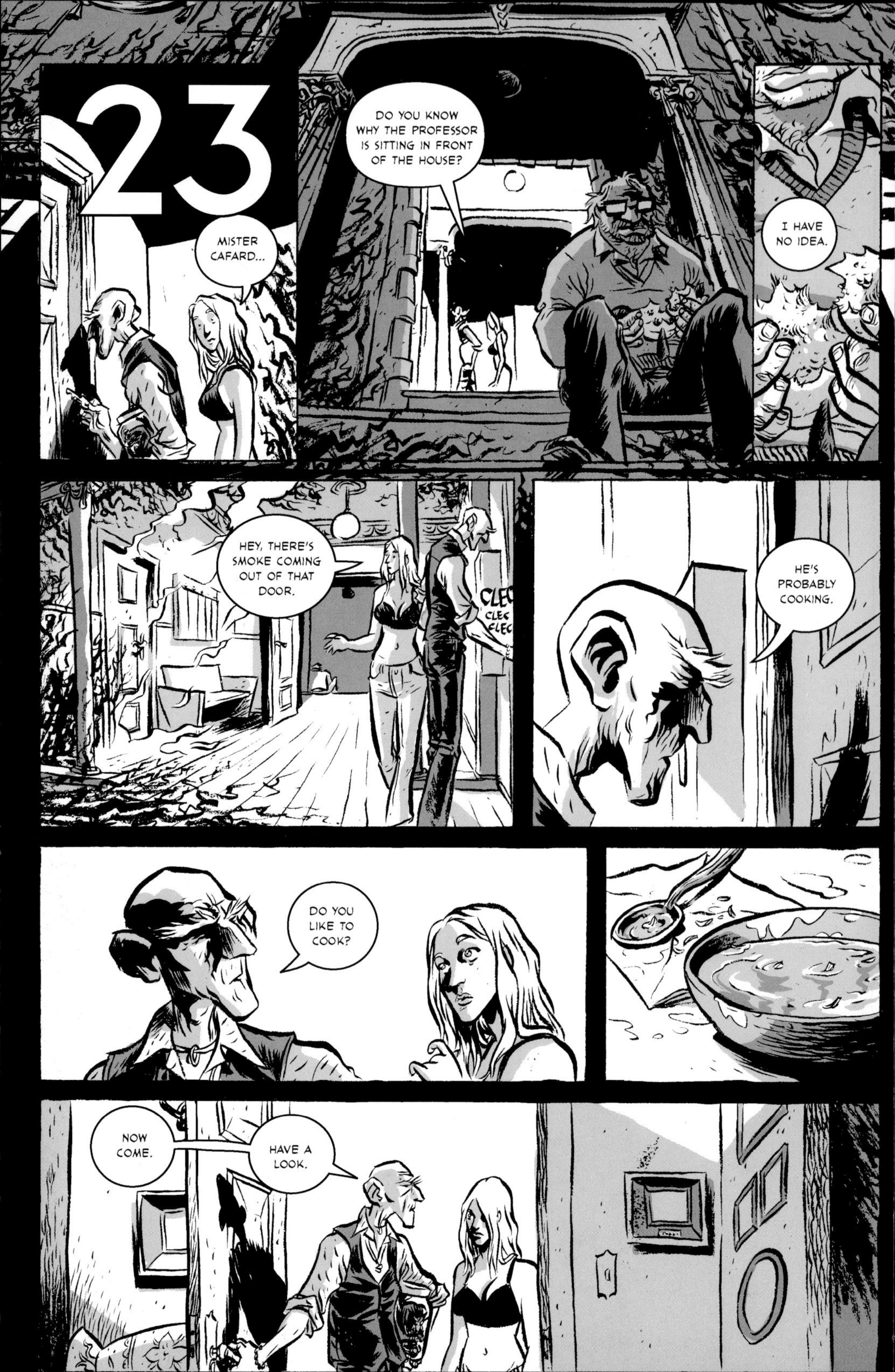
23
MISTER CAFARD...
DO YOU KNOW WHY THE PROFESSOR IS SITTING IN FRONT OF THE HOUSE?
I HAVE NO IDEA.
HEY, THERE'S SMOKE COMING OUT OF THAT DOOR.
CLEC CLEC CLEC
HE'S PROBABLY COOKING.
DO YOU LIKE TO COOK?
NOW COME.
HAVE A LOOK.

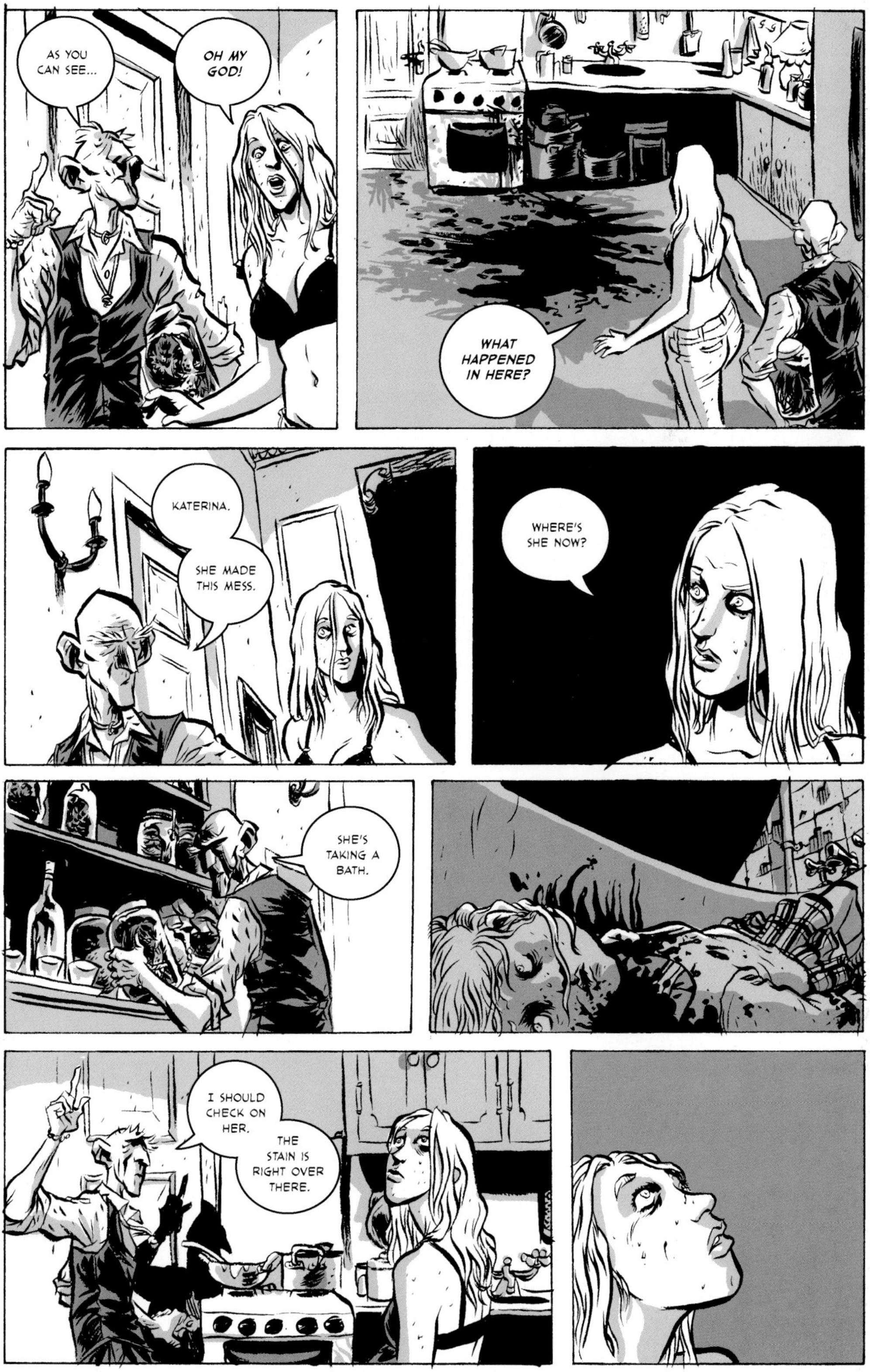
AS YOU CAN SEE...
OH MY GOD!
WHAT HAPPENED IN HERE?
KATERINA.
SHE MADE THIS MESS.
WHERE'S SHE NOW?
SHE'S TAKING A BATH.
I SHOULD CHECK ON HER.
THE STAIN IS RIGHT OVER THERE.

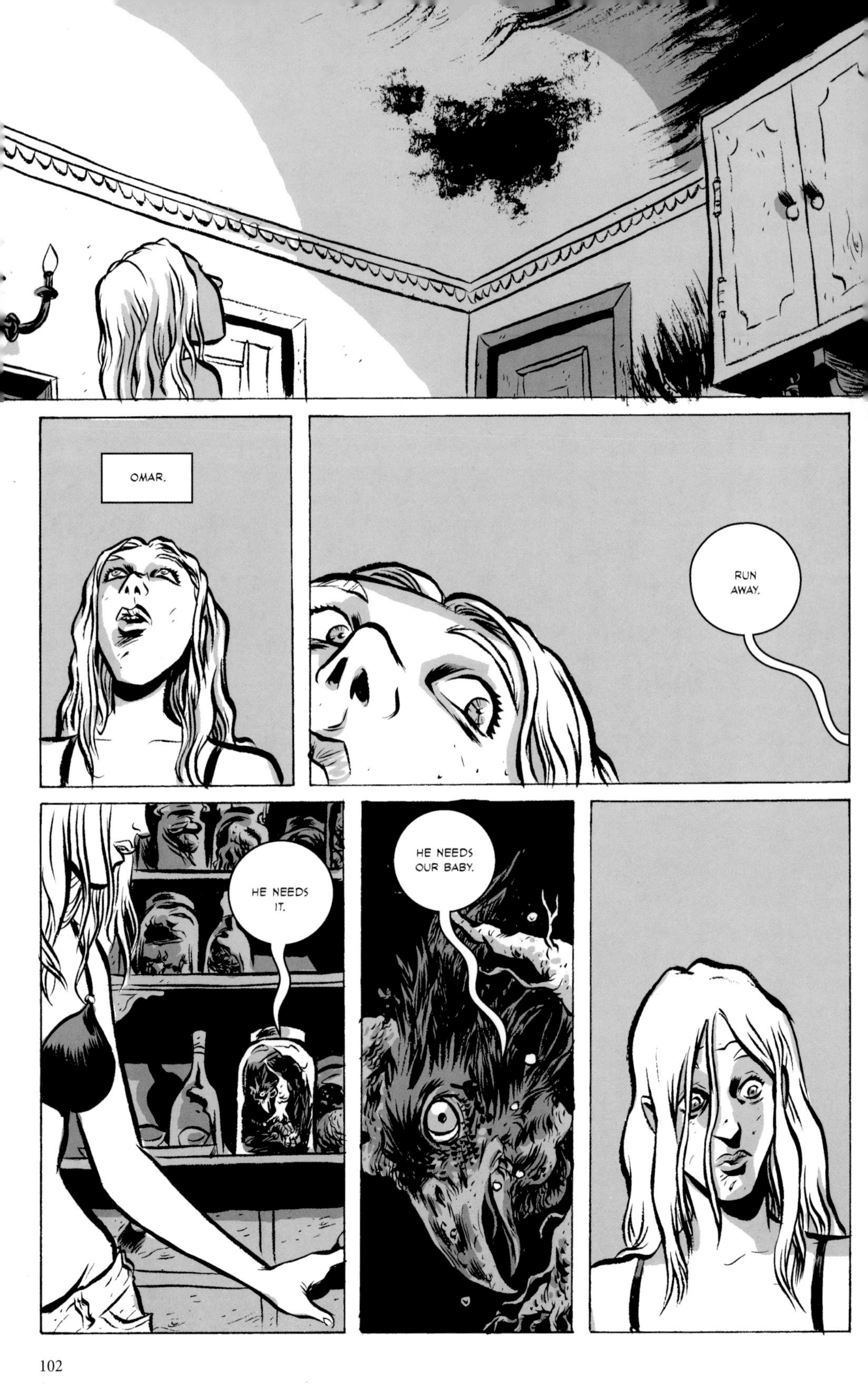
OMAR.
RUN AWAY.
HE NEEDS IT.
HE NEEDS OUR BABY.

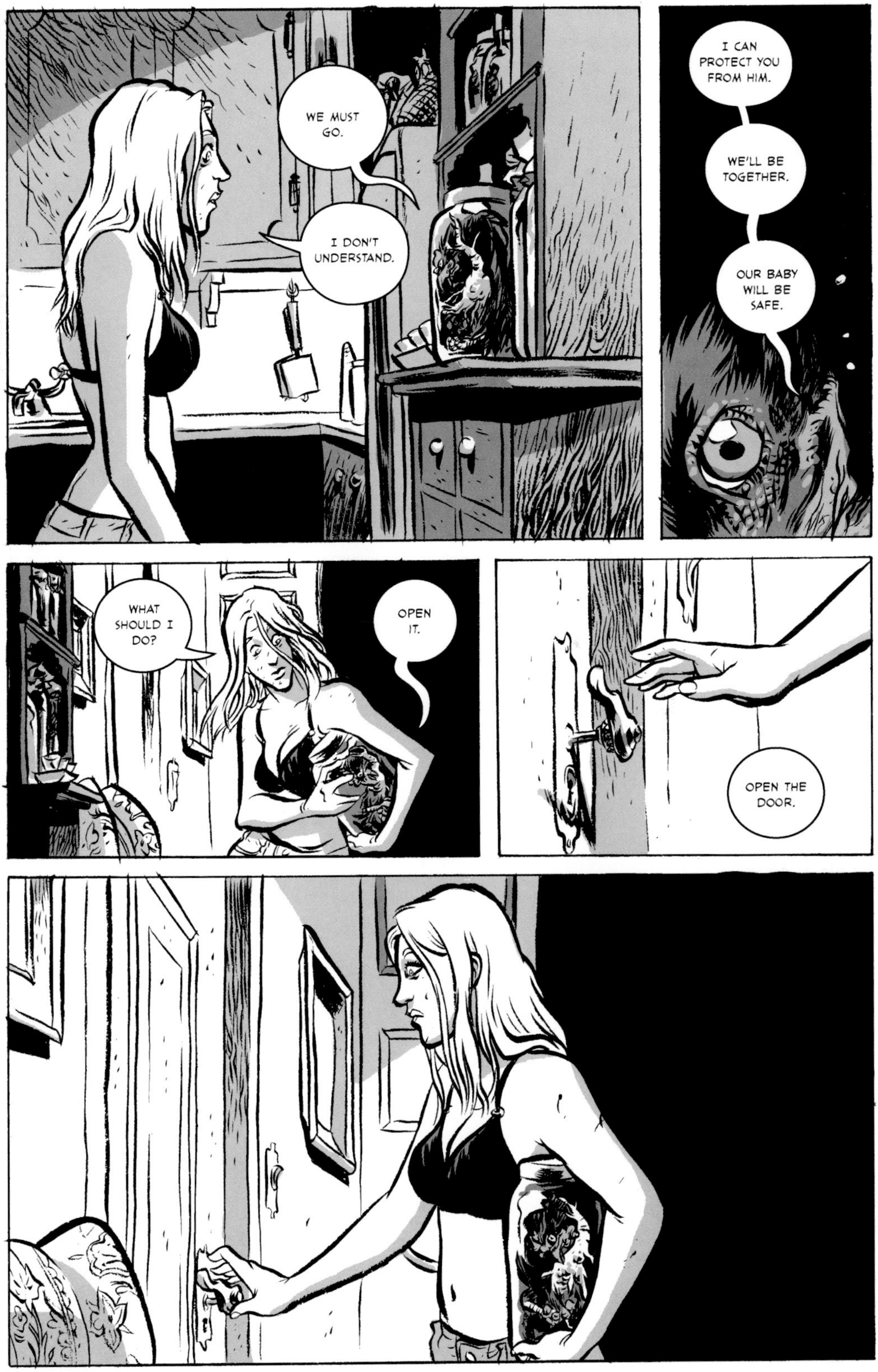
WE MUST GO.
I DON'T UNDERSTAND.
I CAN PROTECT YOU FROM HIM.
WE'LL BE TOGETHER.
OUR BABY WILL BE SAFE.
WHAT SHOULD I DO?
OPEN IT.
OPEN THE DOOR.

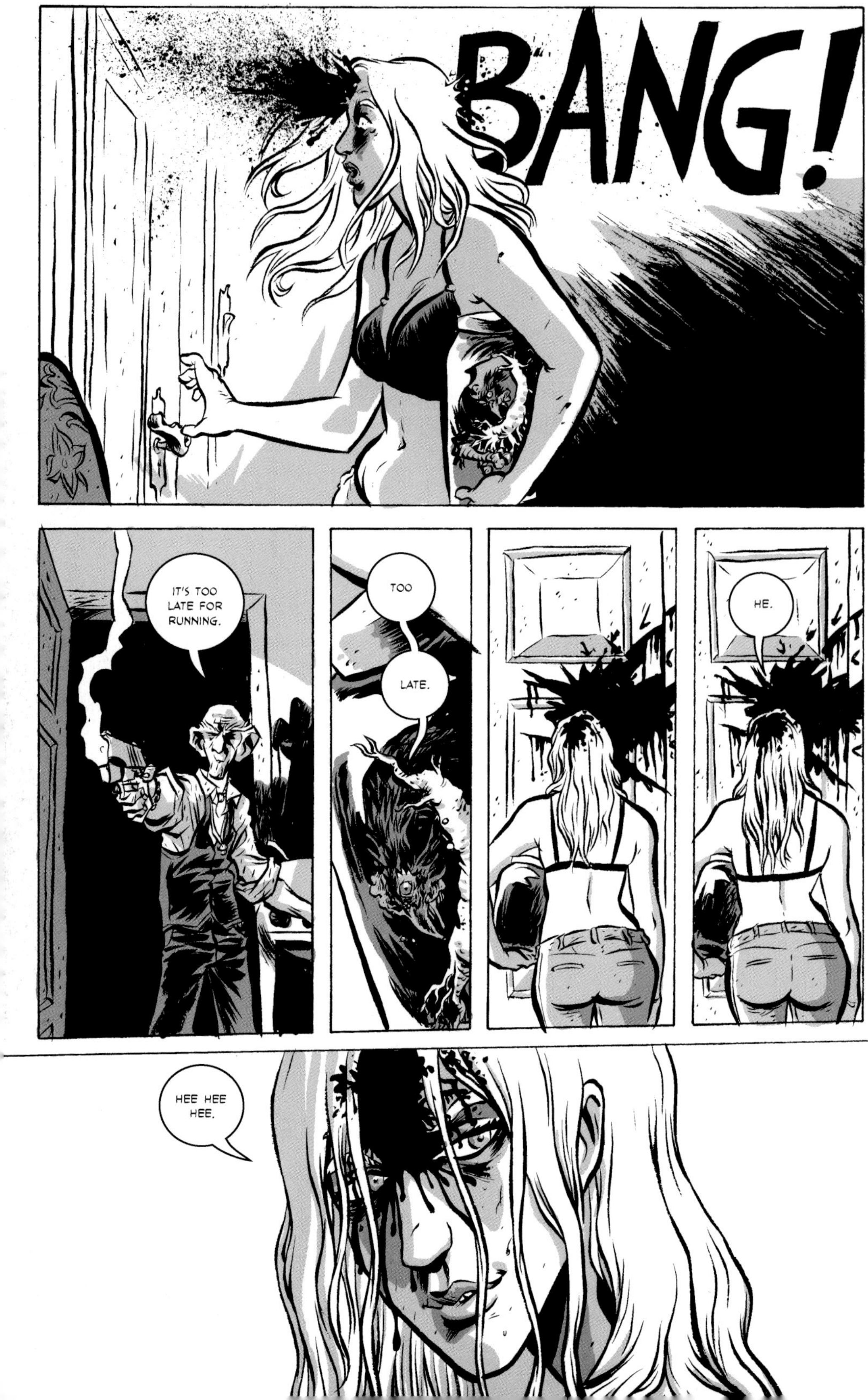
BANG!
IT'S TOO LATE FOR RUNNING.
TOO
LATE.
HE.
HEE HEE HEE.

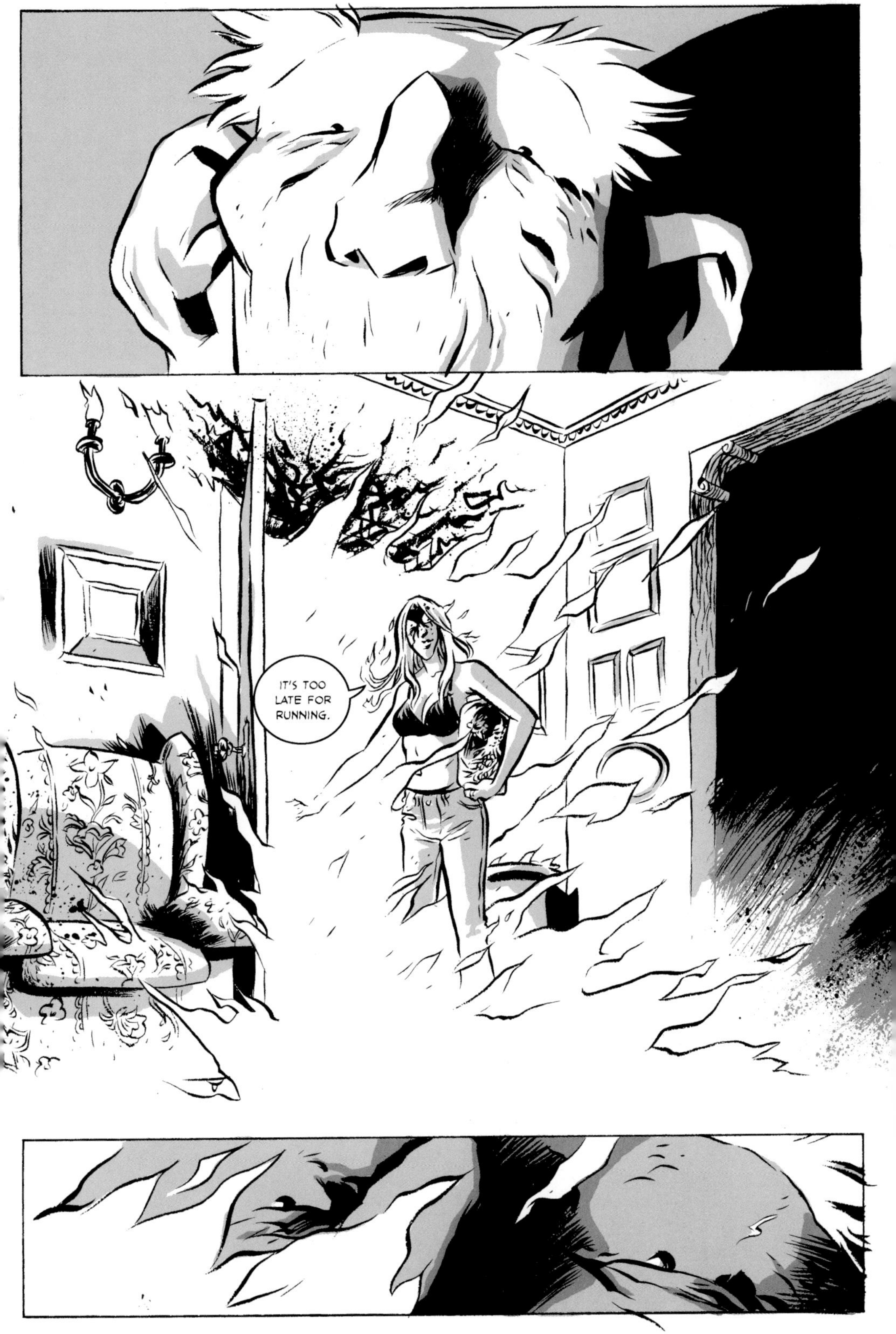
IT'S TOO LATE FOR RUNNING.

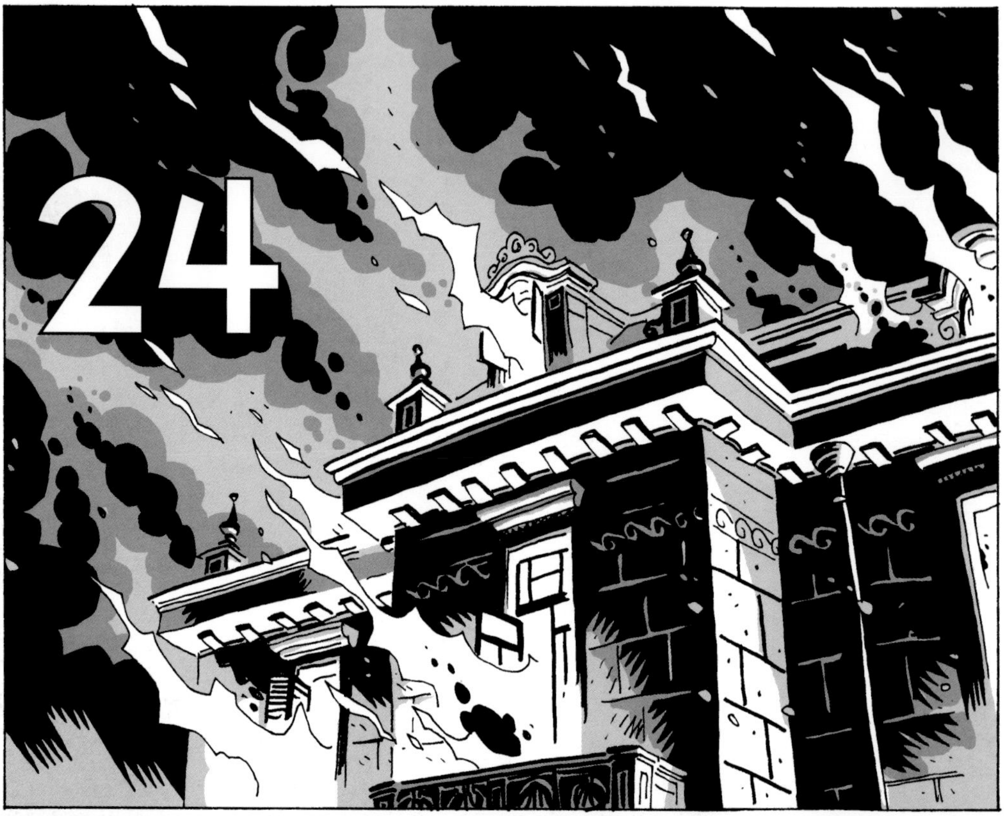
24

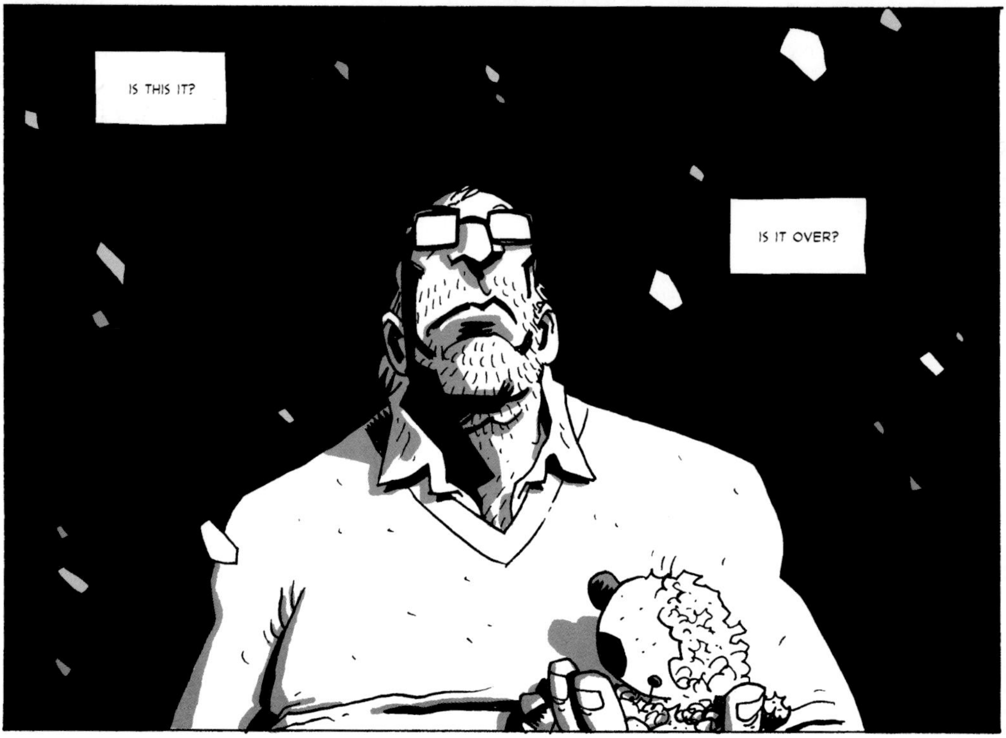
IS THIS IT?
IS IT OVER?

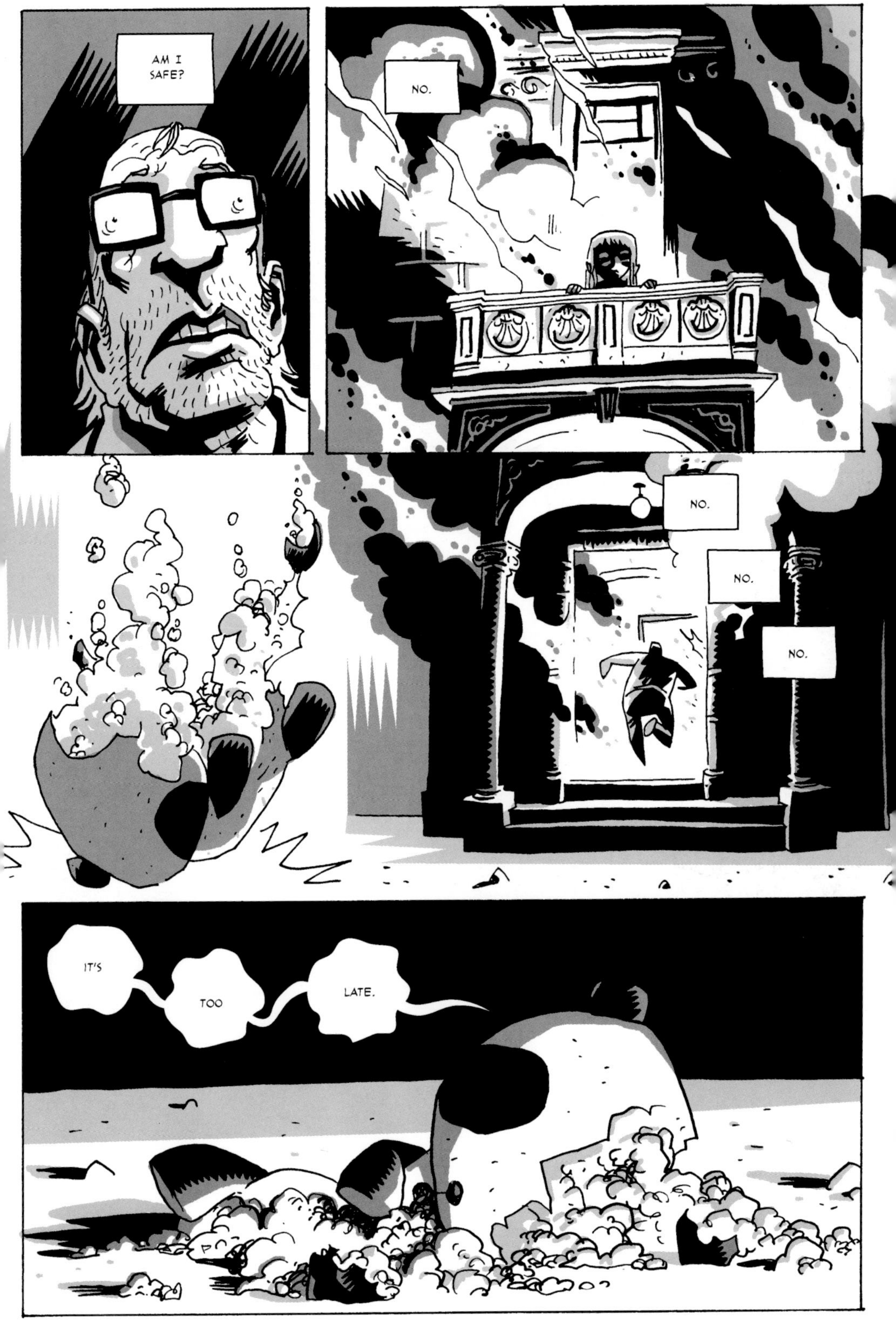
AM I SAFE?
NO.
NO.
NO.
NO.
IT'S
TOO
LATE.

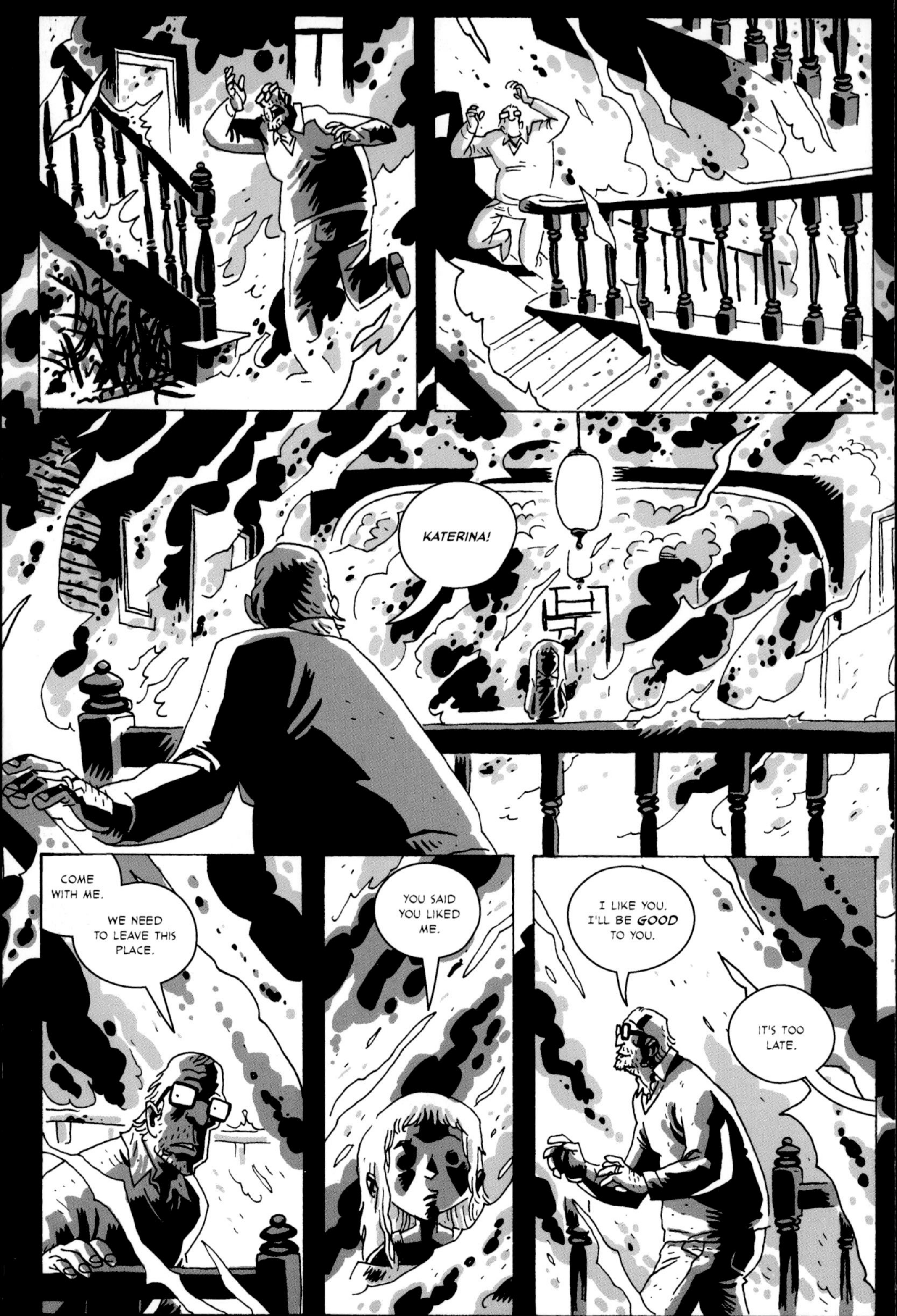
KATERINA!
COME WITH ME.
WE NEED TO LEAVE THIS PLACE.
YOU SAID YOU LIKED ME.
I LIKE YOU. I'LL BE GOOD TO YOU.
IT'S TOO LATE.

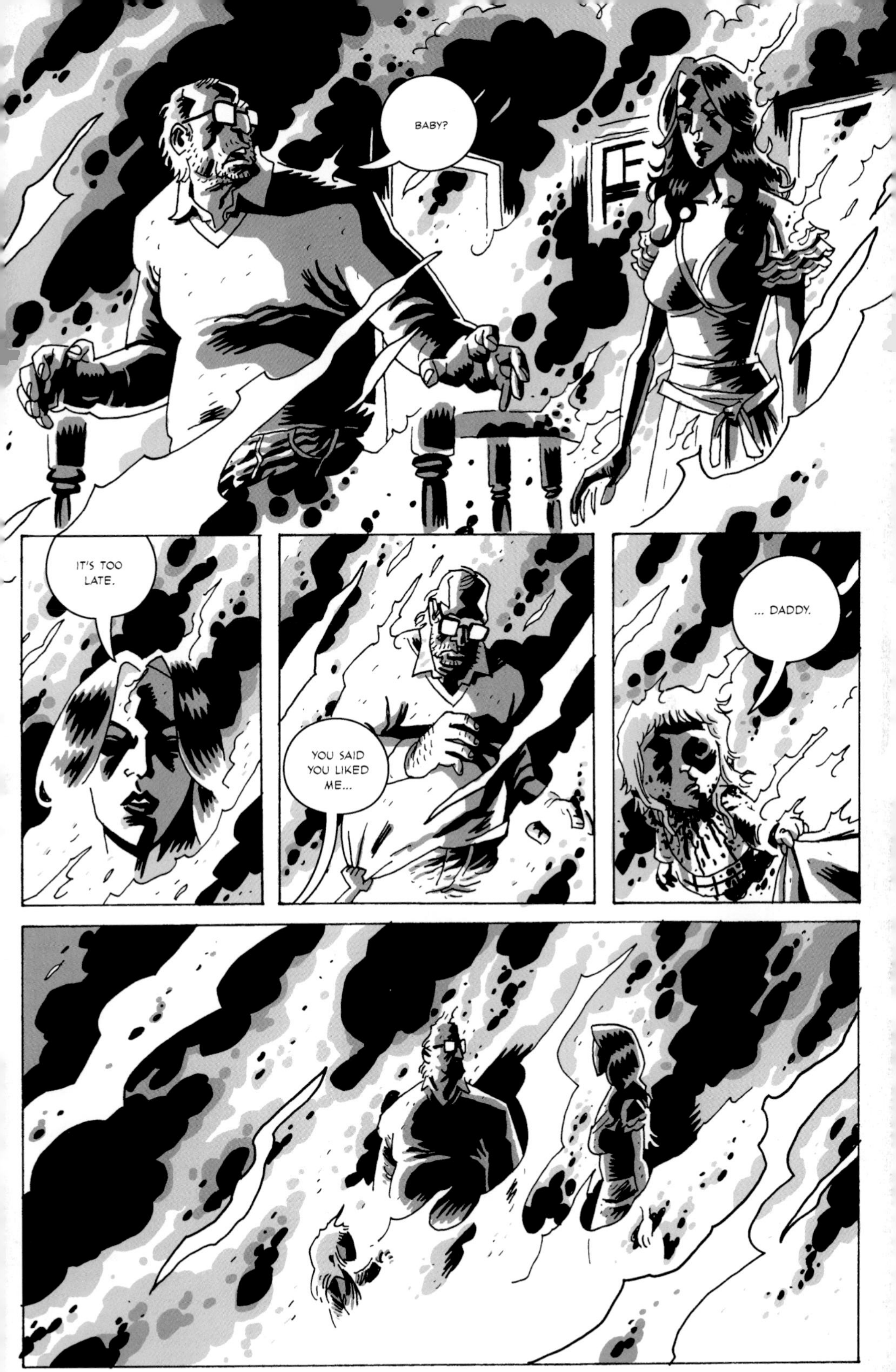
BABY?
IT'S TOO LATE.
YOU SAID YOU LIKED ME...
... DADDY.

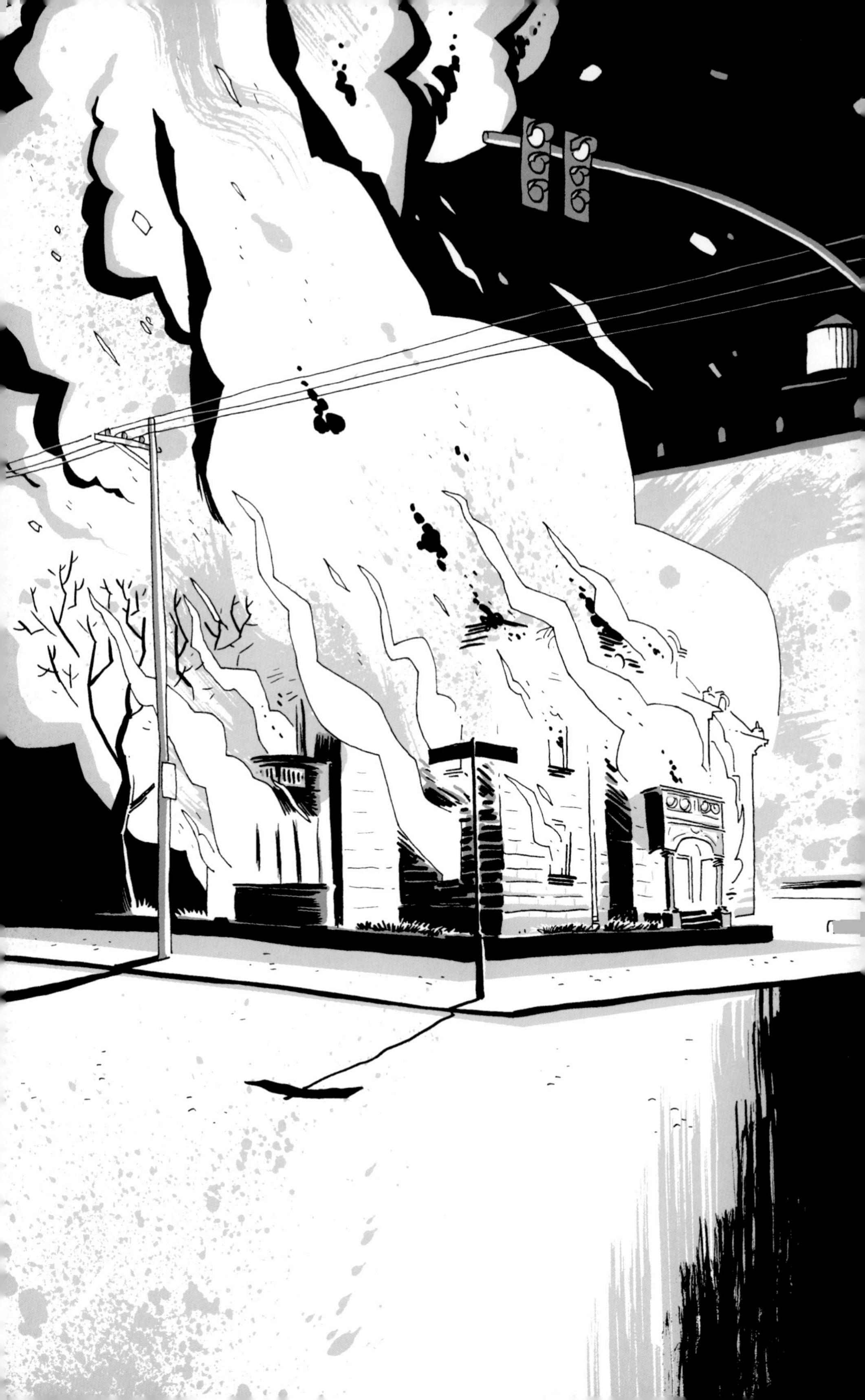

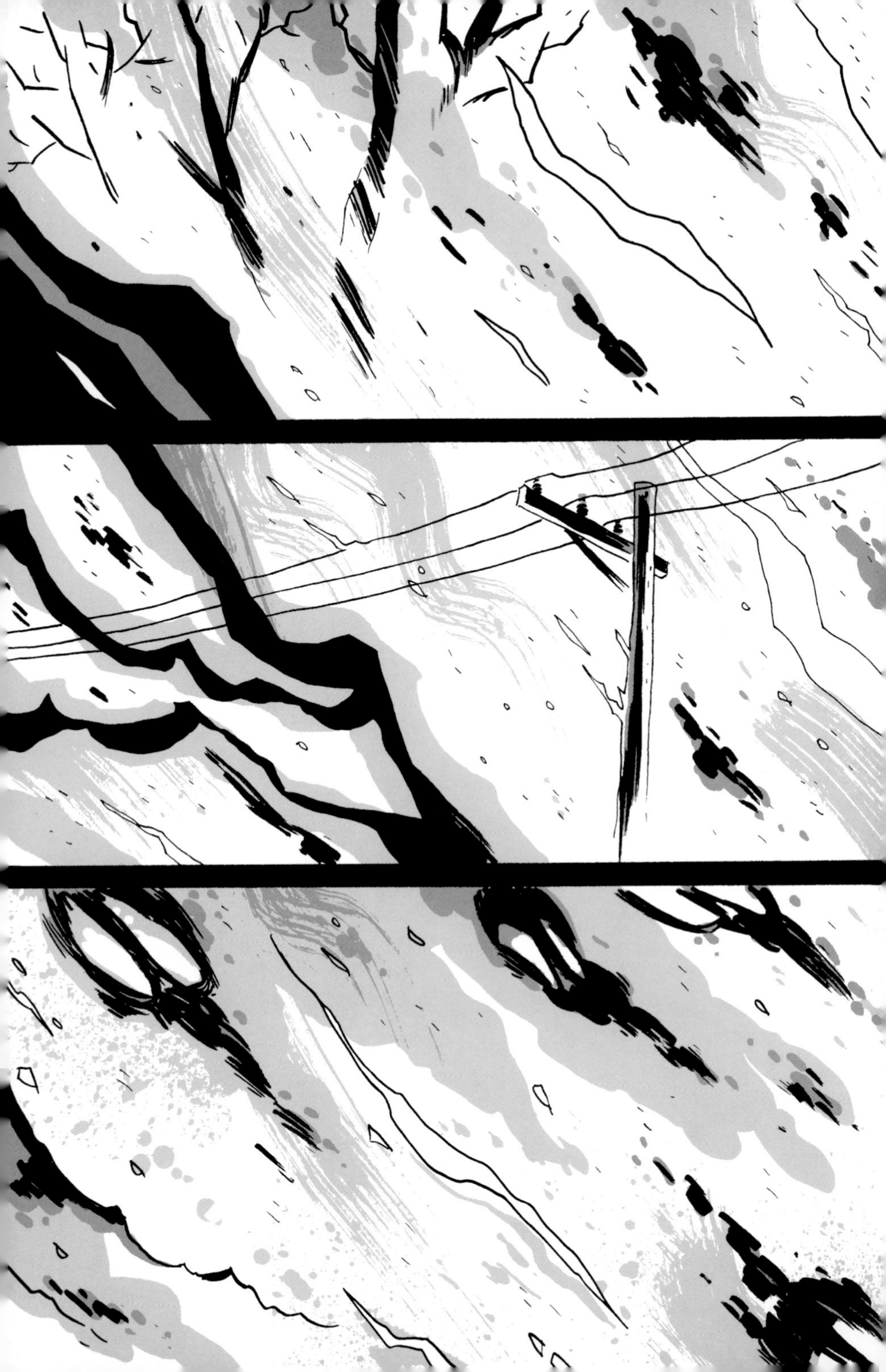

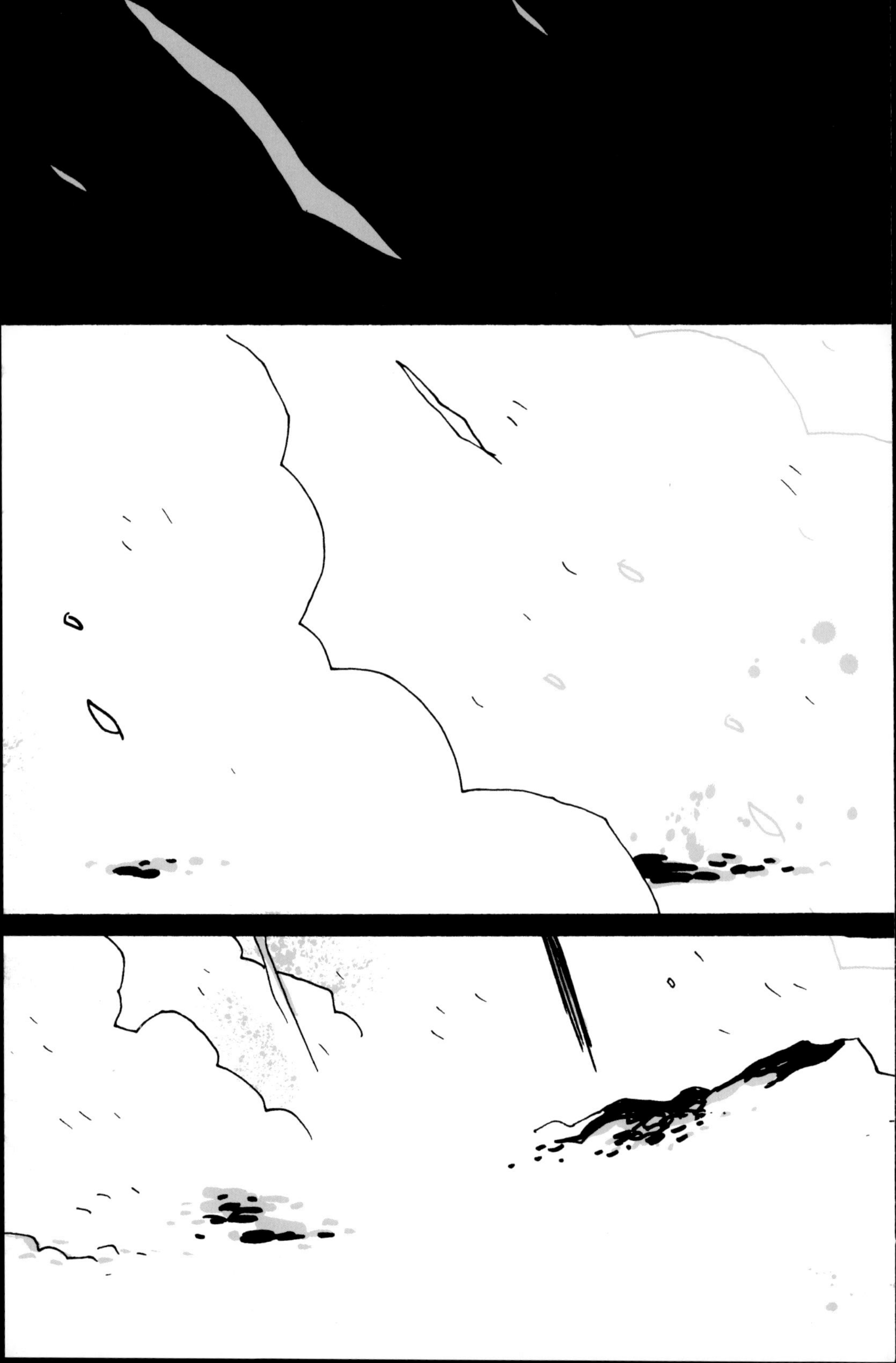

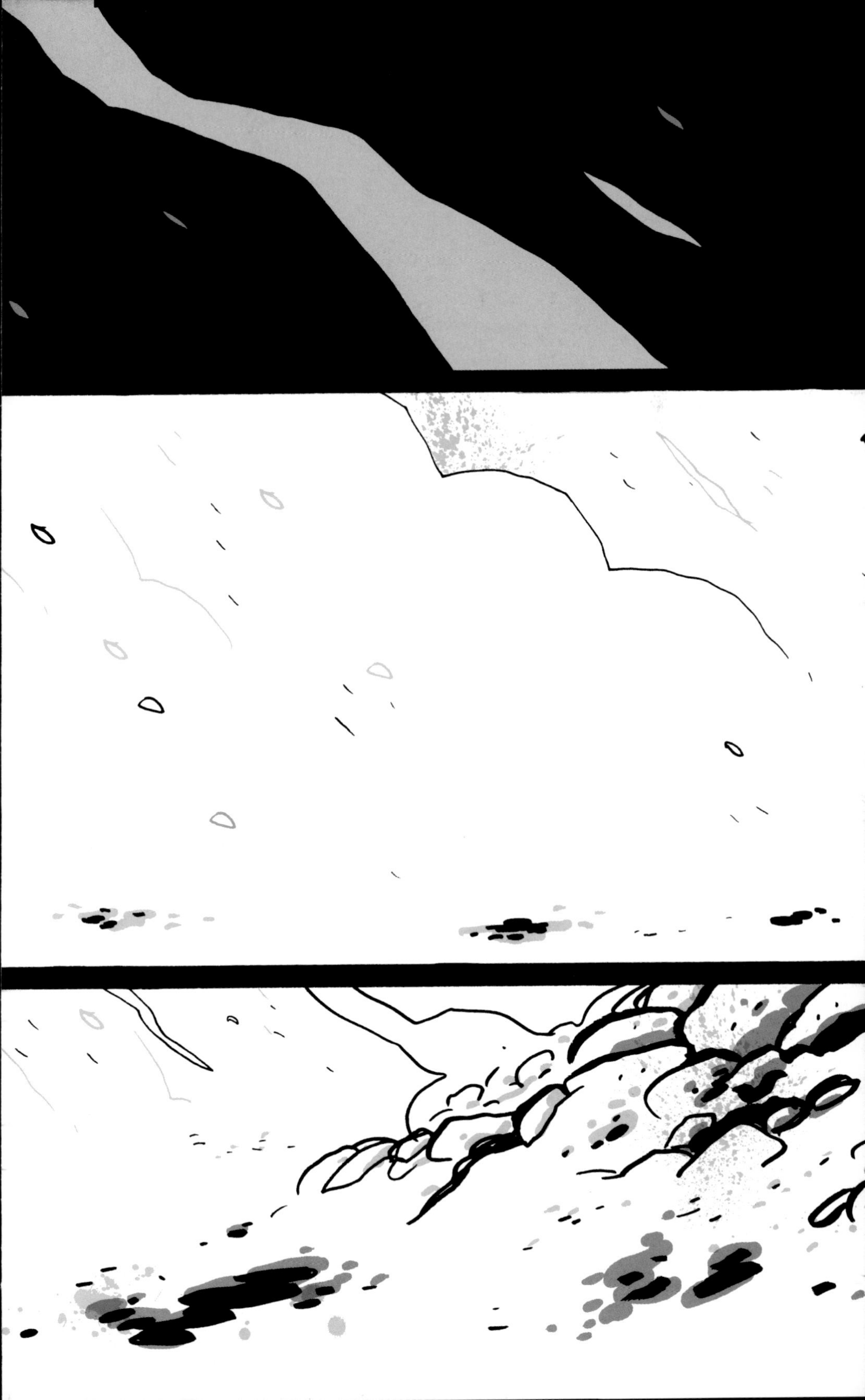

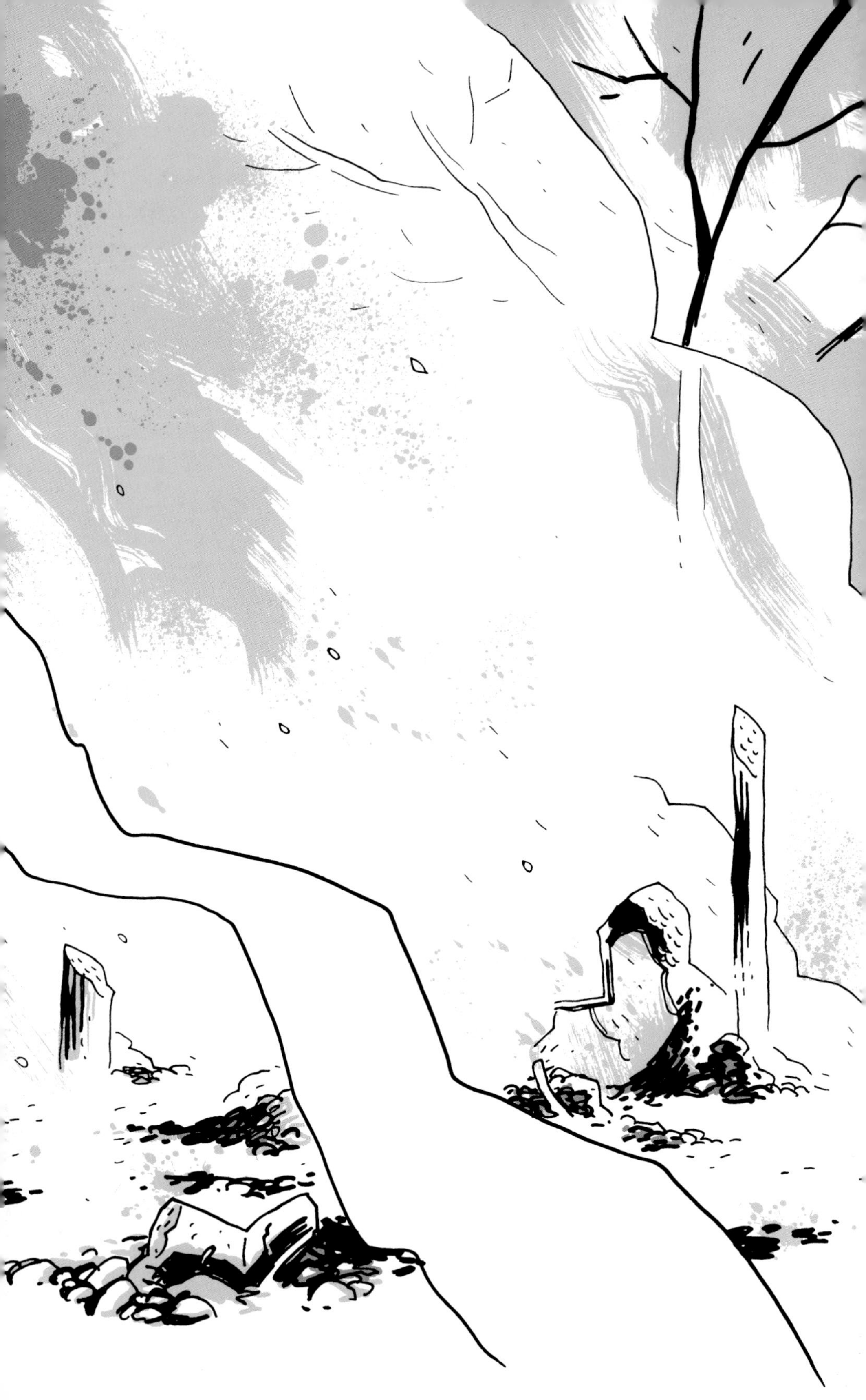

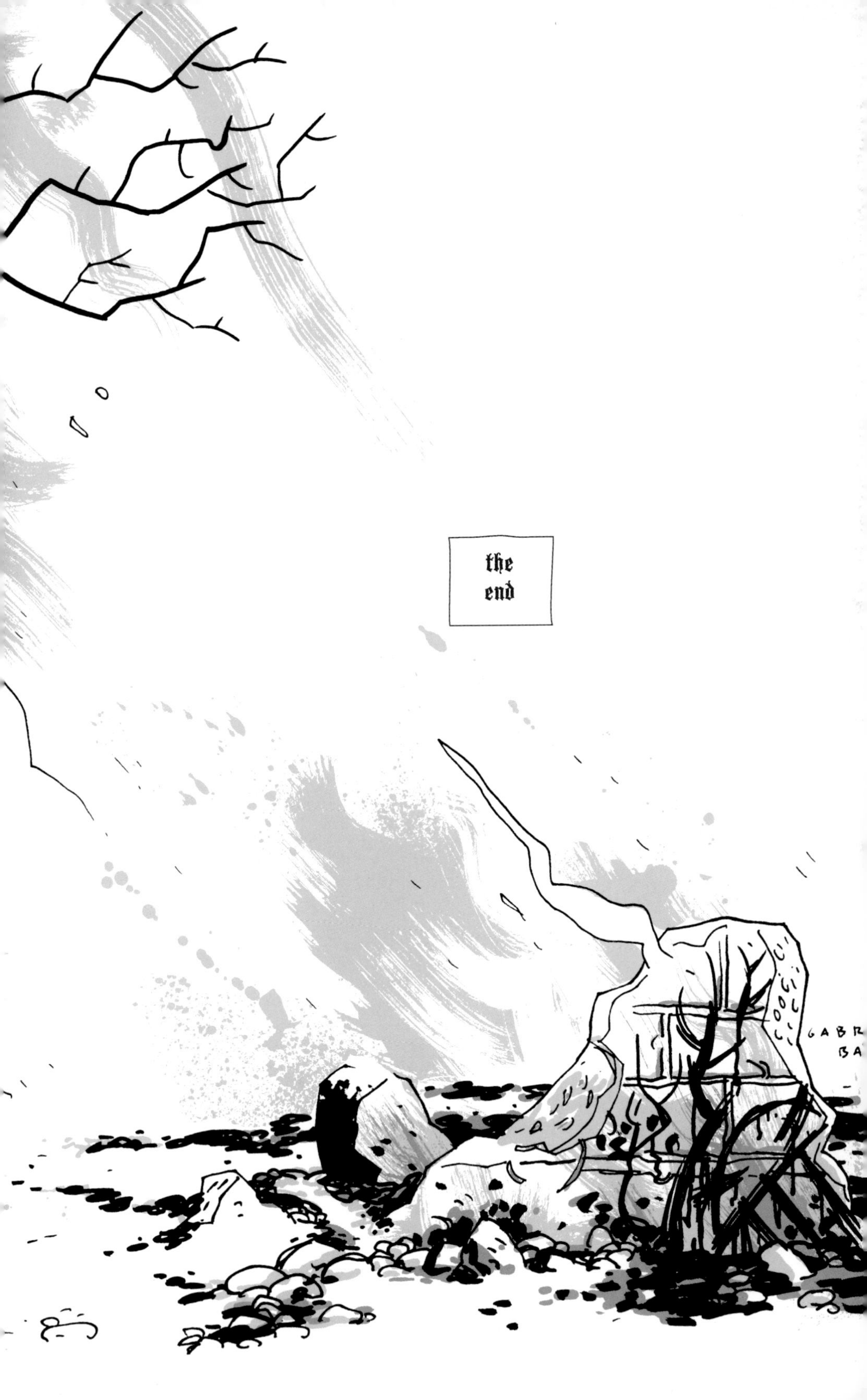
the end
GABR
BA

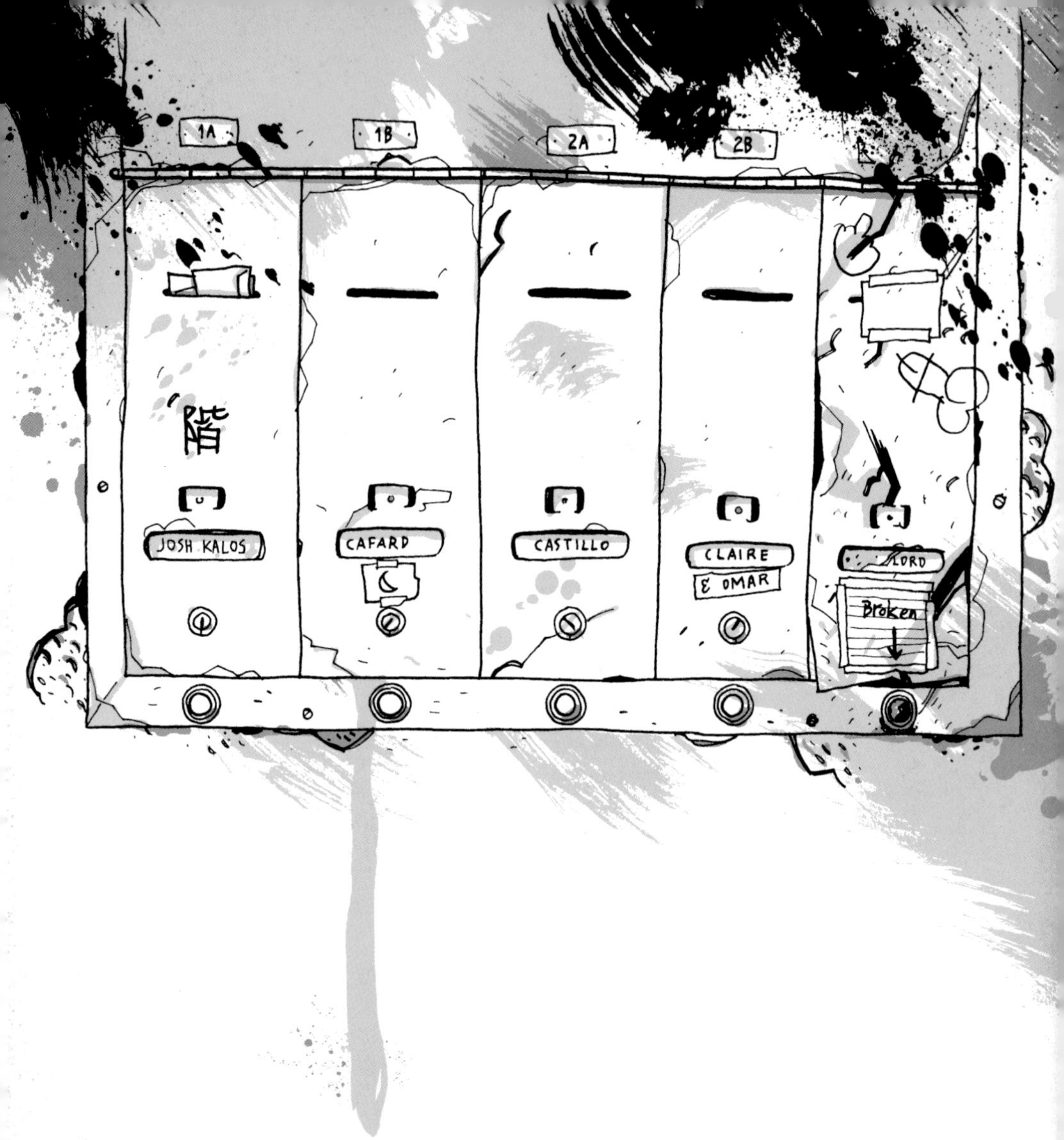
1A
1B
2A
2B
JOSH KALOS
CAFARD
CASTILLO
CLAIRE
& OMAR
LORD
Broken

Concept Designs for *Pixu*

by Gabriel Bá, Becky Cloonan, Vasilis Lolos, Fábio Moon

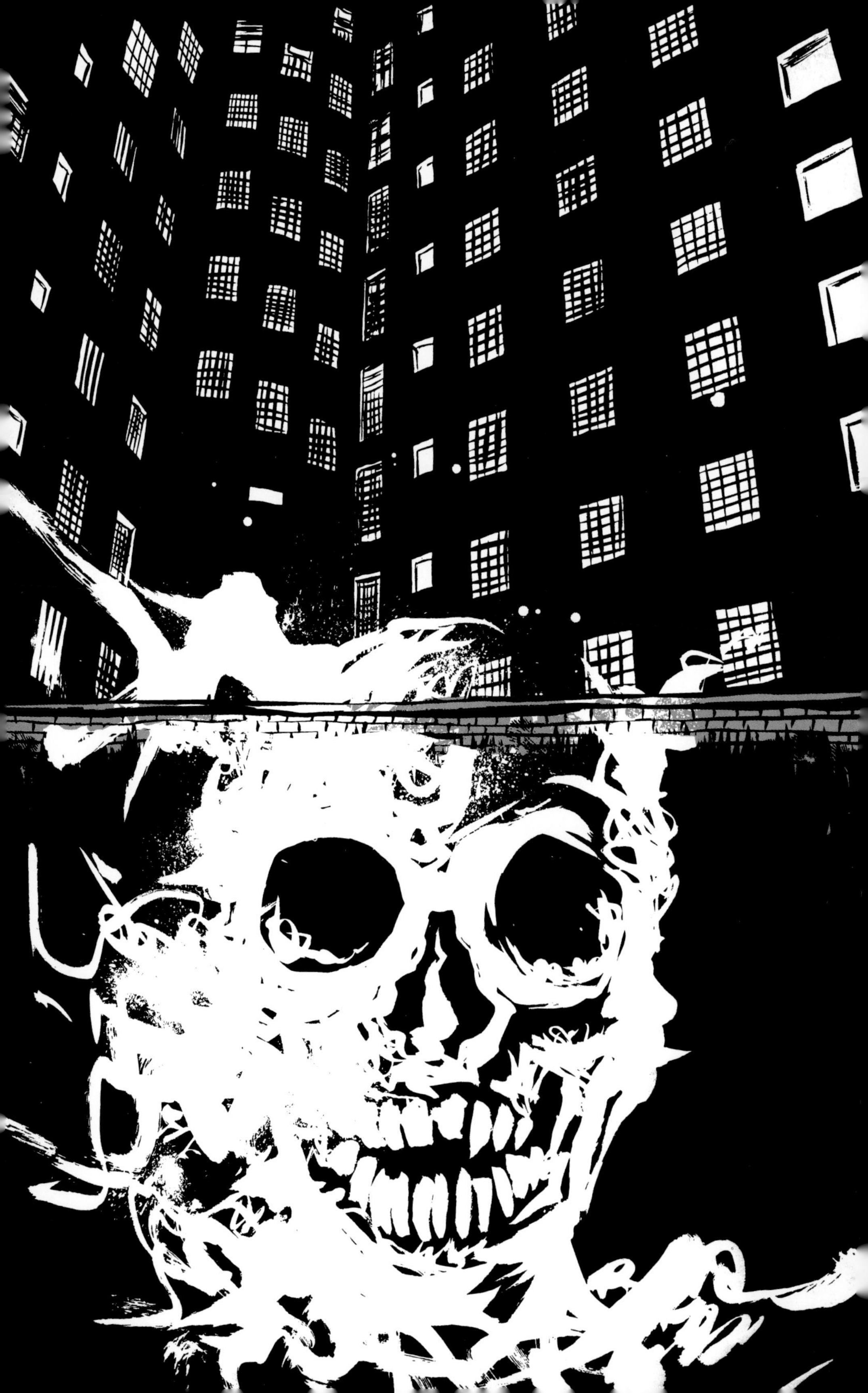

BC
08

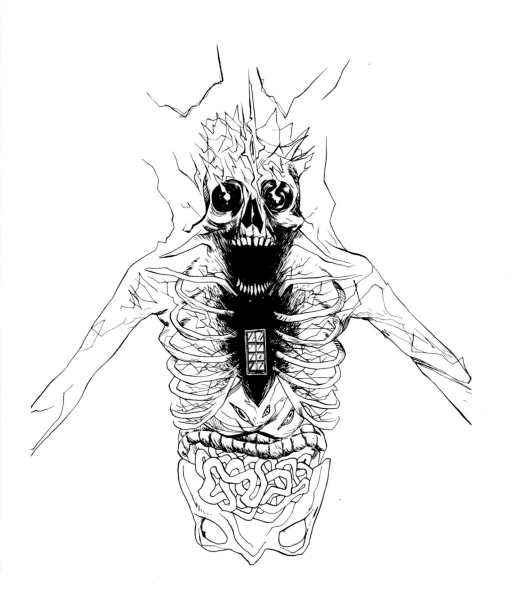

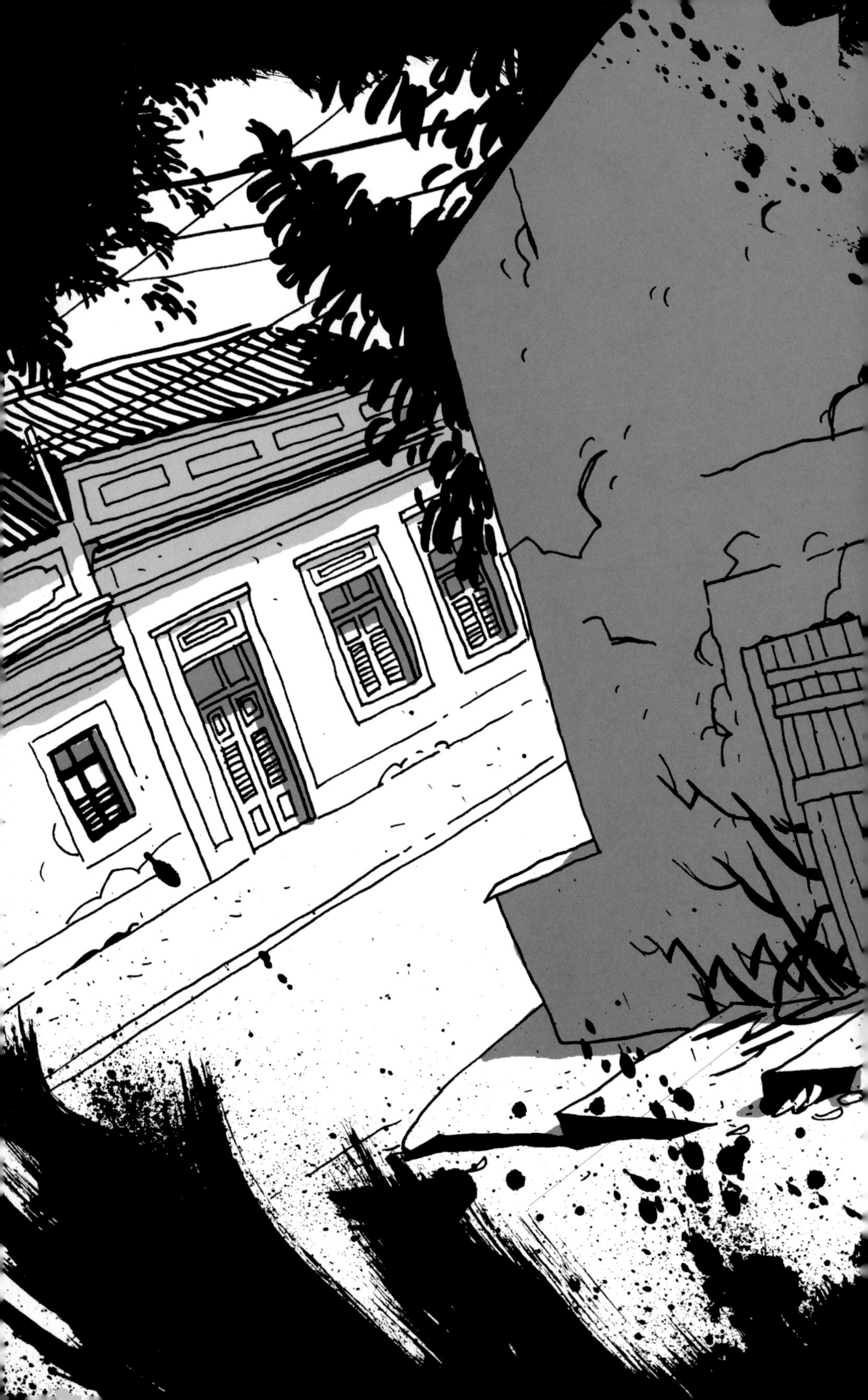

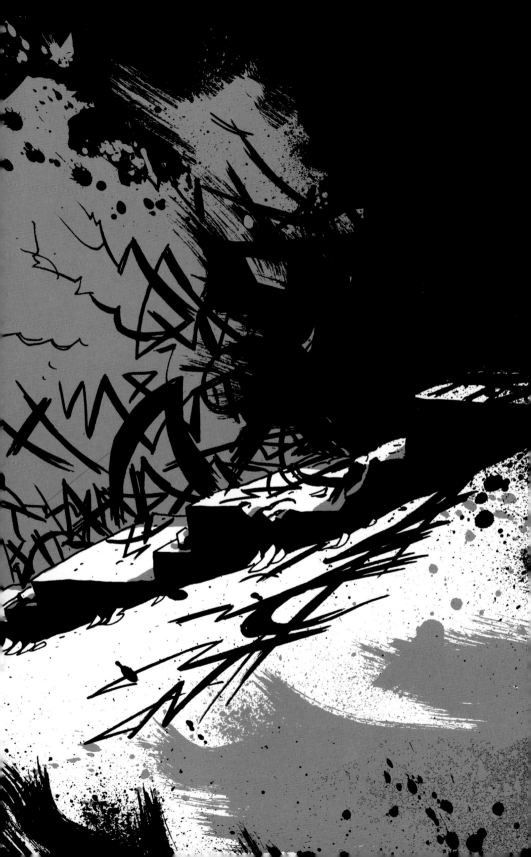

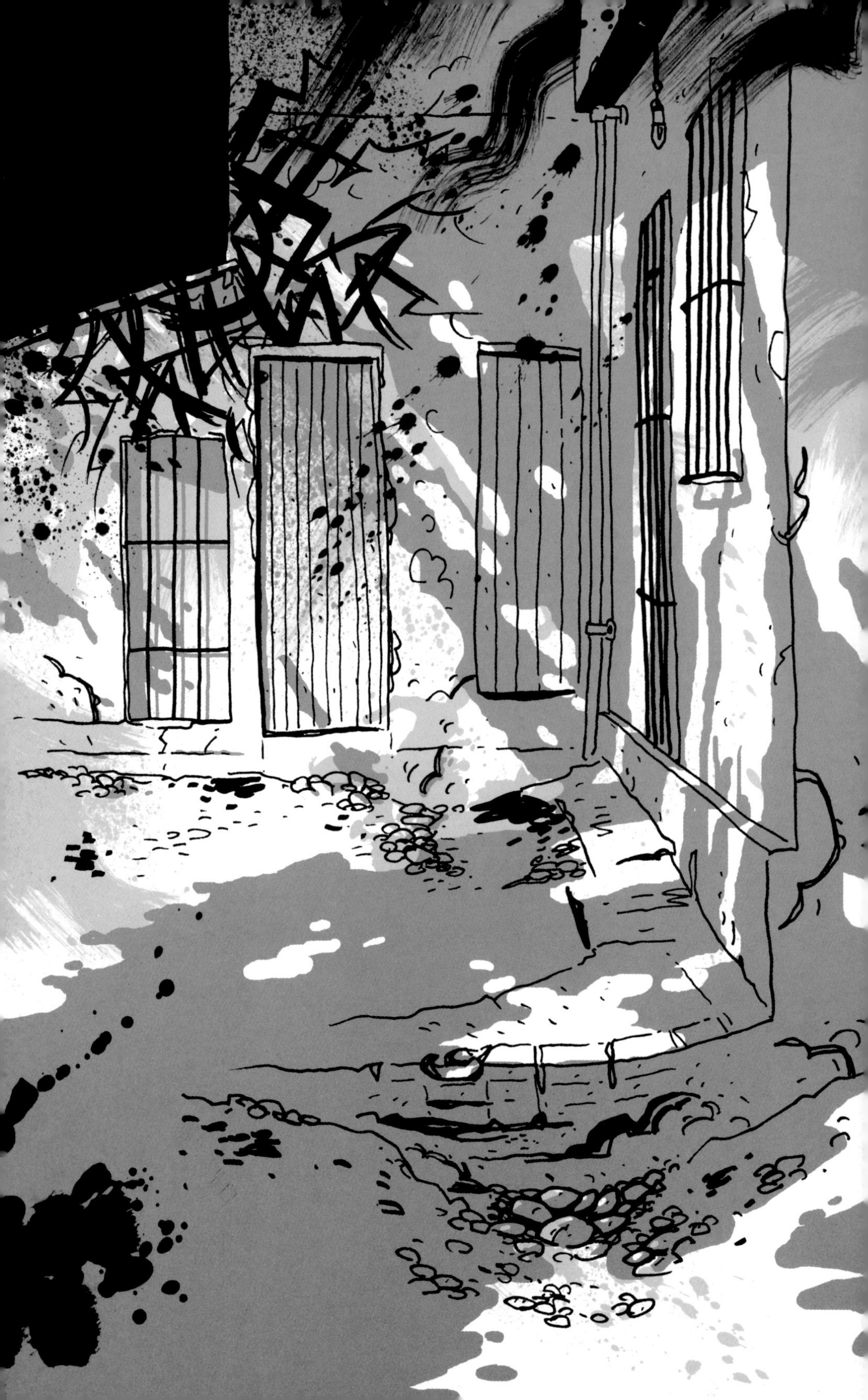

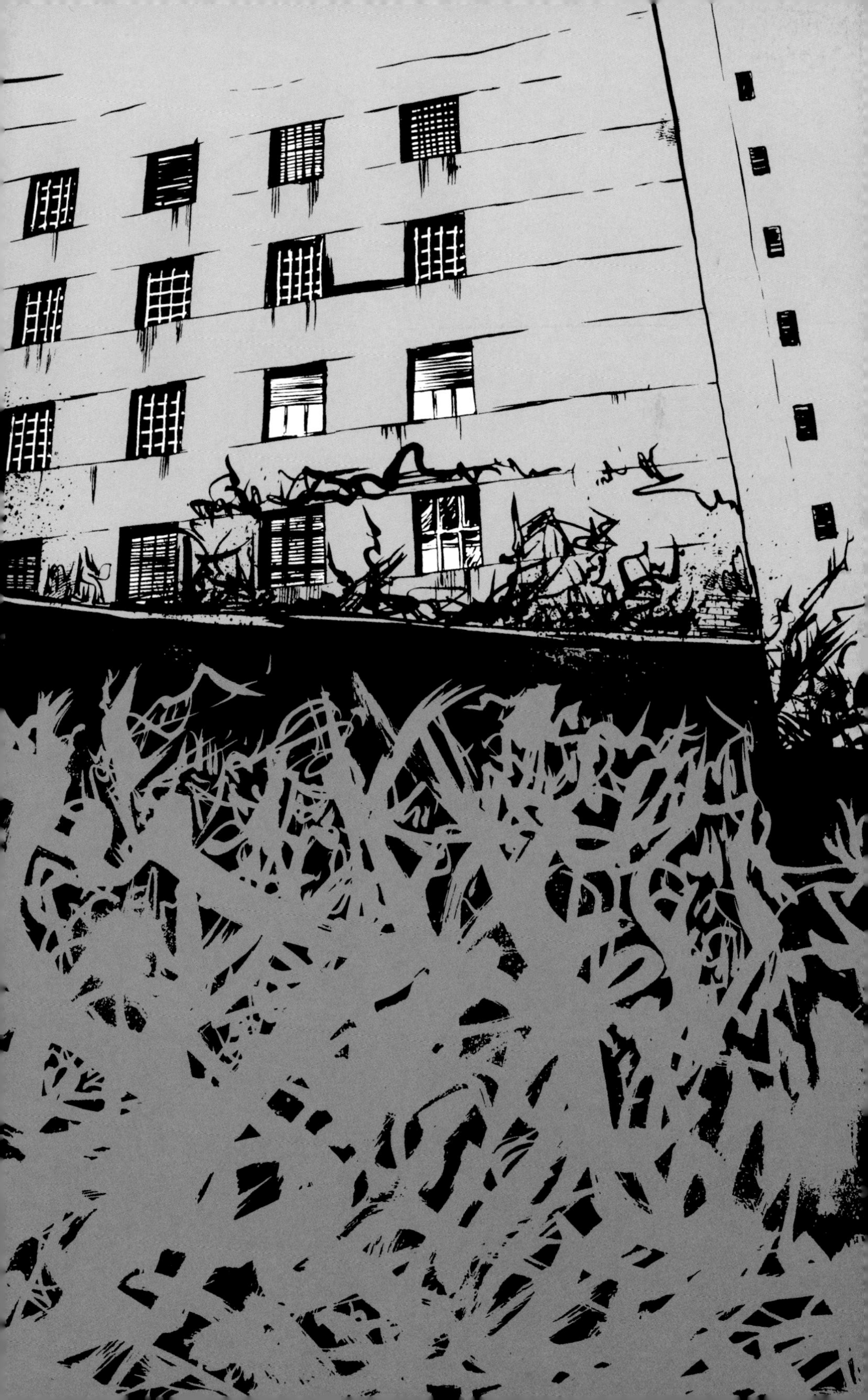

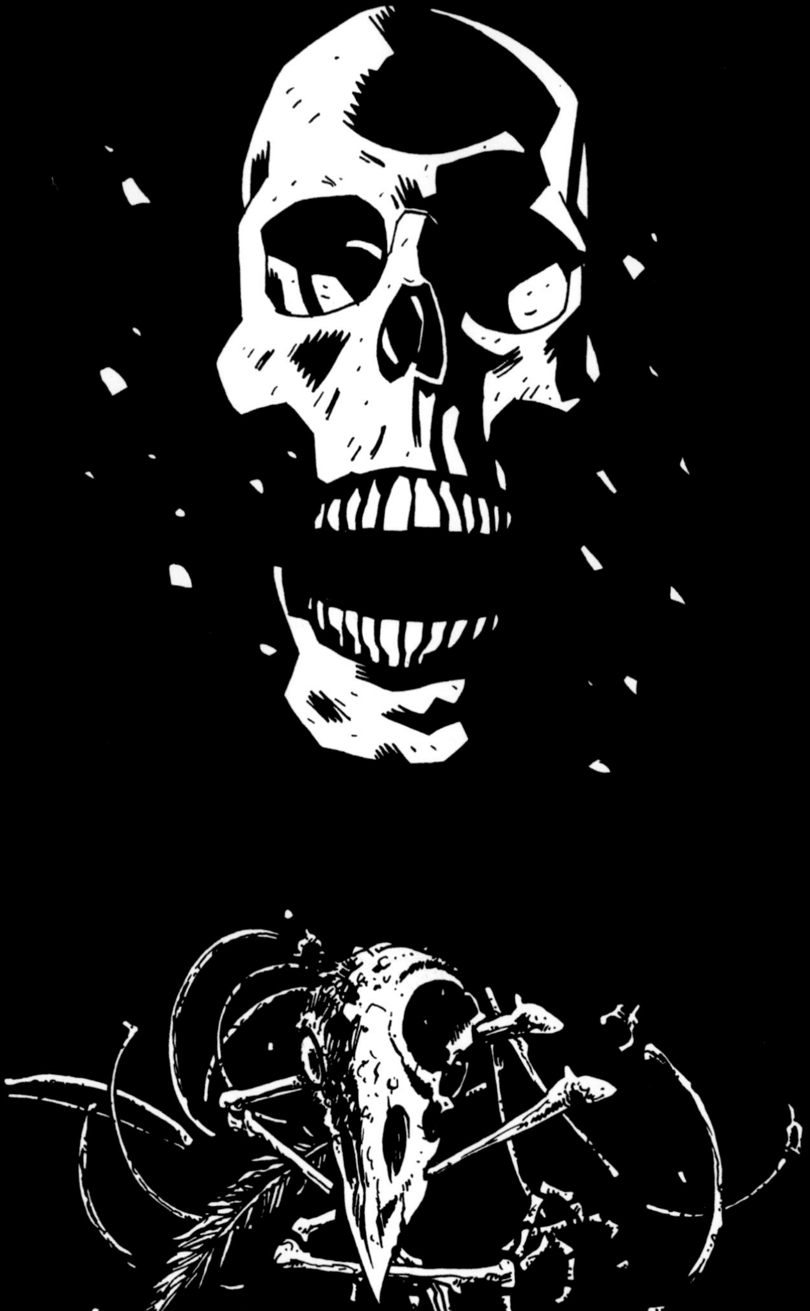

Creator Biographies . . .

Vasilis Lolos

Vasilis Lolos hails from Athens, Greece. His work includes an impressive amount of scattered short stories and a few graphic novels. In 2008 he won, along with his *Pixu* co-creators and Rafael Grampá, the Eisner Award for Best Anthology for *5*.

Later that same year he won a Harvey Award for his graphic novel *The Last Call*. He currently resides on the moon and is working hard on volume two.

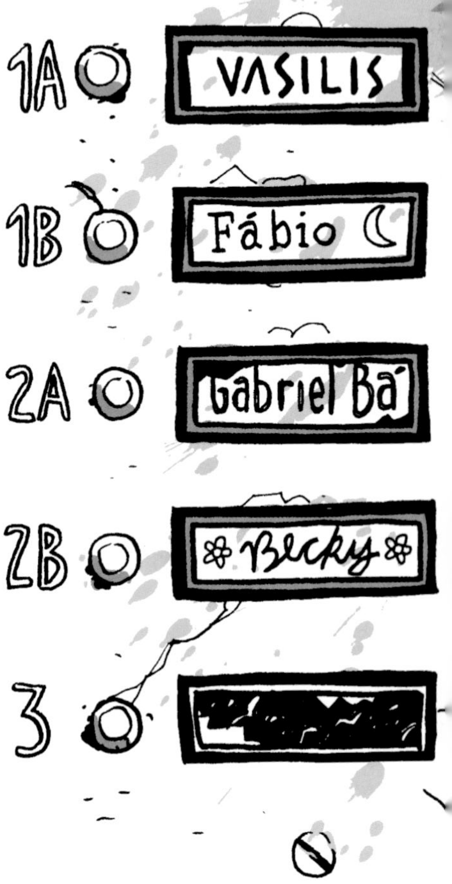
1A
VASILIS
1B
Fábio
2A
Gabriel Bá
2B
Becky
3

Fábio Moon and Gabriel Bá

Born in Brazil in 1976, twins Fábio Moon and Gabriel Bá decided, right then and there, that if they were going to follow the lonely path of the reclusive comic-book artist, they wouldn't have to do it alone. Working together for more then ten years, they set out to make comics look good and, so far, they've been doing it just fine. Widely known for their collaborations with other creators in books like *The Umbrella Academy*, *Casanova*, and the early days of the B.P.R.D. and a young Hellboy in *B.P.R.D.: 1947*, they often return to their fantastic stories of the strange life of creative people in their São Paulo hometown in books like *De:TALES* and *Daytripper*.

They've won a lot of awards, but they don't like to brag about it, because what they really want to do is spread their love for comics and for good stories. And to spread the word on how awesome Becky is.

When they were kids, they were afraid of horror movies, and especially afraid of the dark, and they still think the scariest things are those you can't really see.

Becky Cloonan

Born in Italy in 1980, Becky Cloonan began her comic-book career self-publishing mini-comics. Since then she has worked on a ton of comics, including the critically acclaimed series *Demo*, *American Virgin,* and *East Coast Rising*. She loves coffee, adventure, and period pieces, and still tries to self-publish one book a year. Currently living in Brooklyn, she wishes Brazil, Greece, and the moon weren't so far away.

Recommended Dark Horse Reading . . .

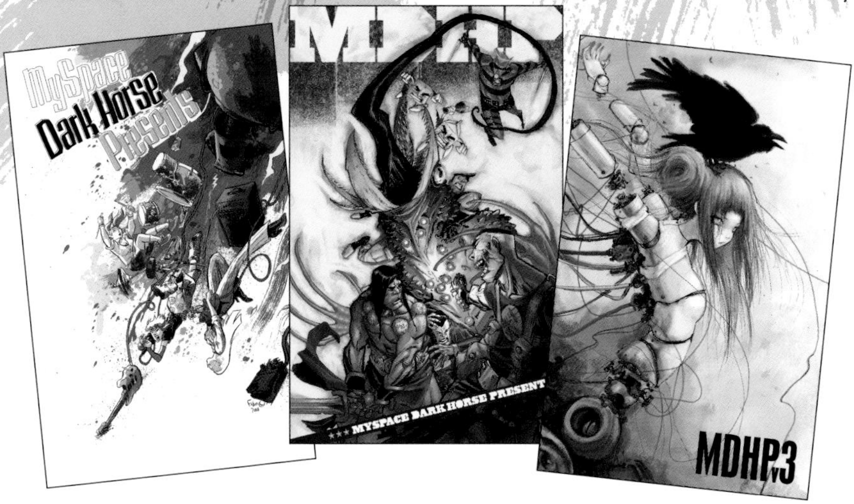
MySpace
Dark Horse
Presents
MYSPACE DARK HORSE PRESENT
MDHPv3

MySpace Dark Horse Presents

Fábio Moon, Gabriel Bá, Becky Cloonan, Gerard Way, Mike Mignola, Joss Whedon, and others

The online comics anthology *MySpace Dark Horse Presents* sees print in these three volumes! Top talents from the industry like Mike Mignola, Joss Whedon, Eric Powell, Adam Warren, John Arcudi, and many others are joined by some of the freshest new talent—found only on MySpace! myspace.com/darkhorsepresents

$19.95 EACH Vol 1 ISBN 978-1-59307-998-7 Vol 2 ISBN 978-1-59582-248-2 Vol 3 ISBN 978-1-59582-327-4

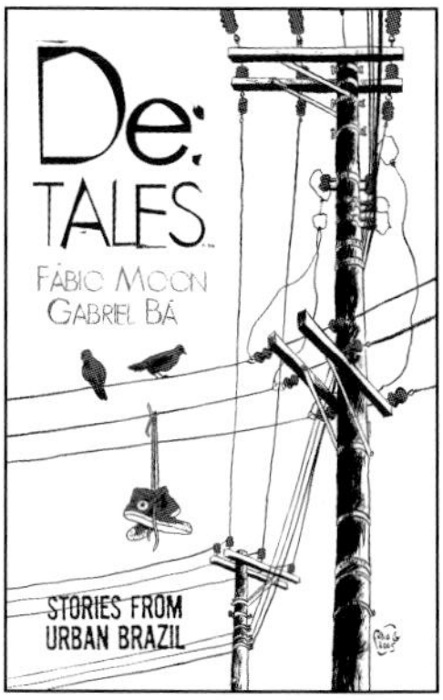
De:
TALES
Fábio Moon
Gabriel Bá
STORIES FROM
URBAN BRAZIL

De:TALES

Fábio Moon and Gabriel Bá

Brazilian twins Fábio Moon and Gabriel Bá share an award-winning talent for comics and an abiding love of the medium with this collection of short stories brimming with all the details of human life and the urban reality of their home in São Paulo.

$14.95 ISBN 978-1-59307-485-2

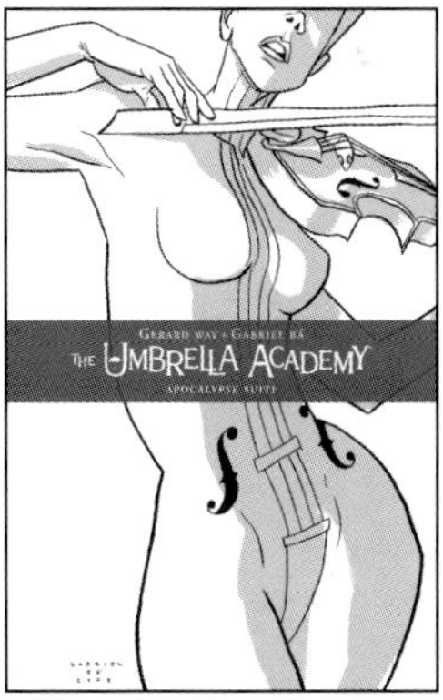
Gerard Way • Gabriel Bá
The Umbrella Academy
Apocalypse Suite

The Umbrella Academy Volume 1: Apocalypse Suite

Gerard Way, Gabriel Bá, and Dave Stewart

In an inexplicable worldwide event, forty-seven extraordinary children were spontaneously born. Millionaire inventor Reginald Hargreeves adopted seven of the children; when asked why, his only explanation was, "To save the world."

$17.95 ISBN 978-1-59307-978-9

AVAILABLE AT YOUR LOCAL COMICS SHOP OR BOOKSTORE

To find a comics shop in your area, call 1-888-266-4226.

For more information or to order direct, visit darkhorse.com or call 1-800-862-0052 • Mon.–Fri. 9 AM to 5 PM Pacific Time.

*Prices and availability subject to change without notice.

DARK HORSE BOOKS

Also from Dark Horse Comics . . .

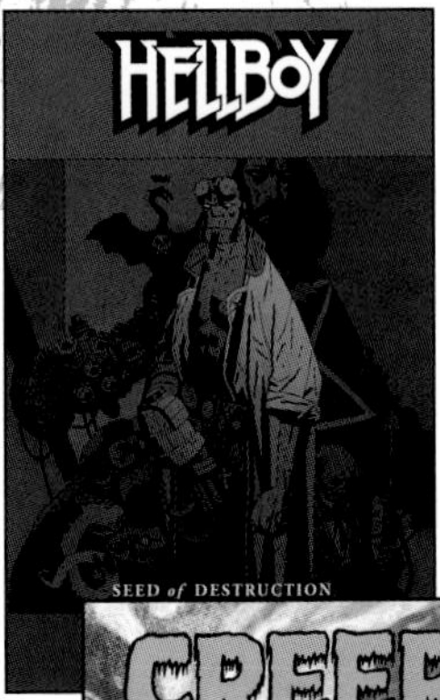
HELLBOY
SEED of DESTRUCTION

Hellboy: Seed of Destruction
Mike Mignola, John Byrne

When strangeness threatens to engulf the world, a strange man will come to save it. Hellboy, the world's greatest paranormal investigator, is the only thing standing between sanity and insanity as he battles the mystical forces of the netherworld and a truly bizarre plague of frogs. And if he fails, we all fail with him!
$17.95 ISBN 978-1-59307-094-6

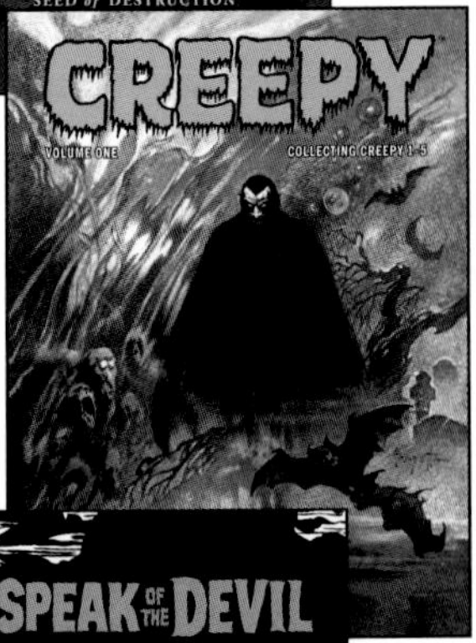
CREEPY
VOLUME ONE
COLLECTING CREEPY 1-5

Creepy Archives Volume 1
Alex Toth, Frank Frazetta, Bernie Wrightson, and others

Gather up your wooden stakes, your blood-covered hatchets, and all the skeletons in the darkest depths of your closet, and prepare for a horrifying adventure into the darkest corners of comics history. Dark Horse Comics further corners the market on high-quality horror storytelling with one of the most anticipated releases of the decade, a hardcover archive collection of legendary *Creepy* magazine.
$49.95 ISBN 978-1-59307-973-4

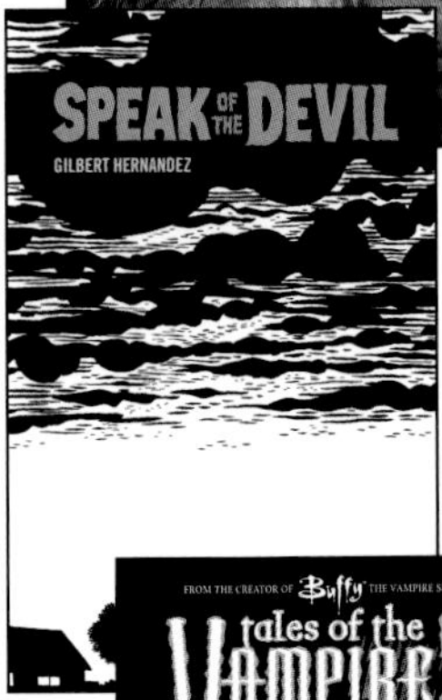
SPEAK OF THE DEVIL
GILBERT HERNANDEZ

Speak of the Devil
Gilbert Hernandez

This is the story of Val Castillo, a promising gymnast with a strange hobby. She is secretly the neighborhood peeping Tom. At first she is alone in this, but when a male friend discovers her doings, he joins her in a dark journey of spying and making discoveries about their neighbors that may have been better left alone. This snowballs into a journey darker than even the most cynical would care to endure.
$19.95 ISBN 978-1-59582-193-5

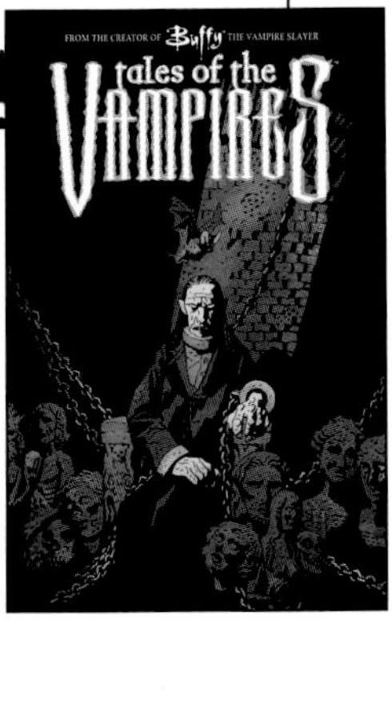
FROM THE CREATOR OF Buffy THE VAMPIRE SLAYER
tales of the VAMPIRES

Tales of the Vampires
Joss Whedon, Ben Edlund, Jane Espenson, Drew Goddard, Tim Sale, and others

The creator of *Buffy the Vampire Slayer* reunites with the writers from his hit TV shows for an imaginative and frightening look into the history of vampires in the world of the Slayer. Intricately woven around a central story by Whedon featuring a group of young Watchers in training meeting their first undead, Whedon's staff of writers present stories ranging from medieval times, to the Depression, to today, as well as Buffy's rematch with Dracula and Angel's ongoing battle with his own demons.
$15.95 ISBN 978-1-56971-749-3

AVAILABLE AT YOUR LOCAL COMICS SHOP OR BOOKSTORE
To find a comics shop in your area, call 1-888-266-4226.
For more information or to order direct, visit darkhorse.com or call 1-800-862-0052 • Mon.–Fri. 9 AM to 5 PM Pacific Time.
*Prices and availability subject to change without notice.